Lecture Notes in Computer Science　　　9147

Commenced Publication in 1973
Founding and Former Series Editors:
Gerhard Goos, Juris Hartmanis, and Jan van Leeuwen

More information about this series at http://www.springer.com/series/7409

Sebastian Maneth (Ed.)

Data Science

30th British International Conference
on Databases, BICOD 2015
Edinburgh, UK, July 6–8, 2015
Proceedings

 Springer

Editor
Sebastian Maneth
University of Edinburgh
Edinburgh
UK

ISSN 0302-9743   ISSN 1611-3349   (electronic)
Lecture Notes in Computer Science
ISBN 978-3-319-20423-9   ISBN 978-3-319-20424-6   (eBook)
DOI 10.1007/978-3-319-20424-6

Library of Congress Control Number: 2015941362

LNCS Sublibrary: SL3 – Information Systems and Applications, incl. Internet/Web, and HCI

Printed on acid-free paper

Springer International Publishing AG Switzerland is part of Springer Science+Business Media (www.springer.com)

Preface

This volume contains the papers presented at BICOD 2015: the 30th British International Conference on Databases held during July 6–8, 2015, in Edinburgh.

The BICOD Conference (formerly known as BNCOD) is a venue for the presentation and discussion of research papers on a broad range of topics related to databases and data-centric computation. The theme of BICOD 2015 was "Data Science", i.e., the extraction of meaning from big data. The conference featured three invited lectures and three invited keynotes, all centered around the theme of data science.

This year, BICOD attracted 37 complete submissions from 14 different countries, namely, Austria, China, Egypt, France, Germany, Ireland, Italy, The Netherlands, Pakistan, Sweden, Switzerland, Tunisia, Turkey, and the UK. Each submission was reviewed by at least three Program Committee members. The committee decided to accept 19 papers on such topics as benchmarking, data integration, data replication, deep learning, graph processing, linked data, log processing, main memory processing, NoSQL querying, and social network analysis.

We would like to thank the authors for submitting their work to this year's BICOD conference, the Program Committee members for their help in selecting an excellent conference program, and the distinguished speakers and lecturers for accepting our invitation. We also thank Linda Hope and Magdalena Mazurczak for their involvement in the local organization of the conference.

May 2015   Sebastian Maneth

Organization

Program Committee

Philippe Bonnet	IT University of Copenhagen, Denmark
Jan Van den Bussche	University of Hasselt, Belgium
Bogdan Cautis	University of Paris-Sud 11, France
James Cheney	University of Edinburgh, UK
Barry Eaglestone	University of Sheffield, UK
Wenfei Fan	University of Edinburgh, UK
Alvaro Fernandes	University of Manchester, UK
George Fletcher	TU Eindhoven, The Netherlands
Georg Gottlob	University of Oxford, UK
Anne James	Coventry University, UK
Sebastian Maneth	University of Edinburgh, UK (PC Chair)
Ioana Manolescu	Inria Saclay, France
Peter McBrien	Imperial College London, UK
Hannes Muehleisen	CWI Amsterdam, The Netherlands
David Nelson	University of Sunderland, UK
Dan Olteanu	University of Oxford, UK
Norman Paton	University of Manchester, UK
Peter Pietzuch	Imperial College London, UK
Alex Poulovassilis	Birkbeck College, University of London, UK
Juan Reutter	PUC Chile, Chile
Tore Risch	Uppsala University, Sweden
Mark Roantree	Dublin City University, Ireland
Kai-Uwe Sattler	TU Ilmenau, Germany
Sławek Staworko	Inria and University of Lille, France
Jens Teubner	TU Dortmund, Germany
John Wilson	University of Strathclyde, UK
Peter Wood	Birkbeck College, University of London, UK

Sponsoring Institutions

University of Edinburgh, Edinburgh, UK
EPSRC Centre for Doctoral Training in Data Science
sicsa: The Scottish Informatics and Computer Science Alliance

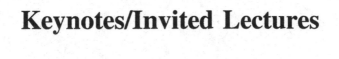

Keynotes/Invited Lectures

Keynote Invited Lectures

Big Data Curation

Renée J. Miller

Department of Computer Science, University of Toronto
miller@cs.toronto.edu
http://cs.toronto.edu/~miller

Keynote Abstract. More than a decade ago, Peter Buneman used the term *curated databases* to refer to databases that are created and maintained using the (often substantial) effort and domain expertise of humans. These human experts clean the data, integrate it with new sources, prepare it for analysis, and share the data with other experts in their field. In *data curation*, one seeks to support human curators in all activities needed for maintaining and enhancing the value of their data over time. Curation includes data provenance, the process of understanding the origins of data, how it was created, cleaned, or integrated. Big Data offers opportunities to solve curation problems in new ways. The availability of massive data is making it possible to infer semantic connections among data, connections that are central to solving difficult integration, cleaning, and analysis problems. Some of the nuanced semantic differences that eluded enterprise-scale curation solutions can now be understood using evidence from Big Data. Big Data Curation leverages the human expertise that has been embedded in Big Data, be it in general knowledge data that has been created through mass collaboration, or in specialized knowledge-bases created by incentivized user communities who value the creation and maintenance of high quality data.

In this talk, I describe our experience in Big Data Curation. This includes our experience over the last five years curating NIH Clinical Trials data that we have published as Open Linked Data at linkedCT.org. I overview how we have adapted some of the traditional solutions for data curation to account for (and take advantage of) Big Data.

Keywords: Data Curation · Big Data · Data Integration · Data Provenance

R.J. Miller—Supported by Bell Canada, NSERC and the NSERC Business Intelligence Network.

Dealing with a Web of Data

Nigel Shadbolt

Web and Internet Science, University of Southampton,
Southampton, SO17 1BJ, UK
nrs@ecs.soton.ac.uk
http://users.ecs.soton.ac.uk/nrs/

Keynote Abstract. We live in an age of superabundant information. The Internet and World Wide Web have been the agents of this revolution. A deluge of information and data has led to a range of scientific discoveries and engineering innovations. Data at Web scale has allowed us to characterise the shape and structure of the Web itself and to efficiently search its billions of items of contents. Data published on the Web has enabled the mobilisation of hundreds of thousands of humans to solve problems beyond any individual or single organisation.

The last five years have seen increasing amounts of open data being published on the Web. Open data published on the Web is improving the efficiency of our public services and giving rise to open innovation. In particular, governments have made data available across a wide range of sectors: spending, crime and justice, education, health, transport, geospatial, environmental and much more. The data has been published in a variety of formats and has been reused with varying degrees of success. Commercial organisations have begun to exploit this resource and in some cases elected to release their own open data.

Data collected at scale by public and private agencies also gives rise to concerns about its use and abuse. Meanwhile, data science is emerging as an area of competitive advantage for individuals, companies, universities, public and private sector organisations and nation states. A Web of data offers new opportunities and challenges for science, government and business. These include issues of provenance and security, quality and curation, certification and citation, linkage and annotation.

Statistical Thinking in Machine Learning

Padhraic Smyth

Department of Computer Science, University of California,
Irvine, CA 92607-3435, USA
http://www.ics.uci.edu/~smyth

Abstract. Machine learning began as a subfield of artificial intelligence several decades ago but has grown to become a major research area within computer science in its own right. In particular, in the past few years machine learning has played a key role in making progress on a variety of application problems in areas such as image recognition, speech recognition, online advertising, and ranking of Web search results. The field is enjoying continued attention with the resurgent interest in neural network models via deep learning, and the broad interest outside computer science in topics such as "data science" and "big data."

In this talk we will discuss the role of statistics in the success of machine learning. Statistical theories and models have long provided a foundational basis for many of the techniques used in machine learning, particularly in models with explicit probabilistic semantics such as logistic regression, hidden Markov models, and so on. But even for models which appear on the surface to have no explicit probabilistic or statistical semantics, such as neural networks or decision trees, there are fundamental statistical trade-offs at play, lurking beneath the surface of problems that appear to be more closely related to optimization than they are to statistical modeling. Focusing primarily on predictive modeling (classification and regression) we will explore how *statistical thinking* is fundamental to machine learning even when statistical models do not appear to be involved.

Keywords: Machine learning · Statistics · Classification · Regression

Streaming Methods in Data Analysis

Graham Cormode

University of Warwick
G.Cormode@Warwick.ac.uk

Abstract. A fundamental challenge in processing the massive quantities of information generated by modern applications is in extracting suitable representations of the data that can be stored, manipulated and interrogated on a single machine. A promising approach is in the design and analysis of compact summaries: data structures which capture key features of the data, and which can be created effectively over distributed, streaming data. Popular summary structures include the count distinct algorithms, which compactly approximate item set cardinalities, and sketches which allow vector norms and products to be estimated. These are very attractive, since they can be computed in parallel and combined to yield a single, compact summary of the data. This talk introduces the concepts and examples of compact summaries.

The Power of Visual Analytics: Unlocking the Value of Big Data

Daniel Keim

Data Analysis and Visualization Group,
University of Konstanz, Konstanz, Germany
keim@uni-konstanz.de
http://www.vis.uni-konstanz.de/mitglieder/keim/

Keynote Abstract. Never before in history data is generated and collected at such high volumes as it is today. For the analysis of large data sets to be effective, it is important to include the human in the data exploration process and combine the flexibility, creativity, and general knowledge of the human with the enormous storage capacity and the computational power of today's computers. Visual Analytics helps to deal with the flood of information by integrating the human in the data analysis process, applying its perceptual abilities to the large data sets. Presenting data in an interactive, graphical form often fosters new insights, encouraging the formation and validation of new hypotheses for better problem-solving and gaining deeper domain knowledge. Visual analytics techniques have proven to be of high value in exploratory data analysis. They are especially powerful for the first steps of the data exploration process, namely understanding the data and generating hypotheses about the data, but they also significantly contribute to the actual knowledge discovery by guiding the search using visual feedback.

In putting visual analysis to work on big data, it is not obvious what can be done by automated analysis and what should be done by interactive visual methods. In dealing with massive data, the use of automated methods is mandatory - and for some problems it may be sufficient to only use fully automated analysis methods, but there is also a wide range of problems where the use of interactive visual methods is necessary. The presentation discusses when it is useful to combine visualization and analytics techniques and it will also discuss the options how to combine techniques from both areas. Examples from a wide range of application areas illustrate the benefits of visual analytics techniques.

Differential Privacy and Preserving Validity in Adaptive Data Analysis

Aaron Roth

University of Pennsylvania

In this talk, we briefly introduce *differential privacy*, a rigorous privacy solution concept developed over the last decade [DMNS06], and explain how it allows various sorts of accurate data analyses to be performed while giving very strong privacy guarantees to the individuals in the data set. Among other things, we will describe recent work which allows the private generation of synthetic data, accurate for large numbers of statistics, even on very high dimensional data sets [GGH+14]. We then explain a very recent and surprising connection between *differential privacy* and *statistical validity* in adaptive data analysis, in which the guarantees of differential privacy can actually *improve* the accuracy of an analysis!

Machine learning and hypothesis testing in empirical science share a common goal: to identify generalizable facts about the distribution from which data points were drawn, while avoiding what is called *overfitting the data-set* in machine learning and *false discovery* in empirical science. The theory of how to do this is well developed when the analysis being performed is *non-adaptive* – i.e. when the set of hypotheses to be tested, the set of models to be fit, or the set of queries to be made to the data are fixed before the data is gathered, and do not change as a function of the outcomes observed. For example, standard sample complexity bounds in learning theory (see e.g. [KV94]) guarantee that for any set of k hypotheses, their value on a dataset sampled i.i.d. from a distribution will be very close to their value on the underlying distribution, so long as the data set contains a number of samples that scales with $\log k$. In contrast, the practice of data-analysis and scientific research is by its nature *adaptive*. Within a single study, new hypotheses are suggested as a result of the outcome of previous exploratory analysis on the data, and data sets are shared and re-used between studies leading to complex dependencies. Unfortunately, this adaptivity breaks the standard generalization guarantees in both machine learning and in the theory of hypothesis testing – in fact, it is not hard to demonstrate that it is *easy* to over-fit the data when adaptive data analysis is done using direct access to the data set.

We have given the first technique for performing arbitrary adaptive data analyses together with rigorous generalization guarantees, that requires a number of data points comparable to what would be required for *non-adaptive* data analyses [DFH+15]. Our result derives from a powerful transfer theorem, which informally states: *any analysis performed on a data-set subject to the guarantees of differential privacy automatically generalizes to the distribution from which the data was drawn.* This connection, which seems surprising at first blush, is in fact natural – differential privacy is an algorithmic stability guarantee, and algorithmic stability is known to prevent overfitting – informally because over-fitting is not a stable operation. The connection has important implications for adaptive data analysis precisely because we know how to perform adaptive data analysis subject to differential privacy! Our original result has since been improved upon, both quantitatively and in terms of generality [BSSU15, NS15].

References

[BSSU15] Bassily, R., Smith, A., Steinke, T., Ullman, J.: More general queries and less generalization error in adaptive data analysis. arXiv:1503.0484 (2015)

[DFH+15] Dwork, C., Feldman, V., Hardt, M., Pitassi, T., Reingold, O., Roth, A.: Preserving statistical validity in adaptive data analysis. In: Proceedings of the 47th Annual ACM Symposium on Theory of Computing. ACM (2015)

[DMNS06] Dwork, C., McSherry, F., Nissim, K., Smith, A.: Calibrating noise to sensitivity in private data analysis. In: Halevi, S., Rabin, T. (eds.) TCC 2006. LNCS, vol. 3876, pp. 265–284. Springer, Heidelberg (2006)

[GGH+14] Gaboardi, M., Jesús Gallego, E., Hsu, J., Roth, A., Steven Wu, Z.: Dual query: practical private query release for high dimensional data. In: Proceedings of the 31th International Conference on Machine Learning, ICML 2014, Beijing, China, 21–26 June 2014, vol. 32, pp. 1170–1178. JMLR.org (2014)

[KV94] Kearns, M.J., Vazirani, U.V.: An introduction to computational learning theory. MIT Press (1994)

[NS15] Nissim, K., Stemmer, U.: On the generalization properties of differential privacy. arXiv:1504.05800 (2015)

Contents

Invited Lectures

Streaming Methods in Data Analysis

Graham Cormode[✉]

University of Warwick, Coventry, UK
G.Cormode@Warwick.ac.uk

Abstract. A fundamental challenge in processing the massive quantities of information generated by modern applications is in extracting suitable representations of the data that can be stored, manipulated and interrogated on a single machine. A promising approach is in the design and analysis of compact summaries: data structures which capture key features of the data, and which can be created effectively over distributed, streaming data. Popular summary structures include the count distinct algorithms, which compactly approximate item set cardinalities, and sketches which allow vector norms and products to be estimated. These are very attractive, since they can be computed in parallel and combined to yield a single, compact summary of the data. This talk introduces the concepts and examples of compact summaries.

1 Introduction

Business and scientific communities all agree that "big data" holds both tremendous promise, and substantial challenges [8]. There is much potential for extracting useful intelligence and actionable information from the large quantities of data generated and captured by modern information processing systems. Big data challenges involve not only the sheer volume of the data, but the fact that it can represent a complex variety of entities and interactions between them, and new observations that arrive, often across multiple locations, at high velocity. Examples of applications that generate big data include:

- *Physical Data* from sensor deployments and scientific experiments—astronomy data from modern telescopes generates terabytes of data each night, while the data collected from a single particle physics experiment is too big to store;
- *Medical Data*, as we can now sequence whole genomes economically, generating data sets of the order of 200TB in one example [7];
- *Activity Data*, as human activity data is captured and stored in ever greater quantities and detail: interactions from online social networks, locations from GPS, Internet activity etc.

Across all of these disparate settings, certain common themes emerge. The data in question is large, and growing. The applications seek to extract patterns, trends or descriptions of the data. Ensuring the scalability of systems, and the timeliness and veracity of the analysis is vital in many of these applications. In order to realize the promise of these sources of data, we need new methods that can handle them effectively.

© Springer International Publishing Switzerland 2015
S. Maneth (Ed.): BICOD 2015, LNCS 9147, pp. 3–6, 2015.
DOI: 10.1007/978-3-319-20424-6_1

While such sources of big data are becoming increasingly common, the resources to process them (chiefly, processor speed, fast memory and slower disk) are growing at a slower pace. The consequence of this trend is that there is an urgent need for more effort directed towards capturing and processing data in many critical applications. Careful planning and scalable architectures are needed to fulfill the requirements of analysis and information extraction on big data. In response to these needs, new computational paradigms are being adopted to deal with the challenge of big data. Large scale distributed computation is a central piece: the scope of the computation can exceed what is feasible on a single machine, and so clusters of machines work together in parallel. On top of these architectures, parallel algorithms are designed which can take the complex task and break it into independent pieces suitable for distribution over multiple machines.

A central challenge within any such system is how to compute and represent complex features of big data in a way that can be processed by many single machines in parallel. A vital component is to be able to build and manipulate a *compact summary* of a large amount of data. This powerful notion of a small summary, in all its many and varied forms, is the subject of this tutorial. The idea of a summary is a natural and familiar one. It should represent something large and complex in a compact fashion. Inevitably, a summary must dispense with some of the detail and nuance of the object which it is summarizing. However, it should also preserve some key features of the object in a very accurate fashion. Effective compact summaries are often *approximate* in their answers to queries and *randomized*.

The theory of compact summaries can be traced back over four decades. A first example is the Morris Approximate Counter, which approximately counts quantities up to magnitude n using $O(\log \log n)$ bits, rather than the $\lceil \log n \rceil$ bits to count exactly [15]. Subsequently, there has been much interest in summaries in the context of *streaming algorithms*: these are algorithms that process data in the form of a stream of updates, and whose associated data structures can be seen as a compact summary [16]. More recently, the more general notion of *mergeable summaries* has arisen: summaries that can be computed on different portions of a dataset in isolation, then subsequently combined to form a summary of the union of the inputs [1]. It turns out that a large number streaming algorithms entail a mergeable summary, hence making this class of objects a large and interesting one.

There has been much effort expended on summary techniques over recent years, leading to the invention of powerful and effective summaries which have found applications in Internet Service Providers [5], Search Engines [12,17], and beyond.

2   Outline

The accompanying talk will introduce the notion of summaries, and outline ideas behind some of the most prominent examples, which include:

– Counts, approximate counts [15], and approximate frequencies [14]
– Count distinct, set cardinality, and set operations [9,10]

- Random projections with low-independence vectors to give *sketch* data structures [3,4,6]
- Summaries for medians and order statistics [11,13]
- Linear summaries for graphs: connectivity, bipartiteness and sparsification [2]
- Summaries for matrix and linear algebra operations [18]
- Problems for which no compact summary can exist, via communication complexity lower bounds.

Acknowledgments. This work supported in part by a Royal Society Wolfson Research Merit Award, funding from the Yahoo Research Faculty Research and Engagement Program, and European Research Council (ERC) Consolidator Grant ERC-CoG-2014-647557.

References

1. Agarwal, P., Cormode, G., Huang, Z., Phillips, J., Wei, Z.: Mergeable summaries. ACM Principles Database Sys. **38**(4), 1–28 (2012)
2. Ahn, K.J., Guha, S., McGregor, A.: Analyzing graph structure via linear measurements. In: ACM-SIAM Symposium on Discrete Algorithms (2012)
3. Alon, N., Matias, Y., Szegedy, M.: The space complexity of approximating the frequency moments. ACM Symp. Theor. Comput. **46**(2), 20–29 (1996)
4. Charikar, M., Chen, K., Farach-Colton, M.: Finding frequent items in data streams. In: Proceedings of the International Colloquium on Automata, Languages and Programming (ICALP) (2002)
5. Cormode, G., Korn, F., Muthukrishnan, S., Johnson, T., Spatscheck, O., Srivastava, O.: Holistic UDAFs at streaming speeds. In: ACM SIGMOD International Conference on Management of Data, pp. 35–46 (2004)
6. Cormode, G., Muthukrishnan, S.: An improved data stream summary: the Count-Min sketch and its applications. J. Algorithms **55**(1), 58–75 (2005)
7. Cravedi, K., Randall, T., Thompson. L.: 1000 genomes project data available on Amazon Cloud. NIH News, March 2012
8. Cukier, K.: Data, data everywhere. The Economist, February 2010
9. Flajolet, P., Martin, G.N.: Probabilistic counting algorithms for database applications. J. Comput. Syst. Sci. **31**, 182–209 (1985)
10. Flajolet, P., Fusy, É., Gandouet, O., Meunier, F.: Hyperloglog: the analysis of a near-optimal cardinality estimation algorithm. In: International Conference on Analysis of Algorithms (2007)
11. Greenwald, M., Khanna, S.: Space-efficient online computation of quantile summaries. In: ACM SIGMOD International Conference on Management of Data (2001)
12. Melnik, S., Gubarev, A., Long, J.J., Romer, G., Shivakumar, S., Tolton, M., Vassilakis, T.: Dremel: interactive analysis of web-scale datasets. In: International Conference on Very Large Data Bases, pp. 330–339 (2010)
13. Metwally, A., Agrawal, D., El Abbadi, A.: Efficient computation of frequent and top-k elements in data streams. In: International Conference on Database Theory (2005)
14. Misra, J., Gries, D.: Finding repeated elements. Sci. Comput. Program. **2**, 143–152 (1982)

15. Morris, R.: Counting large numbers of events in small registers. Commun. ACM **21**(10), 840–842 (1977)
16. Muthukrishnan, S.: Data Streams: Algorithms and Applications. Now Publishers, Norwell (2005)
17. Pike, R., Dorward, S., Griesemer, R., Quinlan, S.: Interpreting the data: parallel analysis with sawzall. Dyn. Grids Worldwide Comput. **13**(4), 277–298 (2005)
18. Woodruff, D.: Sketching as a tool for numerical linear algebra. Found. Trends Theor. Comput. Sci. **10**(1–2), 1–157 (2014)

Data Integration

A Framework for Scalable Correlation of Spatio-temporal Event Data

Stefan Hagedorn[1]($\boxtimes$), Kai-Uwe Sattler[1], and Michael Gertz[2]

[1] Technische Universität Ilmenau, Ilmenau, Germany
{Stefan.Hagedorn,Kai-Uwe.Sattler}@tu-ilmenau.de
[2] Heidelberg University, Heidelberg, Germany
gertz@informatik.uni-heidelberg.de

Abstract. Spatio-temporal event data do not only arise from sensor readings, but also in information retrieval and text analysis. However, such events extracted from a text corpus may be imprecise in both dimensions. In this paper we focus on the task of event correlation, i.e., finding events that are similar in terms of space and time. We present a framework for Apache Spark that provides correlation operators that can be configured to deal with such imprecise event data.

1 Introduction

An event is often described as "something that happens at some place at some time". Thus, events inherently have a spatial and a temporal component. These spatio-temporal events do not only origin from sensor readings, but can also be extracted from text corpora like news, weblogs, and tweets.

The task we focus on in this paper is to find events that are correlated to a given event in terms of its time and place of occurrence. The result is, e.g., a list of pointers to documents in which similar events have been detected. For such correlation tasks, we are facing the following problems:

- First, event specifications are often imprecise. For example, for the event extracted from the sentence "Obama visited Germany in April 2009", we do not know (using only the text source) which part of Germany Obama visited or at what exact dates he visited Germany.
- Second, for comparing events in terms of their similarity solely based on their temporal and geographic components, we need a distance measure.
- Third, depending on the specific application different correlation techniques are needed: for finding similar events, nearest neighbor or skyline queries are an appropriate approach, whereas for determining hot spots, clustering (such as DBSCAN) might be a better choice.
- Finally, because (extracted) event data can be large datasets, scalable techniques are required. Modern data processing frameworks such as Apache Hadoop or Spark provide a suitable platform for addressing this challenge. In [2] an adaption of DBSCAN to MapReduce is proposed, whereas in [1] and [4] adaptions of the skyline algorithm are shown.

© Springer International Publishing Switzerland 2015
S. Maneth (Ed.): BICOD 2015, LNCS 9147, pp. 9–15, 2015.
DOI: 10.1007/978-3-319-20424-6_2

In this paper, we propose a framework that addresses the problem of determining the correlation between events. For this, we introduce an event model and indicate different distance measures for both the temporal and geographic components of events. We further introduce a set of basic operators for preparing as well as exploring and analyzing event data correlations. These operators are provided as transformation operators in Apache Spark and allow to define application-specific spatio-temporal event analysis pipelines including top-k and skyline processing as well as (density-based) clustering.

2   Event Data Model

We assume an event model in which information about events has been extracted from some document and is represented by a temporal and a geographic component along with other information like an ID and metadata such as the origin. The expressions underlying these components are based on concept hierarchies for time and space.

Temporal expressions can be of different granularities, with days being the finest and years the coarsest level of granularity. Although further granularities such as weeks or centuries can be included. For the sake of simplicity, in the following, we only focus on days, months, and years. We denote the corresponding domains as $T = \{T_{day}, T_{month}, T_{year}\}$.

Analogously, geographic expressions are taken from the domains in $G = \{G_{city}, G_{state}, G_{country}\}$. We assume that with each expression a spatial object in the form of a single polygon (without holes) is associated.

Definition 1. *(Event) Given concept hierarchies T and G for temporal and geographic expressions, respectively. An event $e = \langle t, g \rangle$ consists of a temporal expression t with $t.type \in T$ and a geographic expression g with $g.type \in G$.*

Examples of (imprecise) event specifications are (2013-09-02, Munich), (1955, Germany), or (2000-04, Bavaria). To account for these types of imprecision, in our framework we make the following assumptions:

1. Temporal and geographic expressions of the finest granularity are certain.
2. Every temporal (resp. geographic) expression of type P' that refines a given temporal (resp. geographic) expression of type P, with P' being of finer granularity than P, is equally likely.

Distance Measures. To compute correlations between events, we need a distance measure that takes both the temporal and the geographic component of an event into account, both of which can be imprecise. For the most fine-grained, point-based locations (e.g., cities) and days, this is trivial, resulting in a scalar value for time (e.g., distance in days) and location (e.g., distance in kilometers), which can be combined into some single (weighted) distance value. For events having an imprecise temporal or geographic expressions, different types of distance functions are meaningful and can be specified accordingly.

In general, there are two approaches for realizing a distance function for imprecise event data. First, dates representing a month or year can be mapped to intervals of days (e.g., "2014-05" can be mapped to [2014-05-01, 2014-05-30]) with each subinterval being valid instance of "2014-05". Similarly, a country can be mapped to a polygon or minimum bounding box. Then, a function is devised that determines the distance between intervals (for time) and boxes/polygons (for regions). Each such a function can either yield a single scalar value (e.g., the average distance between points of two intervals/boxes), or an interval, giving the minimum and maximum distance between two intervals/boxes. In our current framework, we only consider the former case where single scalar values for both the temporal and geographic component are determined and linearly combined using a weight. That is, for two events e_1 and e_2, we assume a distance function $dist(e_1, e_2) := w_t \ dist_t(e_1, e_2) + w_g \ dist_g(e_1, e_2)$, with $dist_e$ and $dist_g$ functions for determining the distance between intervals and regions/boxes, respectively, and $w_t, w_g \in [0, 1], w_t + w_g = 1$.

3   Techniques for Correlating Event Data

Correlating events means to find events in the dataset that have something in common or which have the same or a similar context. In this paper, we focus on the spatio-temporal aspect of events, which means we consider the similarity of events in terms of their spatial and/or temporal properties. Depending on the specific application different approaches can be used to determine correlations.

Nearest Neighbor Queries. Nearest neighbor queries represent the most straight-forward solution. Given a set of events $\mathcal{E}$, a reference event e_r and a distance function $dist$, the task is to find the set $kNN(e_r)$ of the k nearest events. In the case of our spatio-temporal event data this requires a single distance measure, which is usually defined using weights for the spatial and temporal distances.

Skyline. Defining appropriate weights is often difficult. Skyline queries avoid this problem. Adapted to our scenario, the notion of the Skyline algorithm is to find those events in $\mathcal{E}$ that "match" a query event $q = \langle t_q, g_q \rangle$ best. Since we consider two dimension for events, time and space, it is thus intuitive to employ a skyline-based approach as there might be events that match t_q well but not g_q, and vice versa. A core concept of skylines is the dominance relationship. The skyline S_q consists of all events that are not dominated by any other event in $\mathcal{E}$ with respect to q. Because the dominance of an event with respect to another event is decided by their respective distances to q, the distance function outlined in the previous section come into play.

Clustering. Clustering represents another useful technique for correlating event data. Applied to the problem of event correlation we can form clusters of events on their distance values and, in this way, events belonging to the same cluster are considered to be correlated. Focusing only on the spatial and temporal dimension results in clusters of events that occur in close proximity in terms of space and time.

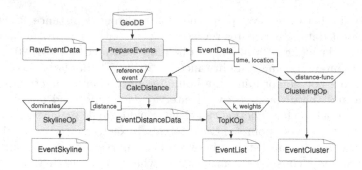

Fig. 1. Framework showing operators and event analysis pipeline

4   A Spark-Based Correlation Framework

Given the event data model, the distance functions, and the set of correlation functions described above, the goal of our work is to provide a framework for scalable event data correlation. As the underlying platform we have chosen Apache Spark[1], but our framework can be easily ported to other platforms providing a similar (Scala-based) API such as the Apache Flink[2] project. Figure 1 shows the components of the framework and their role in an event analysis pipeline.

The core components are the following operators implemented as transformations on Spark's resilient distributed datasets (RDD):

PrepareEvents: This operator transforms a set of raw (textual) event data into a set of event records $\langle t, q \rangle$ conforming to our framework. This means that textual temporal and spatial properties are normalized into numerical values, i.e., date/time values and points or polygons for the spatial descriptions such as names of cities or locations. For the latter, a service such as GeoNames[3] can be used.

CalcDistance: This implements a transformation operator for calculating the spatial and temporal distance *dist* of each event of a RDD to a given reference event.

TopKOp: This operator computes the top-k list of events from an input RDD produced by CalcDistance. Parameters to this operator are k as well as the weights for the geographic (w_g) and temporal (w_t) distance.

SkylineOp: This operator computes the skyline of event records from a RDD produced by CalcDistance. The dominance relation can be passed as parameter to the operator.

ClusteringOp: Finding groups of correlated events is realized by the ClusteringOp operator implementing a parallel variant of DBSCAN [3] for spatio-temporal data. Parameters are the standard clustering parameters ε

---

[1] http://spark.apache.org.
[2] http://flink.apache.org.
[3] http://www.geonames.org.

and MinPts as well as a global distance function taking both spatial and temporal distances into account.

While the implementation of `PrepareEvents`, `CalcDistance`, and – a sort-based – `TopKOp` operator is rather straightforward, efficient skyline processing and density-based clustering require more effort. As mentioned in Sect. 1, there already exist some proposals for MapReduce-based implementations of these operators that have inspired our Spark implementations.

Both `SkylineOp` and `ClusteringOp` are based on a grid partitioning, where the dimensions of the grid are either the spatial and temporal dimensions (in case of skyline processing) or longitude, latitude, and time in case of clustering. For simplicity, we assume – non-optimal – equally-sized grid cells representing partitions of Spark's RDDs.

Our skyline operator implements the idea presented in [4] by computing in a first phase bitstrings representing grid cells containing data points. This can be done in parallel without moving data. By combining these bitstrings in a reduce step, dominated as well as empty cells can be pruned. In the second phase, all nodes compute a local skyline of their data by taking the information from this global bitstring into account. Finally, the local skylines are merged.

For density-based clustering, grid cells must not be disjoint in order to determine the neighborhood for objects at the border of cells. Thus, we compute an overlap between neighboring cells and assign objects in this overlap area to its neighbor cells, too. Next, for each cell a local DBSCAN is performed. Note that compared to the skyline processing strategy, this requires to repartition data according their grid cell membership. Finally, we build a global graph of all local clusters in order to merge clusters from different cells.

5 Use Cases

In this section, we show the outcome of the skyline and top-k operations. Due to space limitations we do not present a full performance evaluation. Our test dataset was crawled from the website `eventful.com` and contains 122,467 events. It consists only of events that took place in Germany where the earliest event appeared on 2007-06-30 and the latest on 2020-06-30. For the test of our operators, we manually removed all events in the eastern part of Germany (which is the federal state of Saxony).

Figure 2 shows the spatial distribution of all events in our dataset. On the left, the skyline (marked with +) is shown. The right figure shows the result of the top-k query ($k = 10$; marked with ●). The reference point for both queries is shown as ◆. One can see that the spatio-temporal skyline not only finds correlated events that have both a small spatial and temporal distance to the reference event, but also considers events as correlated that are near to the reference event in at least one dimension. The two shown skyline points in the north and the south have a large spatial distance, but only a small temporal distance and thus, are considered correlated to the reference event. On the other hand, the top-k operator accepts user-defined weights for the spatial and temporal distances

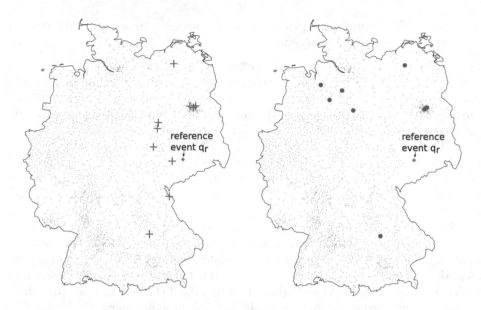

Fig. 2. Left: the skyline (+); right: top-10 result (•) for a reference event (♦).

to express a desired preference over one or the other dimension. In the given example these weights are $w_g = 0.10$ for the geographic and $w_t = 0.90$ for the temporal dimension, i.e., the temporal distance is considered more important. As Fig. 2 shows, the resulting points have a large geographic distance, but are near to the reference event in the temporal dimension. Note, there are events that take place at the exact same position, so that they cover each other in the figure and appear as one point. Thus, the figure shows only eight result points. Due to space limitations, we cannot show the results of the spatio-temporal clustering.

6   Conclusions and Ongoing Work

In this paper, we presented a framework for Apache Spark that provides operators for computing correlated events. We provide operators for data import and cleaning as well as operators for the actual correlation tasks. These operators can be configured by their parameters and the distance function - for which we also provide several alternatives. Our ongoing work focuses more on imprecise data and respective distance functions that return intervals instead of scalar values, which will result in, e.g., SkyBands instead of Skylines.

Acknowledgement. This work was funded by the DFG under grant no. SA782/22.

References

1. Chen, L., Hwang, K., Wu, J.: MapReduce skyline query processing with a new angular partitioning approach. In: IPDPSW (2012)
2. Dai, B.-R., Lin, I.-C.: Efficient map/reduce-based DBSCAN algorithm with optimized data partition. In: CLOUD (2012)
3. Ester, M., Kriegel, H.P., Sander, J., Xu, X.: A density-based algorithm for discovering clusters in large spatial databases with noise. In: KDD (1996)
4. Mullesgaard, K., Pederseny, J.L., Lu, H., Zhou, Y.: Efficient skyline computation in MapReduce. In: EDBT (2014)

Towards More Data-Aware
Application Integration

Daniel Ritter (✉)

SAP SE, Technology Development, Dietmar-Hopp-Allee 16,
69190 Walldorf, Germany
daniel.ritter@sap.com

Abstract. Although most business application data is stored in relational databases, programming languages and wire formats in integration middleware systems are not table-centric. Due to costly format conversions, data-shipments and faster computation, the trend is to "pushdown" the integration operations closer to the storage representation. We address the alternative case of defining declarative, table-centric integration semantics within standard integration systems. For that, we replace the current operator implementations for the well-known *Enterprise Integration Patterns* by equivalent "in-memory" table processing, and show a practical realization in a conventional integration system for a non-reliable, "data-intensive" messaging example. The results of the runtime analysis show that table-centric processing is promising already in standard, "single-record" message routing and transformations, and can potentially excel the message throughput for "multi-record" table messages.

Keywords: Datalog · Message-based/Data integration · Integration system

1 Introduction

Integration middleware systems in the sense of EAI brokers [5] address the fundamental need for (business) application integration by acting as a messaging hub between applications. As such, they have become ubiquitous in service-oriented enterprise computing environments. Messages are mediated between applications mostly in wire formats based on XML (e. g., SOAP for Web Services).

The advent of more "data-aware" integration scenarios (observation *O1*) put emphasis on (near) "real-time" or online processing (*O2*), which requires us to revisit the standard integration capabilities, system design and architectural decisions. For instance, in the financial/utilities industry, *China Mobile* generates 5–8 TB of call detail records per day, which have to be processed by integration systems (i. e., mostly message routing and transformation patterns), "convergent charging"[1] (CC) and "invoicing" applications (not further discussed). In addition, the standard XML-processing has to give ground to other

---

[1] Solace Solutions, visited 02/2015; last update 2012: http://www.solacesystems.com/ techblog/deconstructing-kafka.

© Springer International Publishing Switzerland 2015
S. Maneth (Ed.): BICOD 2015, LNCS 9147, pp. 16–28, 2015.
DOI: 10.1007/978-3-319-20424-6_3

formats like JSON and CSV (*O3*). These observations (*O1–3*) are backed by similar scenarios from sports management (e. g., online player tracking) and the rapidly growing amount of data from the *Internet of Things* and *Cyber Physical System* domains. For those scenarios, an architectural setup with systems like *Message Queuing* (MQ) are used as reliable "message buffers" (i. e., queues, topics) that handle "bursty" incoming messages and smoothen peak loads (cf. Fig. 1). Integration systems are used as message consumers, which (transactionally) dequeue, transform (e. g., translation, content enrichment) and route messages to applications. For reliable transport and message provenance, integration systems require relational Database Systems, in which most of the (business) application data is currently stored (*O4*). When looking at the throughput capabilities of the named systems, software-/hardware-based MQ systems like *Apache Kafka* or *Solace*(See footnote 1) are able to process several millions of messages per second. RDBMS benchmarks like TPC-H, TPC-DI measure queries and inserts in PB sizes, while simple, header-based routing benchmarks for integration systems show message throughputs of few thousands of messages per second [2] (*O5*). In other words, MQ and DBMS (e. g., RDBMS, NoSQL, NewSQL) systems are already addressing observations *O1–5*. Integration systems, however, seem to not be there yet.

Compared to MQs, integration systems work on message data, which seems to make the difference in message throughput. We argue that integration operations, represented by *Enterprise Integration Patterns* (EIP) [9], can be mapped to an "in-memory" representation of the table-centric RDBMS operations to profit from their efficient and fast evaluation. Early ideas on this were brought up in our position papers [11,13]. In this work, we follow up to shed light on the observed discrepancies. We revisit the EIP building blocks and operator model of integration systems, for which we define RDBMS-like table operators (so far without changing their semantics) as a symbiosis of RDBMS and integration processing, e. g., by using Datalog [17]. We choose Datalog as example of an efficiently computable, table-like integration co-processing facility close to the actual storage representation with expressive foundations (e. g., recursion), which we call *Table-centric Integration Patterns* (TIP). To show the applicability of our approach to integration scenarios along observations *O1–5* we conduct an experimental message throughput analysis for selected routing and transformation patterns, where we carefully embed the TIP definitions into the open-source integration system *Apache Camel* [3] that implements most of the EIPs. Not changing the EIP semantics means that table operations are executed on "single-record" table messages. We give an outlook to "multi-record" table message processing.

The remainder of this paper is organized along its main contributions. After a more comprehensive explanation of the motivating CC example and a brief sketch of our approach in Sect. 2, we analyse common integration patterns with respect to their extensibility for alternative operator models and define a table-centric operator/processing model that can be embedded into the patterns (still) aligned with their semantics in Sect. 3. In Sect. 4 we apply our approach to a conventional integration system and briefly describe and discuss our experimental performance analysis, and we draw an experimental sketch of the idea of "multi-record" table message processing. Section 5 examines related work and Sect. 6 concludes the paper.

2   Motivating Example and General Approach

In this section, the motivating "Call Record Detail" example in the context of the "Convergent Charging" application is described more comprehensively along with a sketch of our approach. Figure 1 shows aspects of both as part of a common integration system architecture.

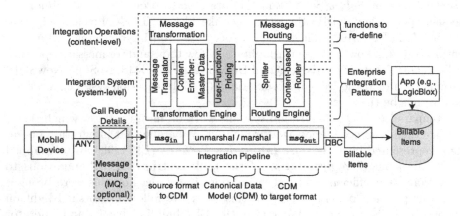

Fig. 1. High-level overview of the convergent charging integration scenario.

2.1   The Convergent Charging Scenario

Mobile service providers like *China Mobile* generate large amounts of "Call Record Details" (CRDs) per day that have been processed by applications like SAP Convergent Charging[2] (CC). As shown in Fig. 1, these CRDs are usually sent from mobile devices to integration systems (optionally buffered in an MQ system), where they are translated to an intermediate (application) format and enriched by additional master data (e. g., business partner, product). The master data helps to calculate pricing information, with which the message is split into several messages, denoting billable items (i. e., item for billing) that are routed to their receivers (e. g., DB). From there applications like *SAP Convergent Invoicing* generate legally binding payment documents. Alternatively, new application and data analytics stacks like *LogicBlox* [7], *WebdamLog* [1], and *SAP S/4 HANA*[3] (not shown) access the data for further processing. Some of these

---

[2] SAP Convergent Charging, visited 04/2015: https://help.sap.com/cc.
[3] SAP S/4 HANA, visited 04/2015: http://discover.sap.com/S4HANA.

"smart" stacks even provide declarative, Datalog-like language for application and user-interface programming, which complements our integration approach. As motivated before, standard integration systems have problems processing the high number and rate of incoming messages, which usually leads to an "offline", multi-step processing using indirections like ETL systems and pushing integration logic to the applications, leading to long-running CC runs.

2.2 General Approach

The *Enterprise Integration Patterns* (EIPs) [9] define "de-facto" standard operations on the header (i. e., payload's meta-data) and body (i. e., message payload) of a message, which are normally implemented in the integration system's host language (e. g., Java, C#). This way, the actual integration operation (i. e., the content developed by an integration expert like mapping programs and routing conditions) can be differentiated from the implementation of the runtime system that invokes the content operations and processes their results. For instance, Fig. 1 shows the separation of concerns within integration systems with respect to "system-related" and "content-related parts" and sketches which pattern operations to re-define using relational table operators, while leaving the runtime system (implementation) as is. The goal is to only change these operations and make integration language additions for table-centric processing within the conventional integration system, while preserving the general integration semantics like *Quality of Service* (e. g., best effort, exactly once) and the *Message Exchange Pattern* (e. g., one-way, two-way). In other words, the content-related parts of the pattern definitions are evaluated by an "in-process" table operation processor (e. g., a Datalog system), which is embedded into the standard integration system and invoked during the message processing.

3   Table-Centric Integration Patterns

Before defining *Table-centric Integration Patterns* (short TIP) for message routing and transformation more formally, let us recall the encoding of some relevant, basic database operations/operators into Datalog: join, projection, union, and selection. The join of two relations $r(x,y)$ and $s(y,z)$ on parameter y is encoded as $j(x,y,z) \leftarrow r(x,y), s(y,z)$, which projects all three parameters to the resulting predicate j. More explicitly, a projection on parameter x of relation $r(x,y)$ is encoded as $p(x) \leftarrow r(x,y)$. The union of $r(x,y)$ and $s(x,y)$ is $u(x,y) \leftarrow r(x,y)$. $u(x,y) \leftarrow s(x,y)$, which combines several relations to one. The selection $r(x,y)$ according to a built-in predicate $\phi(x)$, where $\phi(x)$ can contain constants and free variables, is encoded as $s(x,y) \leftarrow r(x,y), \phi(x)$. Built-in predicates can be binary relations on numbers such as $<, <=, =$, binary relations on strings such as *equals, contains, startswith* or predicates applied to expressions based on binary operators like $+, -, *, /$ (e. g., $x = p(y) + 1$), and operations on relations like $z = max(p(x,y), x), z = min(p(x,y), x)$, which would assign the maximal or the minimal value x of a predicate p to a parameter z.

Although our approach allows each single pattern definition to evaluate arbitrary, recursive Datalog operations and built-in predicates, the Datalog to pattern mapping tries to identify and focus on the most relevant table-centric operations for a specific pattern. An overview of the mapping of all discussed message routing and transformation operations to Datalog constructs is shown in Fig. 2 and is subsequently discussed. Subsequently, we enumerate common EIPs and separate system- from content-related parts more formally for the TIP definition by example of standard Datalog.

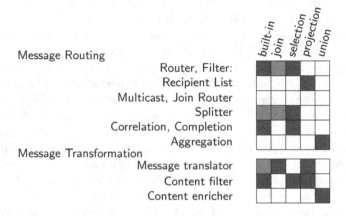

Fig. 2. Message routing and transformation patterns mapped to Datalog. Most common Datalog operations for a single pattern are marked "dark blue", less common ones "light blue", and possible but uncommon ones "white" (Color figure online).

3.1   Canonical Data Model

When connecting applications, various operations are executed on the transferred messages in a uniform way. The arriving message instances are converted into an internal format understood by the pattern implementation, called the *Canonical Data Model* (CDM) [9], before the messages are transformed to the target format. Hence, if a new application is added to the integration solution, only conversions between the CDM and the application format have to be created. Consequently, for a table-centric re-definition of integration patterns, we define a CDM similar to relational database tables as *Datalog programs*, which consists of a collection of facts/a table, optional (supporting) rules as message body and an optional set of meta-facts that describes the actual data as header. For instance, the data-part of an incoming message in JSON format is transformed to a collection of `Open-Next-Close` (ONC)-style table iterators, each representing a table row or fact. These ONC-operators are part of the evaluated execution plan for more efficient evaluation.

3.2   Message Routing Patterns

In this section the message routing pattern implementations are re-defined, which can be seen as control and data flow definitions of an integration channel pipeline. For that, they access the message to route it within the integration system and eventually to its receiver(s). They influence the channel and message cardinality as well as the content of the message.

Content-Based Router/Message Filter. The most common routing patterns that determine the message's route based on its body are the *Content-based Router* and the *Message Filter*. The stateless router has a channel cardinality of $1 : n$, where n is the number of leaving channels, while one channel enters the router, and a message cardinality of $1 : 1$. The entering message constitutes the leaving message according to the evaluation of a *routing condition*. This condition is a function rc, with $\{bool_1, bool_2, ..., bool_n\} := rc(msg_{in}, conds)$, where msg_{in} is the entering message. The function rc evaluates to a list of Boolean output $\{bool_1, bool_2, ..., bool_n\}$ based on a list of conditions $conds$ of the same arity (e. g., Datalog rules in Listing 1.1) for each of the $n \in \mathbb{N}$ leaving channels. In case several conditions evaluate to `true`, only the first matching channel receives the message.

Through the separation of concerns, a system-level routing function provides the entering message msg_{in} to the content-level implementation (i. e., in CDM representation), which is configured by $conds$. Since standard Datalog rules are truth judgements, and hence do not directly produce Boolean values, we decided, for performance and generality considerations, to add an additional function $bool_{rc}$ to the integration system. The function $bool_{rc}$ converts the output list $fact$ of the routing function from a truth judgement to a Boolean by emitting `true` if $fact \neq \emptyset$, and `false` otherwise. Accordingly we define the TIP routing condition as $fact := rc_{tip}(msg_{in}, conds)$, while being evaluated for each channel condition (e. g., selection/built-in predicates). The integration system will then use the function $bool_{rc}$ to convert this into a Boolean value. For the message filter, which is a special case of the router that differs only from its channel cardinality of 1:1 and message cardinality of 1:[0|1], the filter condition is equal to rc_{tip}.

Splitter. The *Splitter* pattern has a channel cardinality of 1:1 and creates new, leaving messages. Thereby the splitter breaks the entering message into multiple (smaller) messages (i. e., message cardinality of 1:n). Hereby, the stateless splitter uses a split condition sc on the content-level, with $\{out_1, out_2, ..., out_n\} := sc(msg_{in}, conds)$, which accesses the entering message's body to determine a list of distinct body parts $\{out_1, out_2, ..., out_n\}$, based on a list of conditions $conds$, that are each inserted to a list of individual, newly created, leaving messages $\{msg_{out1}, msg_{out2}, ..., msg_{outn}\}$ with $n \in \mathbb{N}$ by a splitter function. The header and attachments are copied from the entering to each leaving message.

The re-defined split condition sc_{tip} evaluates a set of Datalog rules as $conds$ (i. e., mostly selection, and sometimes built-in and join constructs; the latter two are marked "light blue"). Each part of the body out_i with $i \in \mathbb{N}$ is a set of facts that is passed to a split function, which wraps each set into a single message.

3.3 Message Transformation Patterns

The transformation patterns exclusively target the content of the messages in terms of format conversations and content modifications.

The stateless *Message Translator* changes the structure or format of the entering message without generating a new one (i.e., channel, message cardinality 1:1). For that, the translator computes the transformed structure by evaluating a mapping program mt (e.g., Datalog rules in Listing 1.2), with $msg_{out}.body := mt(msg_{in}.body)$. Thereby the field content can be altered. The related *Content Filter* and *Content Enricher* patterns can be subsumed by the general *Content Modifier* pattern and share the same characteristics as the translator pattern. The filter evaluates a filter function mt, which only filters out parts of the message structure (e.g., fields or values) and the enricher adds new fields or values as *data* to the existing content structure using an enricher program ep, with $msg_{out}.body := ep(msg_{in}.body, data)$.

The re-definition of the transformation function mt_{tip} for the message translator mainly uses `join` and `projection` (plus `built-in` for numerical calculations and string operations, thus marked "light blue") and `selection`, `projection` and `built-in` (mainly numerical expressions and character operations) for the content filter. While projections allow for rather static, structural filtering, the built-in and selection operators can be used to filter more dynamically based on the content. The resulting Datalog programs are passed as $msg_{out}.body$. In addition, the re-defined enricher program ep_{tip} mainly uses `union` operations to add additional *data* to the message as Datalog programs.

4 Experimental Evaluation

As *System under Test* (SuT) for an experimental evaluation we used the open source, Java-based *Apache Camel* integration system [3] in version 2.14.0, which implements most of the EIPs. The Camel system allows content-level extensions through several interfaces, with which the TIP definitions were implemented and embedded (e.g., own Camel `Expression` definitions for existing patterns, and Camel `Processor` definitions for custom or non-supported patterns). The Datalog system we used for the measurements is a Java-based, standard naïve-recursive Datalog processor (i.e., without stratification) [17] in version 0.0.6 from [14].

Subsequently, the basic setup and execution of the measurements are introduced. However, due to brevity, a more detailed description of the setup, the integration scenarios and more detailed results are provided in the Suppl. Material of the extended version of this paper [12].

4.1 Setup

In the absence of an EIP benchmark, which we are currently developing on the basis of this paper, we used *Apache JMeter*[4] in version 2.12 as a load generator client that sends messages to the SuT. We implemented a JMeter Sampler, which allows to inject messages directly to the integration pipeline via a Camel `direct` endpoint/adapter. For the throughput measurements, we used the JMeter `jp@gc` transaction per second listener plugin from the standard package.

To measure the message throughput in a "data-intensive" (cf. *O1*), non-reliable integration scenario, we use the standard TPC-H order, customer and nation data sets. We added additional, unique message identifier and type fields and translate the single records to JSON objects (cf. *O3*), each representing the payload of a single message (i.e., "single-record" table message). In this way we generated 1.5 million order-only messages (i.e., TPC-H scale level 1) and the same amount of "multi-format" customer/nation messages, consisting of one customer and all 25 nation records per message (in the "single-record" table message case). During the measurements these messages are streamed to the Camel endpoint, serialized to either Java Objects for the Camel-Java and to the ONC representation for the Camel-Datalog case (cf. recall ONC-iterators as canonical data model).

All measurements are conducted on a HP Z600 work station, equipped with two Intel processors clocked at 2.67 GHz with a total of 12 cores, 24 GB of main memory, running a 64-bit Windows 7 SP1 and a JDK version 1.7.0. The JMeter Sampler and the integration system pipeline JVM process get 5 GB heap space.

4.2 "Single-Record"/"Multi-Format" Table Message Processing

Instead of testing all discussed patterns, we focus on the identified table-operations (e.g., `selection/built-in`, `projection`, `join`) and show the respective evaluation by example of a representative pattern (cf. Fig. 2). The measurements for selection and projection use the TPC-H `Order`-based, approximately 4 kB messages (i.e., 1.5 million order messages). The `union` operation (e.g., aggregation strategy, content enricher) is not tested.

We measured the selection/built-in operations in a content-based router scenario with a routing condition *tip_rc* (cf. Listing 1.1), which routes the order message to its receiver based on *conds* for {string equality, integer bigger than} on fields {objecttype, ototalprice}. The *bool$_{rc}$* function is implemented in Java to pass the expected value to the runtime system on system-level. The corresponding "hand-coded" content-level Camel-Java implementation uses JSON path statements for $O(1)$ element access and conducts the type-specific condition evaluation. The routing condition is defined to route $904,500$ of the 1.5 million messages to the first and the rest to the second receiver. Similarly, the projection operation is measured using a message translator. The translator projects the fields of the incoming order message to a target format (cf. Listing 1.2) using

---

[4] Apache JMeter, visited 02/2015: http://jmeter.apache.org/.

a mt_{tip} implementation or a "hand-coded" projection on the Java Object representation. Now, the "multi-format" customer messages (cf. *O1*) with nation records as processing context are used to measure a routing condition with selection/built-in and join operations (cf. Listing 1.3). The customer message is routed, if and only if, the customers balance (ACCTBAL) is bigger than 3,000 and the customer is from the European region determined through join via nation key.

Listing 1.1. Routing condition: tip_rc

```
1 cbr−order ( id , − ,OTOTALPRICE, − ): −
2 order ( id , otype , − ,
3 OTOTALPRICE, −OPRIORITY, − ) ,
4 =(OPRIORITY, ”1−URGENT” )
5 >(OTOTALPRICE, 1 0 0 0 0 0.00 ).
```

Listing 1.2. Message translation program: mt_{tip}

```
1 conv−order ( id , otype ,
2 ORDERKEY, CUSTKEY, SHIPPRIORITY): −
3 order ( id , otype ,ORDERKEY,
4 CUSTKEY, − ,SHIPPRIORITY, − ).
```

Listing 1.3. Routing condition with join over "multi-format" message

```
1 cbr−cust (CUSTKEY, − ): −
2 customer ( cid , ctype ,CUSTKEY, − ,
3 CNATIONKEY, − ,ACCTBAL, − ) ,
4 nation ( nid , ntype ,NATIONKEY, − ,
5 NREGIONKEY, − ) ,
6 >(ACCTBAL, 3 0 0 0.0 ) ,
7 =(CNATIONKEY, NATIONKEY)
8 =(NREGIONKEY, 3 ).
```

Table 1. Throughput measurements for format conversion, message routing and tranformation patterns based on 4 kB messages generated from 1.5 million standard TPC-H orders records.

Format		Content-based Routing			Message Transformation	
Conv. (msec)	Time (sec)	Mean (tps)	Time (sec)	Mean (tps) (Join)	Time (sec)	Mean (tps)
Camel- 7,239.60	108	**13,761.47**	126	11,904.76	**103**	**14,423.08**
Datalog +/-152.69		+/-340.08		+/-261.20		+/-228.74
Camel- **6,648.50**	115	12,931.03	**117**	**12,633.26**	107	13,888.89
Java +/-143.55		+/-304,90		+/-176.89		+/-247.40
Datalog- 7,239.60	12	122,467.58	13	116,780.00	11	133,053.20
Bulk +/-152.69		+/-		+/-		+/-
(size=10)		2,532.42		1714,92		1,645.39

The throughput test streams all 1.5 million order/customer messages to the pipeline. The performance measurement results are depicted in Table 1 for a single thread execution. Measurements with multiple threads show a scaling up to factor 10 of the results, with a saturation around 36 threads (i. e., factor of number of cores; not shown). The stream conversion to JSON object aggregated for all messages is slightly faster than for ONC. However, in both order messages cases the TIP-based implementation reaches a slightly higher transaction per second rate (tps), which lets the processing end 7 s and 4 s earlier respectively, due to the natural processing of ONC iterators in the Datalog engine. Although the measured 99 % confidence intervals do not overlap, the execution times are similar. The rather theoretical case of increasing the number of selection/built-in operations on the order messages (e. g., date before/after, string contains) showed a stronger impact for the Camel-Java case than the Camel-Datalog case (not shown). In general, the Camel-Java implementation concludes with a routing decision as soon as a logical conjunction is found, while the conjunctive Datalog implementation currently evaluates all conditions before returning. In the context of integration operations this is not necessary, thus could be improved by adapting the Datalog evaluation for that, which we could experimentally show (not shown; out of scope for this paper). The measured throughput of the content-based router with `join` processing on "multi-format" the 1.5 million TPC-H customer/nation messages again shows similar results. Only this time, the too simple `NestedLoopJoin` implementation in the used Datalog engine causes a loss of nine seconds compared to the "hand-coded" JSON join implementation.

4.3 Outlook: "Multi-record" Table Message Processing

The discussed measurements assume that a message has a "single-record" payload, which results in 1.5 million messages with one record/message identifier each. So far, the JSON to ONC conversion creates ONC collections with only one table iterator (to conform with EIP semantics). However, the nature of our approach allows us to send ONC collections with several entries (each representing a unique message payload with message identifier). Knowing that this would change the semantics of several patterns (e. g., the content-based router), we conducted the same test as before with "multi-record" table messages of bulk size 10, which reduces the required runtime to 12 s for the router and 11 s for the translator, which can still be used with its original definition (cf. Table 1). Increasing the bulk size to 100 or even 1,000 reduces the required time to 1 s, which means that all 1.5 million messages can be processed with one step in one single thread. Hereby, increasing the bulk size means reducing the number of message collections, while increasing the rows in the single collection. The impressive numbers are due to the efficient table-centric Datalog evaluation on fewer, multi-row message collections. The higher throughput comes with the cost of a higher latency. The noticed join performance issue can be seen in the Datalog-bulk case as well, which required 13 steps/seconds to process the 1.5 million customer/nation messages.

5 Related Work

The application of table-centric operators to current integration systems has not been considered before, up to our knowledge, and was only recently introduced by our position paper [13], which discusses the expressiveness of table-centric/logic programming for integration processing on the content level.

The work on Java systems like Telegraph Dataflow [16], and Jaguar [19]) can be considered related work in the area of programming languages on application systems for faster, data-aware processing. These approaches are mainly targeting to make Java more capable of data-processing, while mainly dealing with threading, garbage collection and memory management. None of them considers the combination of the host language with table-centric processing.

Declarative XML Processing. Related work can be found in the area of declarative XML message processing (e. g., [4]). Using an XQuery data store for defining persistent message queues (i. e., conflicting with *O3*), the work targets a complementary subset of our approach (i. e., persistent message queuing).

Data Integration. The data integration domain uses integration systems for querying remote data that is treated as local or "virtual" relations. Starting with SQL-based approaches (e. g., using `Garlic` [8]), the data integration research reached relational logic programming, summarized by [6]. In contrast to such remote queries, we define a table-centric, integration programming approach for application integration, while keeping the current semantics (for now).

Data-Intensive and Scientific Workflow Management. Based on the data patterns in workflow systems described by Russel et al. [15], modeling and data access approaches have been studied (e. g., by Reimann et al. [10]) in simulation workflows. The basic data management patterns in simulation workflows are ETL operations (e. g., format conversions, filters), a subset of the EIP and can be represented among others by our approach. The (map/reduce-style) data iteration pattern can be represented by combined EIPs like *scatter/gather* or *splitter/gather*.

Similar to our approach, data and control flow have been considered in scientific workflow management systems [18], which run the integration system optimally synchronized with the database. However, the work exclusively focuses on the optimization of workflow execution, not integration systems, and does not consider the usage of table-centric programming on the application server level.

6   Concluding Remarks

This paper motivates a look into a growing "processing discrepancy" (e. g., message throughput) between current integration and complementary systems (e. g., MQ, RDBMS) based on known scenarios with new requirements and fast growing new domains (*O1–O3*). Towards a message throughput improvement, we extended the current integration processing on a content level by table-centric integration processing (TIP). To remain compliant to the current EIP definitions the TIP-operators work on "single-record" messages, which lets us compare with current approaches using a brief experimental throughput evaluation. Although the results slightly improve the standard processing, not to mention the declarative vs. "hand-coded" definition of integration content, the actual potential of our approach lies in "multi-record" table message processing. However, that requires an adaption of some pattern EIP definitions, which is out of scope for this paper.

Open Research Challenges. For a more comprehensive, experimental evaluation, an EIP micro-benchmark will be developed on an extension of the TPC-H and TPC-C benchmarks. EIP definitions do not discuss streaming patterns/operators, which could be evaluated (complementarily) based on Datalog streaming theory (e. g., [20,21]). Eventually, the existing EIP definitions have to be adapted to that and probably new patterns will be established. Notably, the used Datalog engine has to be improved (e. g., join evaluation) and enhanced for integration processing (e. g., for early-match/stop during routing).

Acknowledgements. We especially thank Dr. Fredrik Nordvall Forsberg, Dr. Norman May and Prof. Dr. Erhard Rahm for proof-reading and valuable discussions on the paper.

References

1. Abiteboul, S., Antoine, E., Miklau, G., Stoyanovich, J., Testard, J.: Rule-based application development using webdamlog. In: ACM SIGMOD (2013)
2. AdroitLogic: Esb performance (2013). http://esbperformance.org/
3. Anstey, J., Zbarcea, H.: Camel in Action. Manning, Stamford (2011)
4. Böhm, A., Kanne, C., Moerkotte, G.: Demaq: a foundation for declarative XML message processing. In: CIDR 2007, pp. 33–43 (2007)
5. Chappell, D.: Enterprise Service Bus. O'Reilly Media Inc., Sebastopol (2004)
6. Genesereth, M.R.: Data Integration: The Relational Logic Approach. Morgan & Claypool Publishers, San Rafael (2010)
7. Green, T.J., Aref, M., Karvounarakis, G.: LogicBlox, platform and language: a tutorial. In: Barceló, P., Pichler, R. (eds.) Datalog 2.0 2012. LNCS, vol. 7494, pp. 1–8. Springer, Heidelberg (2012)
8. Haas, L.M., Kossmann, D., Wimmers, E.L., Yang, J.: Optimizing queries across diverse data sources. In: VLDB, pp. 276–285 (1997)
9. Hohpe, G., Woolf, B.: Enterprise Integration Patterns: Designing, Building, and Deploying Messaging Solutions. Addison-Wesley Longman, Boston (2003)
10. Reimann, P., Schwarz, H.: Datenmanagementpatterns in simulationsworkflows. In: BTW, pp. 279–293 (2013)
11. Ritter, D.: What about database-centric enterprise application integration? In: ZEUS, pp. 73–76 (2014)
12. Ritter, D.: Towards more data-aware application integration (extended version). CoRR abs/1504.05707 (2015). arXiv: 1504.05707
13. Ritter, D., Bross, J.: DatalogBlocks: relational logic integration patterns. In: Decker, H., Lhotská, L., Link, S., Spies, M., Wagner, R.R. (eds.) DEXA 2014, Part II. LNCS, vol. 8645, pp. 318–325. Springer, Heidelberg (2014)
14. Ritter, D., Westmann, T.: Business network reconstruction using datalog. In: Barceló, P., Pichler, R. (eds.) Datalog 2.0 2012. LNCS, vol. 7494, pp. 148–152. Springer, Heidelberg (2012)

15. Russell, N., ter Hofstede, A., Edmond, D., van der Aalst, W.: Workflow data patterns: identification, representation and tool support. In: ER (2005)
16. Shah, M.A., Madden, S., Franklin, M.J., Hellerstein, J.M.: Java support for data-intensive systems: experiences building the telegraph dataflow system. SIGMOD Rec. **30**(4), 103–114 (2001)
17. Ullman, J.: Principles of Database and Knowledge-Base Systems, vol. I. Computer Science Press, New York (1988)
18. Vrhovnik, M., Schwarz, H., Suhre, O., Mitschang, B., Markl, V., Maier, A., Kraft, T.: An approach to optimize data processing in business processes. In: VLDB (2007)
19. Welsh, M., Culler, D.E.: Jaguar: enabling efficient communication and I/O in Java. Concurr. Pract. Exp. **12**(7), 519–538 (2000)
20. Zaniolo, C.: A logic-based language for data streams. In: SEBD 2012 (2012)
21. Zaniolo, C.: Logical foundations of continuous query languages for data streams. In: Barceló, P., Pichler, R. (eds.) Datalog 2.0 2012. LNCS, vol. 7494, pp. 177–189. Springer, Heidelberg (2012)

Applying NoSQL Databases for Integrating Web Educational Stores - An Ontology-Based Approach

Reem Qadan Al Fayez(✉) and Mike Joy

Department of Computer Science, University of Warwick,
Coventry CV4 7AL, UK
{r.qadan-al-fayez,m.s.joy}@warwick.ac.uk

Abstract. Educational content available on the web is playing an important role in the teaching and learning process. Learners search for different types of learning objects such as videos, pictures, and blog articles and use them to understand concepts they are studying in books and articles. The current search platforms provided can be frustrating to use. Either they are not specified for educational purposes or they are provided as a service by a library or a repository for searching a limited dataset of educational content. This paper presents a novel system for automatic harvesting and connecting of medical educational objects based on biomedical ontologies. The challenge in this work is to transform disjoint heterogeneous web databases entries into one coherent linked dataset. First, harvesting APIs were developed for collecting content from various web sources such as YouTube, blogging platforms, and PubMed library. Then, the system maps its entries into one data model and annotates its content using biomedical ontologies to enable its linkage. The resulted dataset is organized in a proposed NoSQL RDF Triple Store which consists of 2720 entries of articles, videos, and blogs. We tested the system using different ontologies for enriching its content such as MeSH and SNOMED CT and compared the results obtained. Using SNOMED CT doubled the number of linkages built between the dataset entries. Experiments of querying the dataset is conducted and the results are promising compared with simple text-based search.

Keywords: Linked Data · Web databases · Ontologies

1 Introduction

The use of web content is increasing because of its accessibility at any time and from any place. Online libraries have started to support open access and professionals are increasingly using Web 2.0 technologies to spread their knowledge. In medical education, although its content should be of a high quality and provided by authorized sources, the web had played an important role in providing such content. Medical communities have a high awareness of the range of educational content available and show substantial interest in using such resources [1].

© Springer International Publishing Switzerland 2015
S. Maneth (Ed.): BICOD 2015, LNCS 9147, pp. 29–40, 2015.
DOI: 10.1007/978-3-319-20424-6_4

Searching for relevant educational content on the web can be challenging for its users. The vast amount of information available and the diversity of its types makes the search process time consuming. The content of any website is usually stored in a relational database with different fields used for describing its records. Therefore, integrating web databases into one data store is a challenging issue. New practices for publishing web content using Linked Data are being adopted by an increasing number of content providers leading to the web of data [2].

In this paper, we present a novel system that adopts Linked Data practices for automatic linking of heterogeneous web stores into one dataset based on biomedical ontologies enrichment. The developed system links some of the high quality User Generated Content (UGC), published on *YouTube* and *blogs* by medical educators and organizations, with content from online medical libraries. Using biomedical ontologies, we enriched the content of these databases by annotating free-text descriptions provided in their metadata records. Ontology-based annotation allows the system to discover keyword terms in web database content and builds dynamic linkages between them. The final linked dataset is represented in RDF/XML format and URIs are used for describing the dataset content.

Researchers in the field of e-learning refer to online educational resources that can be used in the learning process as Learning Objects (LOs). Learning Objects as defined in [3] can be of different types -images, videos, or text-, and differ in granularity from books to small web pages. Since the application domain of this work is medical education, we refer to the educational resources retrieved from the web and used in this system as *Educational Medical Objects (EMOs)*. The result of our work is a linked dataset of EMOs named the *LEMO dataset* and a system for managing them called the *LEMO system*.

The paper is structured as follows. Section 2 presents background and related work about the subject. Section 3 describes the processes applied for harvesting distributed web stores and building the LEMO RDF Triple Store. Section 4 provides more details about the ontologies used in the LEMO system, and explains the use of these ontologies in the annotation and enrichment process. Furthermore, a detailed description of the NoSQL RDF Triple Store components are presented in this section. Section 5 details a comparative analyses for using the LEMO system with the MeSH and SNOMED CT ontologies, and discusses experiments conducted for querying this dataset using ontological-based queries. Finally, Sect. 6 presents the conclusions and future work.

2   Background and Related Work

Using Linked Data and ontologies for data enrichment have been researched heavily in the recent years. The enrichment methods can happen at the server-side or client-side of a system. Both variations have been tested in [4] and the advantages and disadvantages were compared. Enriching queries is another method applied at the server-side of the system, and the work presented in [5] investigated enriching queries made to a collection of medical images provided by one library. The queries have been expanded after enriching the text with MeSH ontology terms.

Data enrichment has also been used with UGC content on the web, because user generated tags or folksonomies describing *YouTube* videos may be poorly chosen. The tag expansion and raking applied in [6] has been shown to enhance the description of the videos on *YouTube*. Enriching the content of a single dataset has been heavily researched, especially in the medical field. This is due to having mature and well maintained biomedical ontologies [7].

Linked Data principles have been adopted in education. Projects have been developed for supporting the use of web educational data [8]. Efforts for linking different educational ICT tools registries are presented in [9]. Another project for publishing datasets of educational medical materials in Linked Data has been developed in [10], which focused on providing a data model for exposing various types of educational materials to the web in order to enhance their interoperability and reuse across the web. It is clear that Linked Data will have a potential in the education field. A project presented in [11] developed a curriculum from Open Educational Resources tailored for teaching and training practitioners to use Linked Data. These days, educational organizations and universities are considering storing and publishing data using a Linked Data format [12].

3   LEMO Triple RDF Store

Before integrating web educational stores, we need to harvest and model distributed Educational Medical Objects (EMOs) into one data model. Our goal is to integrate different types of EMOs into one linked data set that is searchable and queryable.

In order to accomplish this goal, we developed two harvesting endpoints. In the first one, we incorporated the OAI-PMH protocol [13]. The other endpoint is basically an RSS feed reader storing web feeds from websites that provide them. Many online libraries expose their metadata using an OAI-PMH protocol such as the *PubMed* library. Using these harvesting endpoints, developed in the LEMO system, we harvested articles from the *PubMed* library and videos and blogs from *YouTube* and *blogging platforms*. The resulted dataset consisted of 2720 medical educational objects divided into 1000 articles from PubMed library and 1720 blogs and videos harvested from five different blogging websites and 6 YouTube channels. The chosen blogs and YouTube channels are maintained by either medical academics or journals and dedicated to educational purposes.

The harvested metadata records are retrieved in XML formats. The OAI service in PubMed supports DCMI metadata, therefore we can set the format parameter in the OAI requests produced by LEMO to be DCMI for harvesting content. On the other hand, blogs and video RSS feeds are structured XML documents which are machine interpretable and provide access to parts of the website entries such as title, authors, publication date, and content [14]. A fragment of the XML files harvested is illustrated in Fig. 1 along with the processes needed to build LEMO RDF Triple Store.

The heterogeneous metadata structures for all EMOs retrieved are mapped into the LEMO data model using XSLT techniques. The LEMO data model has

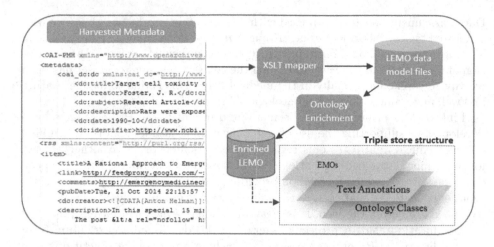

Fig. 1. LEMO RDF Triple Store structure and development process

been proposed in [15] at an earlier stage of developing the LEMO system after conducting a comparative study of existing data model in medical education. It is based on the DCMI metadata schema and implemented in RDF/XML formats. New LEMO properties were introduced for describing the enriched resources in LEMO store which will be discussed in detail in Sect. 4. The mapped files are then sent to the ontology enrichment process which annotates the free-text of EMOs, and discovers possible subjects to categorize them. This will result in having an enriched LEMO Triple Store which consists of EMOs, terms annotated in EMOs, and ontology classes used for annotation, as shown in Fig. 1.

4 Ontology-Based Annotations

Biomedical ontologies are formal representations of knowledge with definition of concepts and their relations [16]. Such ontologies have been used for indexing data produced by researchers in the field to ease its integration [17]. They are also used for indexing articles in medicine libraries such as the use of MeSH ontology for indexing PubMed library articles. In the LEMO system, we use ontologies to annotate free-text in the harvested EMO metadata such as titles and descriptions. Annotating the free-text enables us to discover relations between non related objects on the web. In the LEMO system, we adopt the Linked Data format for building the LEMO Triple Store which is considered the best practice for connecting semantically related data that was not previously linked [2].

The application domain of the LEMO system is medicine education. The BioPortal[1] open repository for biomedical ontologies is used to explore possible ontologies to integrate them with the LEMO system. BioPortal provides access to ontologies developed in different formats via web services which enable its

---

[1] http://bioportal.bioontology.org/.

users to get information about the ontologies or its content [18]. The LEMO system uses additional web services such as the annotator service provided by Bioportal for annotating and linking objects in the dataset. The ontologies used in the LEMO system so far are the Systematized Nomenclature of Medicine - Clinical Terms SNOMED CT and the Medical Subject Headings MeSH.

4.1 SNOMED CT and MeSH Ontologies

The SNOMED CT ontology has been developed by specialized organizations in both the USA and the UK and offers a standardized healthcare terminology which is comprehensive, scientifically validated, with relationships built into its core concepts [19]. This ontology was released in 2002 and since then new versions of it have been released semi-annually. SNOMED CT has been designated as the preferred clinical terminology to use in 19 countries [20]. Its application in medical information systems is expected to increase. The popularity and broad use of this ontology in the field of medicine was the main reason for applying SNOMED CT in the LEMO system.

As for the second ontology applied in the LEMO system, MeSH has been used for indexing PubMed Library content. Therefore, we applied it in the LEMO system to annotate and link EMOs based on its classes and relations. MeSH has been developed by the National Library of Medicine (NLM) in the USA and is considered the controlled vocabulary set used for indexing its articles. It consists of a set of terms naming descriptors organized in a hierarchical structure from general to more specific descriptors [21].

4.2 EMOs Annotation Enrichment

The LEMO RDF Triple Store consists of collections of linked resources describing its content and organized as illustrated in Fig. 2. Each resource is identified by a unique URI and a set of predicates to describe its properties. The major component in the LEMO RDF Triple Store is *EMOs*. After applying ontology enrichment, additional *term annotations* resources are added to the collection of EMOs' *title* and *description* resources to enrich them. The smallest component of the LEMO store is *ontology classes*. Each annotation made in the free-text points to a class in the ontology used for annotation. The classes of an ontology are arranged in a graph structure where relations exist to identify the class hierarchy. The collection of classes used in annotating the LEMO RDF Triple Store forms a subset of the original ontology graph.

The resources of the LEMO RDF Triple Store are described using the LEMO data model. The model is based on DCMI properties enhanced with new properties proposed for representing the annotations in LEMO. Such new properties are defined using the prefix "*lemo*". As shown in the XML fragment of Fig. 2, EMOs are described using only DCMI properties. The values of their **title** and **description** predicates are new resources created, rather than textual values, used for linking the EMOs to annotations using the *lemo:lemoTitleAnnotation* and *lemo:lemoDescAnnotation* properties. The *term annotations* are described

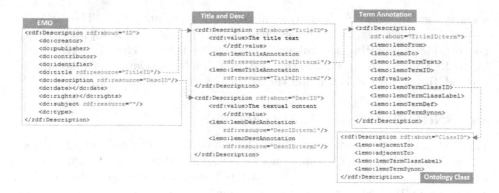

Fig. 2. Snippet of LEMO RDF Triple Store components

in detail using LEMO properties that store details about the original text annotated, its indices and content along with details about the class it was annotated
to using a specific ontology, its ID, label, definition, and synonyms if they exist.
The terms' annotated classes are nodes in the original ontology used for enriching
the dataset. Hence, a sub graph of the original ontology can be built using the
collection of *ontology classes* used for annotating its terms. The class relations
are stored using the *lemo:adjacentTo* property. These class resources will enable
further processing of the LEMO Triple Store to discover subjects or categories
for EMOs and build dynamic linkages between its resources.

In the annotation process, free-text of EMOs is sent for the BioPortal annotator service and an ontology is specified in the request parameter. Then, the
response is read and terms' annotated resources are created and linked to EMOs
stored in the LEMO RDF Triple Store. After the annotation process, each EMO
is represented by a set of keywords which are the terms annotated in its title
and description. Each set of keywords representing an EMO forms a smaller
sub graph of linked ontology classes based on their adjacency lists stored in the
LEMO Triple Store. For discovering subjects for an EMO, we apply a simple
term filtering technique to identify a smaller set of keywords which represent the
EMO subject property and stored as the value of the *dc:subject* predicate for
that EMO. In term filtering, we assign weights for the keywords based on their
position and co-occurrence in an EMO term annotation set. Then, the accu-
mulated weight for each keyword is calculated based on its hierarchical level in
ontology. If the term annotated class is a parent of many terms annotated for
the same EMO, then it will be more important than a term that is leaf in the
ontology. The final weight value for each term annotated is stored in the *rdf:value*
property of the term annotation resource. After normalizing the weights of the
keywords, the top ranked keywords are selected as *subjects* of an EMO.

We tested the LEMO system against two biomedical ontologies: MeSH and
SNOMED. Comparison of annotation results, term filtering, and linkage discovery of these two experiments are detailed in the following section. The results of

Table 1. Number of terms annotated for the set of EMOs using different ontologies

Type of EMOs	Number of EMOs	MeSH annotations			SNOMED CT annotations		
		Title	Description	Total	Title	Description	Total
Article	1000	3887	12192	16079	6166	29859	36025
Video	1259	3027	4304	7331	3677	5710	9387
Blog	461	754	4720	5474	1572	9756	11328
Total	2720	7668	21216	28884	11415	45325	56740

the comparisons helps to decide which ontology to use in LEMO system based on the larger number of annotations created.

5   Results and Discussion: MeSH vs. SNOMED Ontology

The components of the dataset, harvested from the web for testing this system, are detailed in Table 1. The table details the numbers of resources harvested grouped by its type. It also details the number of keywords discovered after annotating its textual content whether annotated in the *title* or the *description* based on MeSH and SNOMED CT ontologies.

We notice that the number of terms annotated using the SNOMED CT ontology is greater than the number of keywords annotated using the MeSH ontology. The difference is not significant for video and blog EMOs compared to article EMOs. This is due to the short text provided in the metadata of blogs and videos compared to the longer text provided for articles in the online libraries. The collection of terms annotated for the dataset is used for building linkages between the EMOs and discovering subjects for categorizing the EMOs.

5.1   Discovering Subjects Using Ontologies

After processing the keyword set for each EMO, *subjects* were selected from the keywords annotated for categorizing each EMO. The resulting sets of subjects selected for each EMO are variable in size. We calculated the total numbers of subjects selected in the LEMO dataset and compared them against the keywords set sizes. The results are detailed in Fig. 3a and b for the MeSH and SNOMED CT subject selections respectively. The percentage of keywords chosen as subject terms from the SNOMED CT annotated terms is less than the percentage from the MeSH annotated collection. In both experiments, the subjects discovered are mainly chosen from the keywords annotated in the titles of EMOs. This indicates that the term filtering techniques have succeed in this matter. We can notice that in SNOMED CT, only 11 % of the keywords annotated in the description were chosen as a subject, compared to a higher percentage of 26 % keywords in the description using MeSH.

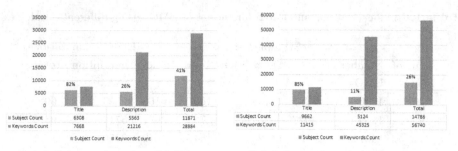

(a) Subjects based on MeSH   (b) Subjects based on SNOMED

Fig. 3. Subject selection

The LEMO dataset consists of different types of EMOs. Video and blog EMOs usually have shorter descriptions in their metadata fields if any. This affects the number of keywords annotated for EMOs from such types and that reflects on the number of subjects selected. Using MeSH and SNOMED CT annotations, the results of discovering subjects for video and blog EMOs are not enhanced in both experiments. Figure 4a and b illustrate the relation between the counts of subjects discovered in MeSH and SNOMED CT annotated EMOs and their types. In both experiments, video and blog EMOs have low subject counts. This is due to the low numbers of terms annotated in this type of EMOs. Comparing the subject selection process based on MeSH and SNOMED CT, we notice that in the SNOMED CT based dataset, very few EMOs did not have any subject count, while in the MeSH based dataset, more than 150 EMOs from articles, videos or blog types have subject counts equal to zero.

5.2 Links Analysis

After the subject selection process, we analysed and compared the dynamically built links in the LEMO dataset. We consider that there exists a link between two EMOs if they have a similar annotated class in their subjects or keywords set. Also, we count a link between two EMOs as directed links. Therefore, if there is a link from node a to node b the link count will be two not one. We compared the number of links built in the dataset in the two experiments conducted. Table 2 illustrates the number of links built in LEMO dataset in both experiments; MeSH and SNOMED CT annotations. As detailed in the table, the number of links based on SNOMED CT ontology is greater than ones based on MeSH ontology. The results are almost doubled in the links count. This is due to the large number of annotation discovered using SNOMED CT ontology.

5.3 Ontology-Based Access

We provided a user interface for querying the LEMO Triple Store enriched with SNOMED CT ontology classes since it resulted in higher number of annotations

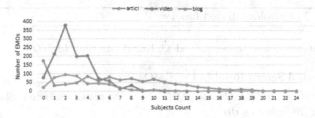

(a) EMOs annotated in MeSH and their subjects

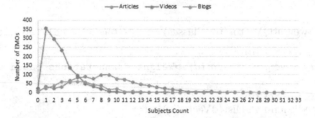

(b) EMOs annotated in SNOMED and their subjects

Fig. 4. Relation between Subjects count and EMOs types

Table 2. Links count in LEMO dataset based of MeSH And SNOMED CT ontologies

	Number of Links based on		
Based on Ontology	Title	Desc	Subject
MeSH	352029	867636	248704
SNOMED CT	464876	1443667	418782

in LEMO content. The system binds the user with choosing ontological classes rather than writing a free-text in the search box. Figure 5 illustrates the auto-complete feature presented in LEMO for ontological based access. The auto-complete text box retrieves SNOMED CT ontology classes used in LEMO store. Algorithm 1 explains the ontological-based technique for searching and ranking the results of searching for a selected class.

The algorithm developed in LEMO is based on the NoSQL structure for LEMO store explained previously in Fig. 2. As explained in the ontology-based query algorithm, the search process starts with one ontology class Q. Then, a query vector is built based on the class adjacency properties stored in LEMO store. Now, we start searching for EMOs annotated with any of the ontology classes related to the query class Q. So far the search results are not ranked according to its relevance to the query initiated. Hence, the related classes retrieved are weighted according to their co-occurrences with Q class in the search result set. Then, the weights are normalized according to the length of the search result size and the class Q in the vector will have a weight of 1. For each EMO in the search result, the weights of its annotations found in QVecor

---

Algorithm 1: Ontology-based Query

---

inputs :

        Ontology class to be queried Q, LEMO dataset $LEMO$

output:

        Ranked Search Result set of EMOs

$RelClasses \leftarrow getRelatedClasses(Q)$ ▷Stores related classes to Q

foreach $c \in RelClasses$ **do**

   | $qResults \leftarrow getEMOsAnnotatedWith(c)$

   | add $qResults$ to $ResSet$ ▷ResSet is the final search results

end

QVector $\leftarrow$ weightQVector(RelClasses)   ▷Weight related classes to Q

foreach $d \in ResSet$ **do**

   | $dVector \leftarrow weightDVector(d)$ ▷Weight d annotations based on QVector

end

foreach $d \in ResSet$ **do**

   | calculatedEucildeanDist(dVector,qVector)

end

Sort(ResSet)   ▷Sort results ascendingly

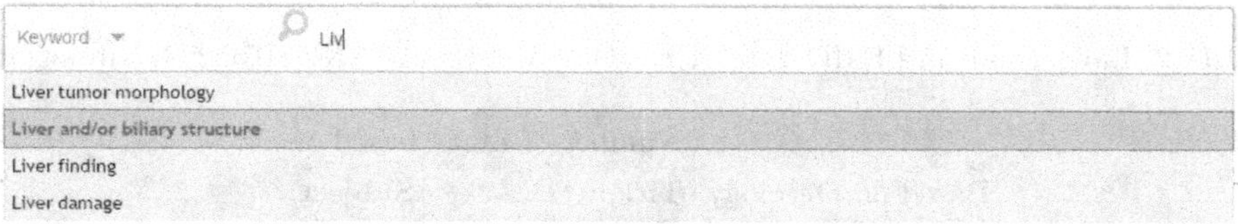

Fig. 5. The ontology-based LEMO search user interface

are retrieved from **rdf:value** in LEMO store which is used to store the weight of an annotated class as explained in the previous sections. In order to have more accurate weights for EMOs' classes, the weights are normalized based on the length of their annotation list. Finally, the search results are ranked based on its euclidean distance from the query vector as shown in the algorithm. In order to test this algorithm, we conducted random queries of 5 classes found in LEMO Triple Store. The results are shown in Table 3 and compared with exact text matching search.

From the sample of classes queried in this experiments, we can notice that the ontological-based search always retrieved higher number of results than text-based access. The overlap coefficient always indicated a percentage higher than 90 % for all the queries tested. In other words, the ontological access covers almost all the search results of text-based access. We calculated the Jaccard Similarity coefficient to emphasize the case in the last query "*RENAL DIS-EASE*". In this query, the text-based results are only 4 EMOs since we used exact text matching. Hence, the jaccard similarity is very low between the two search results. The query vector resulted from searching for "*RENAL DISEASE*"

Table 3. Ontological-based vs. Text-based search results in LEMO Store

Query Class	Size of Ontology-based Result set (O)	Size of Text-based Result set (T)	Overlap Coefficient $O \cap T$	Jaccard Similartiy Coef
HEPATITIS	27	21	100 %	0.78
INFLUENZA	30	25	92 %	0.71
MUSCLE	66	65	95 %	0.89
BRAIN	61	49	100 %	0.80
RENAL DISEASE	36	4	100 %	0.11

included 24 other classes related to it based on SNOMED CT ontology as stored in LEMO dataset. The list of related classes include: (Renal vascular disorder, Nephritis, nephrosis and nephrotic syndrome, Renal impairment, Infectious disorder of kidney and, $\cdots$, others). The algorithm of ontological-based query gives higher weight for the class queried Q which results in having EMOs containing the class Q ranked at the top of the search result set.

6 Conclusions and Future Work

In this paper, we present a system for linking Educational Medical Objects (EMOs) harvested from distributed web databases. The aim of the system was to bridge the gap between UGC content, provided by YouTube and blogging platforms, and online medical libraries such as PubMed. We have tested the system against a sample dataset and compared the results of using MeSH and SNOMED CT ontologies in the enrichment process. The final dataset consisted of 2720 linked EMOs which are annotated, linked, and accessed by the system developed. Using LEMO dataset enriched with SNOMED CT, we tested accessing the dataset using ontological-based approach vs. simple text-based matching. The results indicated the efficiency of ontological-based access in LEMO dataset and the overlapping coefficient between the search results of the two approaches presented values above 90 % in all queries tested. In the future, a more developed user interface will be built with more advanced features for browsing and querying the LEMO dataset presented.

References

1. Sandars, J., Schroter, S.: Web 2.0 technologies for undergraduate and postgraduate medical education: an online survey. Postgrad. Med. J. **83**(986), 759–762 (2007)
2. Bizer, C., Heath, T., Berners-Lee, T.: Linked data-the story so far. Int. J. Seman. Web Inform. Syst. **5**(3), 1–22 (2009)
3. McGreal, R.: Learning objects: a practical definition. Instr. Technol. **1**, 21 (2004)
4. Ritze, D., Eckert, K.: Data enrichment in discovery systems using linked data. In: Spiliopoulou, M., Schmidt-Thieme, L., Janning, R. (eds.) Data Analysis, Machine Learning and Knowledge Discovery, pp. 455–462. Springer, Heidelberg (2014)

5. Díaz-Galiano, M.C., García-Cumbreras, M.Á., Martín-Valdivia, M.T., Montejo-Ráez, A., Ureña-López, L.A.: Integrating MeSH ontology to improve medical information retrieval. In: Peters, C., Jijkoun, V., Mandl, T., Müller, H., Oard, D.W., Peñas, A., Petras, V., Santos, D. (eds.) CLEF 2007. LNCS, vol. 5152, pp. 601–606. Springer, Heidelberg (2008)
6. Choudhury, S., Breslin, J.G., Passant, A.: Enrichment and ranking of the YouTube tag space and integration with the linked data cloud. In: Bernstein, A., Karger, D.R., Heath, T., Feigenbaum, L., Maynard, D., Motta, E., Thirunarayan, K. (eds.) ISWC 2009. LNCS, vol. 5823, pp. 747–762. Springer, Heidelberg (2009)
7. Hoehndorf, R., Dumontier, M., Gkoutos, G.V.: Evaluation of research in biomedical ontologies. Briefings Bioinform. (2012)
8. Domingue, J., Mikroyannidis, A., Dietze, S.: Online learning and linked data: lessons learned and best practices. In: Proceedings of the Companion Publication of the 23rd International Conference on World Wide Web Companion, pp. 191–192 (2014)
9. Ruiz-Calleja, A., Vega-Gorgojo, G., Asensio-Perez, J.I., Bote-Lorenzo, M.L., Gomez-Sanchez, E., Alario-Hoyos, C.: A data approach for the discovery of educational ICT tools in the web of data. Comput. Educ. **59**(3), 952–962 (2012)
10. Mitsopoulou, E., Taibi, D., Giordano, D., Dietze, S., Yu, H.Q., Bamidis, P., Bratsas, C., Woodham, L.: Connecting medical educational resources to the linked data cloud: the meducator RDF schema, store and API. In: Proceedings of Linked Learning 22 (2011)
11. Mikroyannidis, A., Domingue, J., Maleshkova, M., Norton, B., Simperl, E.: Developing a curriculum of open educational resources for linked data. In: Proceedings of 10th Annual OpenCourseWare Consortium Global Conference (OCWC) (2014)
12. d'Aquin, M.: Putting linked data to use in a large higher-education organisation. In: Proceedings of the Interacting with Linked Data (ILD) workshop at Extended Semantic Web Conference (ESWC) (2012)
13. Lagoze, C., Van de Sompel, H.: The making of the open archives initiative protocol for metadata harvesting. Library Hi Tech **21**(2), 118–128 (2003)
14. Gkotsis, G., Stepanyan, K., Cristea, A.I., Joy, M.: Self-supervised automated wrapper generation for weblog data extraction. In: Gottlob, G., Grasso, G., Olteanu, D., Schallhart, C. (eds.) BNCOD 2013. LNCS, vol. 7968, pp. 292–302. Springer, Heidelberg (2013)
15. Al Fayez, R.Q., Joy, M.: A framework for linking educational medical objects: connecting web2.0 and traditional education. In: Benatallah, B., Bestavros, A., Manolopoulos, Y., Vakali, A., Zhang, Y. (eds.) WISE 2014, Part II. LNCS, vol. 8787, pp. 158–167. Springer, Heidelberg (2014)
16. Rubin, D.L., Shah, N.H., Noy, N.F.: Biomedical ontologies: a functional perspective. Briefings Bioinform. **9**(1), 75–90 (2008)
17. Jonquet, C., LePendu, P., Falconer, S., Coulet, A., Noy, N.F., Musen, M.A., Shah, N.H.: NCBO resource index: ontology-based search and mining of biomedical resources. Web Seman. Sci. Serv. Agents World Wide Web **9**(3), 316–324 (2011)
18. Noy, N.F., Shah, N.H., Whetzel, P.L., Dai, B., Dorf, M., Griffith, N., Jonquet, C., Rubin, D.L., Storey, M.A., Chute, C.G., et al.: BioPortal: ontologies and integrated data resources at the click of a mouse. Nucleic Acids Res. **37**, W170–W173 (2009)
19. Elevitch, F.R.: SNOMED CT: electronic health record enhances anesthesia patient safety. AANA J. **73**(5), 361 (2005)
20. Lee, D., de Keizer, N., Lau, F., Cornet, R.: Literature review of SNOMED CT use. JAMIA J. Am. Med. Inform. Assoc. **21**, e11–e19 (2013)
21. Lipscomb, C.E.: Medical subject headings (MeSH). Bull. Med. Libr. Assoc. **88**(3), 265 (2000)

Implementing Peer-to-Peer Semantic Integration of Linked Data

Mirko M. Dimartino[1]([⊠]), Andrea Calì[1,2], Alexandra Poulovassilis[1],
and Peter T. Wood[1]

[1] London Knowledge Lab, Birkbeck, University of London, London, UK
{mirko,andrea,ap,ptw}@dcs.bbk.ac.uk
[2] Oxford-Man Institute of Quantitative Finance, University of Oxford, Oxford, UK

1 Introduction

The World Wide Web has expanded from a network of hyper-linked documents to
a more complex structure where both documents and data are easily published,
consumed and reused. Ideally, users should be able to access this information
as a single, global data space. However, Linked Data on the Web is highly heterogeneous: different datasets may describe overlapping domains, using different
approaches to data modelling and naming. A single global ontological conceptu-
alisation is impracticable, and instead a more extensible approach is needed for
semantic integration of heterogeneous Linked Data sets into a global data space.

In a recent paper [2], we introduced a theoretical framework for the integration of linked data sets, defining the semantic relationships between them
through peer-to-peer mappings. In [2], we specified the semantics of query
answering in this framework, as well as query answering and query rewriting
algorithms. Here, we build on this work by introducing a prototype system that
implements these techniques. After briefly summarising our theoretical framework, we present the architecture of the system and the main tasks that the
system carries out. Finally, we summarise our current research and we establish
some goals for future work.

To motivate our research, we begin by presenting an example. Suppose
two RDF sources describe data in the domain of movies (source 1) and people (source 2). A user wants to retrieve the names and ages of actors in the
movie Mulholland Drive, and poses the following query over their local source
(source 1), hoping for additional information from other relevant sources too:

```
SELECT  ?name ?age
WHERE {db1:Mulholland_Dr_2001 db1:actor ?x . ?x rdfs:label ?name
       . ?x foaf:age ?age }
```

An empty result will be returned because source 1 does not contain foaf data.
The problem can be addressed by using the SPARQL 1.1 SERVICE clause, as
follows:

```
SELECT  ?name ?age
WHERE {db1:Mulholland_Dr_2001 db1:actor ?x . ?x rdfs:label ?name
SERVICE <http://data.people.org/sparql> { ?x foaf:age ?age } }
```

© Springer International Publishing Switzerland 2015
S. Maneth (Ed.): BICOD 2015, LNCS 9147, pp. 41–45, 2015.
DOI: 10.1007/978-3-319-20424-6_5

Even now, it is likely that query evaluation returns an empty result, because real-world entities may be denoted by different IRIs in different sources. In this case, mappings for the variable ?x may not be found. To cope with this issue, Linked Data best practices suggest the adoption of the built-in OWL property sameAs, which states that two linked IRIs represent the same real-world entity. The user can leverage the semantics of the owl:sameAs predicate and submit the following query, so as to perform coreference resolution of the "equivalent" IRIs:

```
SELECT  ?name ?age
WHERE { { db1:Mulholland_Dr_2001 db1:actor ?x . ?x rdfs:label ?name
          . ?x owl:sameAs ?z
    SERVICE <http://data.people.org/sparql> { ?z foaf:age ?age } } }
UNION { db1:Mulholland_Dr_2001 db1:actor ?x . ?x rdfs:label ?name
    SERVICE <http://data.people.org/sparql>
              { ?z owl:sameAs ?x . ?z foaf:age ?age } } }
```

The user may not know whether the owl:sameAs triples are stored in source 1 or source 2, so these two cases need to be taken into consideration by including the UNION operator and two disjuncts in the query pattern. A non-empty result is still not guaranteed since the owl:sameAs triples may be missing.

The drawbacks of this approach are: (1) the user needs to be aware of all the potential sources of information, (2) the user needs to be familiar with the semantic links between sources, and (3) as the number of sources increases, the queries become more complicated to formulate. What is needed is a system that does not require the user to be aware of what other sources are available and where query rewriting is performed automatically in order to obtain as many answers to user queries as possible. We describe such a system in the rest of the paper.

2   Theoretical Foundations

Our approach to semantic integration of heterogeneous Linked Data sources is based on the *RDF Peer System* (RPS) introduced in [2]. This is a framework for peer-based integration of RDF datasets, where the semantic relationships between data at different peers are expressed through mappings. Formally, an RPS $\mathcal{P}$ is defined as a tuple $\mathcal{P} = (\mathcal{S}, G, E)$, where $\mathcal{S}$ is the set of the *peer schemas* in $\mathcal{P}$, G is a set of *graph mapping assertions* and E is a set of *equivalence mappings*. A peer schema in $\mathcal{S}$ is the set of IRIs that a peer (i.e. an RDF data source) adopts to describe its data. The sets of schema-level mappings and instance-level mappings between peers are given by G and E, respectively. G provides semantic linkage between the schemas of different peers and it contains mapping assertions of the form $Q \rightsquigarrow Q'$, where Q and Q' are "conjunctive" SPARQL queries with the same arity over two peers, e.g.

$$Q := q(x, y) \leftarrow (x, actor, y)$$
$$Q' := q(x, y) \leftarrow (x, starring, z) \text{ AND } (z, artist, y)$$

in our earlier example setting. Mappings in E are of the form $c \equiv_e c'$, where c and

c' are IRIs located in the same peer or in two different peers. Each equivalence mapping states that the two IRIs represent the same real-world object. In this sense, equivalence mappings are used to provide coreference resolution during query processing.

A *solution* for an RPS $\mathcal{P}$, denoted by I, is defined as a "global" RDF database which contains: *(i)* all the triples in the peers; *(ii)* triples inferred through the graph mapping assertions, by testing that for each mapping $Q \rightsquigarrow Q'$, Q evaluated over I is contained in Q' evaluated over I; and *(iii)* triples inferred from the equivalence mappings, such that, for each equivalence mapping $c \equiv_e c'$, c appears in I at a certain position in a triple (i.e., subject, predicate or object) if and only if I contains also a triple such that c' appears at the same position. Following this, query answering under RPSs is defined by extending the notion of certain answers [1,2]. For a graph pattern query q, expressed in any peer schema(s), the set of *certain answers* is given by the tuples contained in all the results of q evaluated over all the possible solutions I. In this regard, a query is answered by leveraging the semantics of the mappings so that a more complete answer is given, integrating data from multiple RDF sources. We use the notion of certain answers in RPSs to assess the correctness and completeness of our query processing techniques.

3   Overview of the System

Our system provides a query interface between the user and the Linked Data sources. A unified SPARQL endpoint accepts queries expressed in any source vocabulary. The queries are rewritten with respect to the semantic mappings of the RPS, so as to retrieve the set of certain answers; we envisage that mappings between peers can either be designed manually or automatically inferred. Then, a second rewriting step is performed, generating a SPARQL 1.1 federated query to be evaluated over the sources. The query result is then presented to the user. The system's main components are shown below.

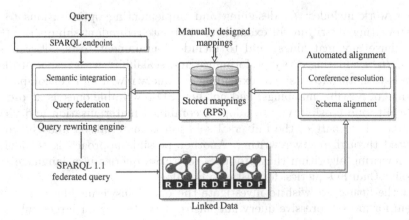

In more detail: The *query rewriting engine* performs query rewriting of the user's query. The rewritten query is then evaluated over the sources and the result is presented to the user. The query rewriting engine is composed of two sub-engines:

(i) The *semantic integration* module generates a "perfect rewriting" of the user's query, that is, a query that preserves a sound and complete answer of the original query based on the semantic mappings in the RPS. Note that, in general, sets of RPS mappings are not FO-rewritable (see [2]), so at present our system is confined to FO-rewritable ones.

(ii) The *query federation* module executes a second rewriting step in order to generate a federated query to be evaluated over multiple RDF sources. Triple patterns in the body of the query are grouped with respect to the RDF sources that can provide a successful graph pattern match. Then, the groups are assigned to the endpoints of the related sources, and evaluated using the SPARQL 1.1 `SERVICE` clause.

The system provides for *automated alignment* of the peer schemas, to link entities and concepts in the Linked Open Data cloud. This part has not yet been implemented, but we envisage that it would extract structural information from the sources, such as the sets of entities, predicates, classes etc. Then, it would perform schema alignment and coreference resolution by:

– *retrieving* mappings between sources, such as `owl:sameAs` or `VoID`[1] triples, and other semantic links between sources;
– *generating* new mappings, using existing ontology matching and instance linkage techniques, such as Falcon-AO [3];
– *translating* these alignments into our peer mapping language; and
– *storing* the mappings in the RPS.

4   Current and Future Work

Current work includes: *(i)* designing and implementing optimisations to the query rewriting algorithm, for example to eliminate redundant sub-queries (that cannot have any matchings) and to include containment tests between sub-queries; *(ii)* evaluating query performance and scalability with respect to large real and synthetic datasets; *(iii)* extending our query rewriting to encompass the full range of possible mappings, and not just FO-rewritable ones as at present. Specifically, one possibility is to adopt a combined materialisation and virtual approach, where part of the universal solution is materialised and the rest is computed through query rewriting. Another possible approach is to devise a query rewriting algorithm that produces rewritten queries in a language more expressive than FO-queries, for instance Datalog.

For the future, we wish to investigate the query answering/query rewriting problem for more expressive query languages, in particular for larger subsets of

---

[1] http://www.w3.org/TR/void/.

SPARQL. Another area of future investigation is automatic discovery of mappings between peers, i.e. implementation of the Automated Alignment module of our system.

References

1. Abiteboul, S., Duschka, O.M.: Complexity of answering queries using materialized views. In: PODS, pp. 254–263 (1998)
2. Dimartino, M.M., Calì, A., Poulovassilis, A., Wood, P.T.: Peer-to-peer semantic integration of linked data. In: EDBT/ICDT Workshops, pp. 213–220 (2015)
3. Hu, W., Qu, Y., Cheng, G.: Matching large ontologies: a divide-and-conquer approach. Data Knowl. Eng. **67**(1), 140–160 (2008)

Graph Data

Virtual Network Mapping: A Graph Pattern Matching Approach

Yang Cao[1,2]($\boxtimes$), Wenfei Fan[1,2], and Shuai Ma[1]

[1] RCBD and SKLSDE Lab, Beihang University, Beihang, China
{caoyang,mashuai}@act.buaa.edu.cn, wenfei@inf.ed.ac.uk
[2] University of Edinburgh, Edinburgh, UK

Abstract. Virtual network mapping (VNM) is to build a network on demand by deploying virtual machines in a substrate network, subject to constraints on capacity, bandwidth and latency. It is critical to data centers for coping with dynamic cloud workloads. This paper shows that VNM can be approached by graph pattern matching, a well-studied database topic. (1) We propose to model a virtual network request as a graph pattern carrying various constraints, and treat a substrate network as a graph in which nodes and edges bear attributes specifying their capacity. (2) We show that a variety of mapping requirements can be expressed in this model, such as virtual machine placement, network embedding and priority mapping. (3) In this model, we formulate VNM and its optimization problem with a mapping cost function. We establish complexity bounds of these problems for various mapping constraints, ranging from PTIME to NP-complete. For intractable optimization problems, we further show that these problems are approximation-hard, *i.e.*, NPO-complete in general and APX-hard even for special cases.

1 Introduction

Virtual network mapping (VNM) is also known as virtual network embedding or assignment. It takes as input (1) a *substrate network* (SN, a physical network), and (2) a *virtual network* (VN) specified in terms of a set of virtual nodes (machines or routers, denoted as VMs) and their virtual links, along with constraints imposed on the capacities of the nodes (*e.g.*, CPU and storage) and on the links (*e.g.*, bandwidth and latency). VNM is to deploy the VN in the SN such that virtual nodes are hosted on substrate nodes, virtual links are instantiated with physical paths in the SN, and the constraints on the virtual nodes and links are satisfied.

VNM is critical to managing big data. Big data is often distributed to data centers [23, 26]. However, data center networks become *the bottleneck* for dynamic cloud workloads of querying and managing the data. In traditional networking platforms, network resources are manually configured with static policies, and new workload provisioning often takes days or weeks [1]. This highlights the need for VNM, to automatically deploy virtual networks in a data center network in response to real-time requests. Indeed, VNM is increasingly employed in industry,

© Springer International Publishing Switzerland 2015
S. Maneth (Ed.): BICOD 2015, LNCS 9147, pp. 49–61, 2015.
DOI: 10.1007/978-3-319-20424-6_6

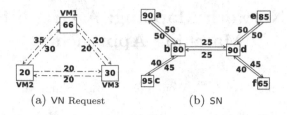

(a) VN Request   (b) SN

Fig. 1. VN requests found in practice

e.g., Amazon's EC2 [2], VMware Data Center [3] and Big Switch Networks [1]. It has proven effective in increasing server utilization and reducing server provisioning time (from days or weeks to minutes), server capital expenditures and operating expenses [1]. There has also been a host of work on virtualization techniques for big data [23] and database systems [7,24].

Several models have been proposed to specify VNM in various settings:

(1) *Virtual machine placement* (VMP): it is to find a mapping f from virtual machines in a VN to substrate nodes in an SN such that for each VM v, its capacity is no greater than that of $f(v)$, *i.e.,* $f(v)$ is able to conduct the computation of the VM v that it hosts [12].

(2) *Single-path* VN *embedding* (VNE$_{SP}$): it is to find
   (a) an injective mapping f_v that maps nodes in VN to nodes in SN, subject to node capacity constraints; and
   (b) a function that maps a virtual link (v, v') in VN to a path from $f_v(v)$ to $f_v(v')$ in SN that satisfies a bandwidth constraint, *i.e.,* the bandwidth of each link in the SN is no smaller than the sum of the bandwidth requirements of all those virtual links that are mapped to a path containing it [20].

(3) *Multi-path* VN *embedding* (VNE$_{MP}$): it is to find a node mapping f_v as in VNE$_{SP}$ and a function that maps each virtual link (v, v') to *a set* of paths from $f_v(v)$ to $f_v(v')$ in SN, subject to bandwidth constraints [14,25].

However, there are a number of VN requests commonly found in practice, which cannot be expressed in any of these models, as illustrated by the following.

Example 1. Consider a VN request and an SN, depicted in Figs. 1(a) and 1(b), respectively. The VN has three virtual nodes VM$_1$, VM$_2$ and VM$_3$, each specifying a capacity constraint, along with a constraint on each virtual link. In the SN, each substrate node bears a resource capacity and each connection (edge) has an attribute, indicating either bandwidth or latency. Consider the following cases.

(1) Mapping with Latency Constraints (VNM$_L$). Assume that the numbers attached to the virtual nodes and links in Fig. 1(a) denote requirements on CPUs and latencies for SN, respectively. Then the VNM problem, denoted by VNM$_L$, aims to map each virtual node to a substrate node with sufficient computational power, and to map each virtual link (v, v') in the VN to a path in the SN such that its latency, *i.e., the sum* of the latencies of the edges on the path, does not

exceed the latency specified for (v, v'). The need for studying VNM_L arises from latency sensitive applications such as multimedia transmitting networks [21], which concern latency rather than bandwidth.

(2) Priority Mapping (VNM_P). Assume that the constraints on the nodes in Fig. 1(a) are CPU capacities, and constraints imposed on edges are bandwidth capacities. Here the VNM problem, denoted by VNM_P, is to map each virtual node to a node in SN with sufficient CPU capacity, and each virtual link (v, v') in the VN to a path in SN such that the *minimum* bandwidth of all edges on the path is no less than the bandwidth specified for (v, v'). The need for this is evident in many applications [4], we want to give different priorities at run time to virtual links that share some physical links, and require the mapping only to provide bandwidth guarantee for the connection with the highest priority.

(3) Mapping with Node Sharing ($VNE_{SP(NS)}$). Assume that the numbers attached to the virtual nodes and links in Fig. 1(a) denote requirements on CPUs and bandwidths for SN, respectively. Then $VNE_{SP(NS)}$ is an extension of the single-path VN embedding (VNE_{SP}) by supporting node sharing, *i.e.*, by allowing mapping multiple virtual nodes to the same substrate node, as needed by X-Bone [6].

There is also practical need for extending other mappings with node sharing, such as virtual machine placement (VMP), latency mapping (VNM_L), priority mapping VNM_P and multi-path VN embedding (VNE_{MP}). We denote such an extension by adding a subscript NS.

Observe that (a) VNM varies from practical requirements, *e.g.*, when latency, high-priority connections and node sharing are concerned; (b) Existing models are not capable of expressing such requirements; indeed, none of them is able to specify VNM_L, VNM_P or $VNE_{SP(NS)}$; And (c) it would be an overkill to develop a model for each of the large variety of requirements, and to study it individually.

As suggested by the example, we need a generic model to express virtual network mappings in various practical settings, including both those already studied (*e.g.*, VMP, VNE_{SP} and VNE_{MP}) and those being overlooked (*e.g.*, VNM_L, VNM_P and $VNE_{SP(NS)}$). The uniform model allows us to characterize and compare VNMs in different settings, and better still, to study generic properties that pertain to all the variants. Among these are the complexity and approximation analyses of VNMs, which are obviously important but have not yet been systematically studied by and large.

Contributions & Roadmap. This work takes a step toward providing a uniform model to characterize VNMs. We show that VNMs, an important problem for managing big data, can actually be tackled by graph pattern matching techniques, a database topic that has been well studied. We also provide complexity and approximation bounds for VNMs. Moreover, for intractable VNM cases, we develop effective heuristic methods to find high-quality mappings.

(1) We propose a generic model to express VNMs in terms of graph pattern matching [18] (Sect. 2). In this model a VN request is specified as a graph

pattern, bearing various constraints on nodes and links defined with aggregation functions, and an SN is simply treated as a graph with attributes associated with its nodes and edges. The decision and optimization problems for VNMs are then simply graph pattern matching problems. We also show that the model is able to express VNMs commonly found in practice, including all the mappings we have seen so far (Sect. 3).

(2) We establish complexity and approximation bounds for VNMs (Sect. 4). We give a uniform upper bound for the VNM problems expressed in this model, by showing that all these problems are in NP. We also show that VNM is polynomial time (PTIME) solvable if only node constraints are present (VMP), but it becomes NP-complete when either node sharing is allowed or constraints on edges are imposed. Moreover, we propose a VNM cost function and study optimization problems for VNM based on the metric. We show that the optimization problems are intractable in most cases and worse still, are NPO-complete in general and APX-hard [10] for special cases. To the best of our knowledge, these are among the first complexity and approximation results on VNMs.

We contend that these results are useful for developing virtualized cloud data centers for querying and managing big data, among other things. By modeling VNM as graph pattern matching, we are able to characterize various VN requests with different classes of graph patterns, and study the expressive power and complexity of these graph pattern languages. The techniques developed for graph pattern matching can be leveraged to study VNMs. Indeed, the proofs of some of the results in this work capitalize on graph pattern techniques. Furthermore, the results of this work are also of interest to *the study of graph pattern matching* [18].

2   Graph Pattern Matching Model

Below we first represent virtual networks (VNs) and substrate networks (SNs) as weighted directed graphs. We then introduce a generic model to express virtual network mapping (VNM) in terms of graph pattern matching [18].

2.1   Substrate and Virtual Networks

An SN consists of a set of substrate nodes connected with physical links, in which the nodes and links are associated with resources of a certain capacity, *e.g.*, CPU and storage capacity for nodes, and bandwidth and latency for links. A VN is specified in terms of a set of virtual nodes and a set of virtual links, along with requirements on the capacities of the nodes and the capacities of the links. Both VNs and SNs can be naturally modeled as weighted directed graphs.

Weighted Directed Graphs. A *weighted directed graph* is defined as $G = (V, E, f_V, f_E)$, where (1) V is a finite set of nodes; (2) $E \subseteq V \times V$ is a set of edges, in which (v, v') denotes an edge from v to v'; (3) f_V is a function defined on V such that for each node $v \in V$, $f_V(v)$ is a positive rational number; and similarly, (4) f_E is a function defined on E.

Substrate Networks. A *substrate network* (SN) is a weighted directed graph $G_S = (V_S, E_S, f_{V_S}, f_{E_S})$, where (1) V_S and E_S denote sets of substrate nodes and physical links (directly connected), respectively; and (2) the functions f_{V_S} and f_{E_S} denote resource capacities on the nodes (*e.g.*, CPU) and links (*e.g.*, bandwidth and latency), respectively.

Virtual Networks. A *virtual network* (VN) is specified as a weighted directed graph $G_P = (V_P, E_P, f_{V_P}, f_{E_P})$, where (1) V_P and E_P denote virtual nodes and links, and (2) f_{V_P} and f_{E_P} are functions defined on V_P and E_P in the same way as in substrate networks, respectively.

Example 2. The SN depicted in Fig. 1(b) is a weighted graph G_S, where (1) the node set is $\{a, b, ..., f\}$; (2) the edges include the directed edges in the graph; (3) the weights associated with nodes indicate CPU capacities; and (4) the weights of edges denote bandwidth or latency capacities. Figure 1(a) shows a VN, where (1) the node set is $\{VM_1, VM_2, VM_3\}$; (2) the edge set is $\{(VM_i, VM_j) \mid i, j = 1, 2, 3\}$; (3) $f_{V_P}(VM_1) = 66$, $f_{V_P}(VM_2) = 20$, $f_{V_P}(VM_3) = 30$; and (4) the function f_{E_P} is defined on the edge labels. As will be seen when we define the notion of VN requests, the labels indicate requirements on deploying the VN in an SN.

Paths. A *path* ρ from node u_0 to u_n in an SN G_S is denoted as $(u_0, u_1, \ldots, u_n)$, where (a) $u_i \in V_S$ for each $i \in [0, n]$, (b) there exists an edge $e_i = (u_{i-1}, u_i)$ in E_S for each $i \in [1, n]$, and moreover, (c) for all $i, j \in [0, n]$, if $i \neq j$, then $u_i \neq u_j$. We write $e \in \rho$ if e is an edge on ρ. When it is clear from the context, we also use ρ to denote the set of edges on the path, *i.e.*, $\{e_i \mid i \in [1, n]\}$.

2.2   Virtual Network Mapping

Virtual network mapping (VNM) from a VN G_P to an SN G_S is specified in terms of a node mapping, an edge mapping and a VN request. The VN request imposes constraints on the node mapping and edge mapping, defining their semantics. We next define these notions.

A *node mapping* from G_P to G_S is a pair (g_V, r_V) of functions, where g_V maps the set V_P of virtual nodes in G_P to the set V_S of substrate nodes in G_S, and for each v in V_P, if $g_V(v) = u$, $r_V(v, u)$ is a positive number. Intuitively, function r_V specifies the amount of resource of the substrate node u that is allocated to the node v.

For each edge (v, v') in G_P, we use $P(v, v')$ to denote the set of paths from $g_V(v)$ to $g_V(v')$ in G_S. An *edge mapping* from G_P to G_S is a pair (g_E, r_E) of functions such that for each edge $(v, v') \in E_P$, $g_E(v, v')$ is a subset of $P(v, v')$, and r_E attaches a positive number to each pair (e, ρ) if $e \in E_P$ and $\rho \in g_E(e)$. Intuitively, $r_E(e, \rho)$ is the amount of resource of the physical path ρ allocated to the virtual link e.

VN Requests. A VN *request* to an SN G_S is a pair $(G_P, \mathcal{C})$, where G_P is a VN, and $\mathcal{C}$ is a set of constraints such that for a pair $((g_V, r_V), (g_E, r_E))$ of node and edge mappings from G_P to G_S, each constraint in $\mathcal{C}$ has one of the forms below:

(1) for each $v \in V_P$, $f_{V_P}(v) \leq r_V(v, g_V(v))$;

(2) for each $u \in V_S$, $f_{V_S}(u) \geq \mathsf{sum}(N(u))$, where $N(u)$ is $\{|r_V(v, u) \mid v \in V_P, g_V(v) = u|\}$, a bag (an unordered collection of elements with repetitions) determined by virtual nodes in G_P hosted by u;

(3) for each $e \in E_P$, $f_{E_P}(e)$ op $\mathsf{agg}(Q(e))$, where $Q(e)$ is $\{|r_E(e, \rho) \mid \rho \in g_E(e)|\}$, a bag collecting physical paths ρ that instantiate e; here op is either the comparison operator $\leq$ or $\geq$, and $\mathsf{agg}()$ is one of the aggregation functions min, max and sum;

(4) for each $e' \in E_S$, $f_{E_S}(e') \geq \mathsf{sum}(M(e'))$, where $M(e')$ is $\{|r_E(e, \rho) \mid e \in E_P, \rho \in g_E(e), e' \in \rho|\}$, a bag collecting those virtual links that are instantiated by a physical link ρ containing e'; and

(5) for each $e \in E_P$ and $\rho \in g_E(e)$, $r_E(e, \rho)$ op $\mathsf{agg}(U(\rho))$ where $U(\rho)$ is $\{|f_{E_S}(e') \mid e' \in \rho|\}$), a bag of all edges on a physical path that instantiate e.

Constraints in a VN request are classified as follows.

Node Constraints: Constraints of form (1) or (2). Intuitively, a constraint of form (1) assures that when a virtual node v is hosted by a substrate node u, u must provide adequate resource. A constraint of form (2) asserts that when a substrate node u hosts (possibly multiple) virtual nodes, u must have sufficient capacity to accommodate all those virtual nodes. When u hosts at most one virtual node, _i.e._, if node sharing is not allowed, then $|N(u)| \leq 1$, where we use $|N(u)|$ to denote the number of virtual nodes hosted by u.

Edge Constraints: Constraints of form (3), (4) or (5). Constraints of form (3) assure that when a virtual link e is mapped to a set of physical paths in the SN, those physical paths together satisfy the requirements (on bandwidths or latencies) of e. We denote by $|Q(e)|$ the number of physical paths to which e is mapped. Those of form (4) assert that for each physical link e', it must have sufficient bandwidth to accommodate those of all the virtual links that are mapped to some physical path containing e'. Those of form (5) assure that when a virtual link e is mapped to a set of paths, for each ρ in the set, the resource of ρ allocated to e must be consistent with the capacities of the physical links on ρ, _e.g._, may not exceed the minimum bandwidth of the physical links on ρ.

VNM. We say that a VN request $(G_P, \mathcal{C})$ can be _mapped to_ an SN G_S, denoted by $G_P \rhd_\mathcal{C} G_S$, if there exists a pair $((g_V, r_V), (g_E, r_E))$ of node and edge mappings from G_P to G_S such that all the constraints of $\mathcal{C}$ are satisfied, _i.e._, the functions g_V and g_E satisfy all the inequalities in $\mathcal{C}$.

The VNM_problem_ is to determine, given a VN request $(G_P, \mathcal{C})$ and an SN G_S, whether $G_P \rhd_\mathcal{C} G_S$.

3   Case Study

All the VNM requirements in the Introduction (Sect. 1) can be expressed in our model, by treating VN request as a pattern and SN as a graph. Below we present a case study.

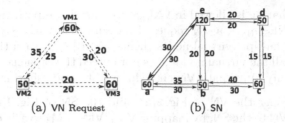

Fig. 2. VN request and SN for case study

Case 1: Virtual Machine Placement. VMP can be expressed as a VN request in which only node constraints are present. It is to find an injective mapping (g_V, r_V) from virtual nodes to substrate nodes (hence $|N| \leq 1$) that satisfies the node constraints, while imposing no constraints on edge mapping.

Case 2: Priority Mapping. VNM_P can be captured as a VN request specified as $(G_P, \mathcal{C})$, where $\mathcal{C}$ consists of (a) node constraints of forms (1) and (2), and (b) edge constraints of form (3) when op is $\leq$ and agg is max, and form (5) when op is $\leq$ and agg is min. It is to find an injective node mapping (g_V, r_V) and an edge mapping (g_E, r_E) such that for each virtual link e, $g_E(e)$ is a single path (hence $|Q(e)| = 1$). Moreover, it requires that the capacity of each virtual node v does not exceed the capacity of the substrate node that hosts v. When a virtual link e is mapped to a physical path ρ, the *bandwidth* of each edge on ρ is no less than that of e, *i.e.*, ρ suffices to serve any connection *individually*, including the one with the highest priority when ρ is allocated to the connection.

Example 3. Consider the VN given in Fig. 1(a) and the SN of Fig. 1(b). Constraints for priority mapping can be defined as described above, using the node and edge labels (on bandwidths) in Fig. 1(a). There exists a priority mapping from the VN to the SN. Indeed, one can map VM_1, VM_2 and VM_3 to b, a and d, respectively, and map the virtual links to the shortest physical paths uniquely determined by the node mapping, *e.g.*, $(\text{VM}_1, \text{VM}_2)$ is mapped to (b, a).

Case 3: Single-Path VN Embedding. A VNE_{SP} request can be specified as $(G_P, \mathcal{C})$, where $\mathcal{C}$ consists of (a) node constraints of forms (1) and (2), and (b) edge constraints of form (3) when op is $\leq$ and agg is sum, and edge constraints of forms (4) and (5) when op is $\leq$ and agg is min. It differs from VNM_P in that for each physical link e', it requires the *bandwidth* of e' to be no less than *the sum of* bandwidths of *all* those virtual links that are instantiated via e'. In contrast to VNM_P that aims to serve the connection with the highest priority at a time, VNE_{SP} requires that each physical link has enough capacity to serve *all connections* sharing the physical link at the same time.

Similarly, multi-path VN embedding (denoted by VNE_{MP}) can be expressed as a VN request. It is the same as VNE_{SP} except that a virtual link e can be mapped to *a set* $g_E(e)$ of physical paths. When taken together, the paths in $g_E(e)$ provide sufficient bandwidth required by e.

When node sharing is allowed in $\mathsf{VNE_{SP}}$, *i.e.*, for single-path embedding with node sharing ($\mathsf{VNE_{SP(NS)}}$), a VN request is specified similarly. Here a substrate node u can host multiple virtual nodes (hence $|N(u)| \geq 0$) such that the sum of the capacities of all the virtual nodes does not exceed the capacity of u. Similarly, one can also specify multi-path VN embedding with node sharing ($\mathsf{VNE_{MP(NS)}}$).

Example 4. Consider the VN of Fig. 2(a), and the SN of Fig. 2(b). There is a $\mathsf{VNE_{SP}}$ from the VN to the SN, by mapping $\mathsf{VM_1}, \mathsf{VM_2}, \mathsf{VM_3}$ to a, b, e, respectively, and mapping the VN edges to the shortest paths in the SN determined by the node mapping. There is also a multi-path embedding $\mathsf{VNE_{MP}}$ from the VN to the SN, by mapping $\mathsf{VM_1}, \mathsf{VM_2}$ and $\mathsf{VM_3}$ to a, c and e, respectively. For the virtual links, $(\mathsf{VM_1}, \mathsf{VM_2})$ can be mapped to the physical path (a, b, c), $(\mathsf{VM_1}, \mathsf{VM_3})$ to (a, e), and $(\mathsf{VM_3}, \mathsf{VM_2})$ to two paths $\rho_1 = (e, b, c)$ and $\rho_2 = (e, d, c)$ with $r_E((\mathsf{VM_3}, \mathsf{VM_2}), \rho_1) = 5$ and $r_E((\mathsf{VM_3}, \mathsf{VM_2}), \rho_2) = 15$; similarly for the other virtual links.

One can verify that the VN of Fig. 2(a) allows no more than one virtual node to be mapped to the same substrate node in Fig. 2(b). However, if we change the bandwidths of the edges connecting a and e in SN from 30 to $f_{V_S}(a, e) = 40$ and $f_{V_S}(e, a) = 50$, then there exists a mapping from the VN to the SN that supports node sharing. Indeed, in this setting, one can map both $\mathsf{VM_1}, \mathsf{VM_2}$ to e and map $\mathsf{VM_3}$ to a; and map the virtual edges to the shortest physical paths determined by the node mapping; for instance, both $(\mathsf{VM_1}, \mathsf{VM_3})$ and $(\mathsf{VM_2}, \mathsf{VM_3})$ can be mapped to (e, a).

Case 4: Latency Constrained Mapping. A $\mathsf{VNM_L}$ request is expressed as $(G_P, \mathcal{C})$, where $\mathcal{C}$ consists of (a) node constraints of forms (1) and (2), and (b) edge constraints of form (3) when op is $\geq$ and agg is min, and of form (5) when op is $\geq$ and agg is sum. It is similar to $\mathsf{VNE_{SP}}$ except that when a virtual link e is mapped to a physical path ρ, it requires ρ to satisfy the *latency* requirement of e, *i.e.*, the sum of the latencies of the edges on ρ does not exceed that of e.

Example 5. One can verify that there is no latency mapping of the VN shown in Fig. 1(a) to the SN in Fig. 1(b). However, if we change the constraints on the virtual links of the VN request to: $(\mathsf{VM_1}, \mathsf{VM_2}) = 50$, $(\mathsf{VM_2}, \mathsf{VM_1}) = 55$, $(\mathsf{VM_1}, \mathsf{VM_3}) = (\mathsf{VM_3}, \mathsf{VM_1}) = 120$ and $(\mathsf{VM_2}, \mathsf{VM_3}) = (\mathsf{VM_3}, \mathsf{VM_2}) = 60$, then there is a mapping from the VN to the SN. We can map $\mathsf{VM_1}, \mathsf{VM_2}, \mathsf{VM_3}$ to c, b, a, respectively, and map the edges to the shortest physical paths determined by the node mapping.

4   Complexity and Approximation

We next study fundamental issues associated with virtual network mapping. We first establish the complexity bounds of the VNM problem in various settings, from PTIME to NP-complete. We then introduce a cost metric for virtual network mapping, formulate optimization problems based on the function, and finally, give the complexity bounds and approximation hardness of the optimization problems. Due to the space constraint, we defer the detailed proofs to [5].

4.1   The Complexity of VNM

We provide an upper bound for the VNM problem in the general setting, by showing it is in NP. We also show that the problem is in PTIME when only node constraints are present. However, when node sharing or edge constraints are imposed, it becomes NP-hard, even when both virtual and substrate networks are directed acyclic graphs (DAGs). That is, node sharing and edge constraints make our lives harder.

Theorem 1. *The virtual network mapping problem is*
(1) in NP regardless of what constraints are present;
(2) in PTIME when only node constraints are present, without node sharing, i.e., VMP *is in PTIME; However,*
(3) it becomes NP-complete when node sharing is requested, i.e., VMP$_{(NS)}$, VNM$_{P(NS)}$, VNM$_{L(NS)}$, VNE$_{SP(NS)}$ *and* VNE$_{MP(NS)}$ *are NP-complete; and*
(4) it is NP-complete in the presence of edge constraints; i.e., VNM$_P$, VNM$_L$, VNE$_{SP}$ *and* VNE$_{MP}$ *are intractable.*

All the results hold when both VNs *and* SNs *are* DAGs.

4.2   Approximation of Optimization Problems

In practice, one typically wants to find a VNM mapping with "the lowest cost". This highlights the need for introducing a function to measure the cost of a mapping and studying its corresponding optimization problems.

A Cost Function. Consider an SN $G_S = (V_S, E_S, f_{V_S}, f_{E_S})$, and a VN request $(G_P, \mathcal{C})$, where $G_P = (V_P, E_P, f_{V_P}, f_{E_P})$. Assume a positive number associated with all nodes v and links e in G_S, denoted by $w(v)$ and $w(e)$, respectively, that indicates the price of the resources in the SN.

Given a pair $((g_V, r_V), (g_E, r_E))$ of node and edge mappings from $(G_P, \mathcal{C})$ to G_S, its *cost* $c((g_V, r_V), (g_E, r_E))$ is defined as
$c((g_V, r_V), (g_E, r_E)) = \sum_{v \in V_P} h_V(g_V, r_V, v) \cdot w(g_V(v)) + \sum_{e' \in E_S} h_E(g_E, r_E, e') \cdot w(e')$,
where (1) $h_V(g_V, r_V, v) = r_V(v, g_V(v)) / f_{V_S}(g_V(v))$,
(2) $h_E(g_E, r_V, e') = \sum_{e \in E_P, \rho \in g_E(e), e' \in \rho} r_E(e, \rho) / f_{E_S}(e')$ when the resource of physical links is bandwidth, and
(3) when latency is concerned, $h_E(g_E, r_V, e')$ is 1 if there exists $e \in E_P$ such that $e' \in g_E(e)$, and 0 otherwise.

Intuitively, h_V indicates that the more CPU resource is allocated, the higher the cost it incurs; similarly for h_E when bandwidth is concerned. When latency is considered, the cost of the edge mapping is determined only by g_E, whereas the resource allocation function r_E is irrelevant.

The cost function is motivated by economic models of network virtualization [13]. It is justified by Web hosting and cloud storage [11], which mainly sell CPU power or storage services of nodes, and by virtual network mapping, which also sells bandwidth of links [14]. It is also to serve cloud provision in virtualized data center networks [19], for which dynamic routing strategy (latency) is critical while routing congestion (bandwidth allocation) is considered secondary.

Minimum Cost Mapping. We now introduce optimization problems for virtual network mapping.

The *minimum cost mapping* problem is to find, given a VN request and an SN, a mapping $((g_V, r_V), (g_E, r_E))$ from the VN to the SN such that its cost based on the function above is minimum among all such mappings.

The decision problem for minimum cost mapping is to decide, given a number (bound) K, a VN request and an SN, whether there is a mapping $((g_V, r_V), (g_E, r_E))$ from the VN to the SN such that its cost is no larger than K.

We shall refer to the minimum cost mapping problem and its decision problem interchangeably in the sequel.

Complexity and Approximation. We next study the minimum cost mapping problem for all cases given before. Having seen Theorem 1, it is not surprising that the optimization problem is intractable in most cases. This motivates us to study their efficient approximation algorithms with performance guarantees.

Unfortunately, the problem is hard to approximate in most cases. The results below tell us that when node sharing is requested or edge constraints are present, minimum cost mapping is beyond reach in practice for approximation.

Theorem 2. *The minimum cost mapping problem is*
(1) in PTIME for VMP *without node sharing; however, when node sharing is requested, i.e., for* VMP$_{(NS)}$, *it becomes NP-complete and is APX-hard;*
(2) NP-complete and NPO-complete for VNM$_P$, VNE$_{SP}$, VNE$_{MP}$, VNM$_L$, VNM$_{P(NS)}$, VNE$_{SP(NS)}$, VNE$_{MP(NS)}$, VNM$_{L(NS)}$; *And*
(3) APX-hard when there is a unique node mapping in the presence of edge constraints. In particular, VNM$_P$ *does not admit* $\ln(|V_P|)$-*approximation, unless $P = NP$.*

The NPO-hardness results remain intact even when both VNs *and* SNs *are* DAGs.

Here NPO is the *class* of all NP optimization problems (cf. [10]). An NPO-complete problem is NP-hard to optimize, and is among the hardest optimization problems. APX is the *class* of problems that allow PTIME approximation algorithms with a constant approximation ratio (cf. [10]).

Heuristic Algorithms. These above results tell us that it is beyond reach in practice to find PTIME algorithms for VNMs with edge constraints such as VNM$_P$ and VNE$_{SP}$, or to find efficient approximation algorithms with decent performance guarantees. In light of these, we study heuristic algorithms.

We develop heuristic algorithms for priority mapping VNM$_P$, with node sharing or not [5]. We focus on VNM$_P$ since it is needed in, *e.g.*, internet-based virtualized infrastructure computing platform (iVIC [4]). Our algorithm reduces unnecessary computation by minimizing VNs requests and utilizing auxiliary graphs of SNs [5]. While several algorithms are available for VN embedding (*e.g.*, [20]), no previous work has studied algorithms for VNM$_P$. We encourage interested readers to look into [5] for the detailed introduction and experimental study of these algorithms.

5   Related Work

Virtualization techniques have been investigated for big data processing [23] and database applications [7,8,24]. However, none of these has provided a systematic study of VNM, by modeling VNM as graph pattern matching. The only exception is [20], which adopted subgraph isomorphism for VNM, a special case of the generic model proposed in this work. Moreover, complexity and approximation analyses associated with VNM have not been studied for cloud computing in database applications.

Several models have been developed for VNM. (a) The VM placement problem (VMP, [12]) is to map a set of VMs onto an SN with constraints on node capacities. (b) Single-path VN embedding (VNE$_{SP}$, [22]) is to map a VN to an SN by a node-to-node injection and an edge-to-path function, subject to constraints on the CPU capacities of nodes and constraints on the bandwidths of physical connections. (c) Different from VNE$_{SP}$, multi-path embedding (VNE$_{MP}$, [14,25]) allows an edge of a VN to be mapped to multiple parallel paths of an SN such that the sum of the bandwidth capacities of those paths is no smaller than the bandwidth of that edge. (d) While graph layout problems are similar to VN mapping, they do not have bandwidth constraints on edges but instead, impose certain topological constraints (see [15] for a survey). In contrast to our work, these models are studied for specific domains, and no previous work has studied generic models to support various VN requests that commonly arise in practice.

Very few complexity results are known for VNM. The only work we are aware of is [9], which claimed that the testbed mapping problem is NP-hard in the presence of node types and some links with infinite capacity. Several complexity and approximation results are established for graph pattern matching (see [18] for a survey). However, those results are for edge-to-edge mappings, whereas VNM typically needs to map virtual links to physical paths. There have been recent extensions to support edge-to-path mappings for graph pattern matching [16,17], with several intractability and approximation bounds established there. Those differ from this work in that either no constraints on links are considered [17], or graph simulation is adopted [16], which does not work for VNM. The complexity and approximation bounds developed in this work are among the first results that have been developed for VNM in cloud computing.

6   Conclusion

We have proposed a model to express various VN requests found in practice, based on graph pattern matching, and we have shown that that the model is able to express VNMs commonly found in practice. We have also established a number of intractability and approximation hardness results in various practical VNM settings. These are among the first efforts to settle fundamental problems for virtual network mapping. A few topics are targeted for future work. We are developing practical heuristic algorithms and optimization techniques for VNM.

We are also exploring techniques for processing VN requests for different applications, as well as their use in graph pattern matching.

Acknowledgments. Fan and Cao are supported in part by NSFC 61133002, 973 Program 2014CB340302, Shenzhen Peacock Program 1105100030834361, Guangdong Innovative Research Team Program 2011D005, EPSRC EP/J015377/1 and EP/M025268/1, and a Google Faculty Research Award. Ma is supported in part by 973 Program 2014CB340304, NSFC 61322207 and the Fundamental Research Funds for the Central Universities.

References

1. http://www.bigswitch.com/
2. http://aws.amazon.com/ec2/
3. http://www.vmware.com/solutions/datacenter/
4. http://frenzy.ivic.org.cn/
5. http://homepages.inf.ed.ac.uk/s1165433/papers/vnm-full.pdf
6. http://www.isi.edu/xbone/
7. Aboulnaga, A., Amza, C., Salem, K.: Virtualization and databases: state of the art and research challenges. In: EDBT (2008)
8. Aboulnaga, A., Salem, K., Soror, A., Minhas, U., Kokosielis, P., Kamath, S.: Deploying database appliances in the cloud. IEEE Data Eng. Bull **32**(1), 13–20 (2009)
9. Andersen, D.: Theoretical approaches to node assignment (2002)(unpublished manuscript)
10. Ausiello, G.: Complexity and Approximation: Combinatorial Optimization Problems and Their Approximability Properties. Springer Verlag, Heidelberg (1999)
11. Bavier, A.C., Feamster, N., Huang, M., Peterson, L.L., Rexford, J.: In VINI veritas: realistic and controlled network experimentation. In: SIGCOMM (2006)
12. Bobroff, N., Kochut, A., Beaty, K.: Dynamic placement of virtual machines for managing sla violations. In: IM (2007)
13. Chowdhury, N., Boutaba, R.: A survey of network virtualization. Comput. Netw. **54**(5), 862–876 (2010)
14. Chowdhury, N., Rahman, M., Boutaba, R.: Virtual network embedding with coordinated node and link mapping. In: INFOCOM (2009)
15. Díaz, J., Petit, J., Serna, M.: A survey of graph layout problems. CSUR **34**(3), 313–356 (2002)
16. Fan, W., Li, J., Ma, S., Tang, N., Wu, Y., Wu, Y.: Graph pattern matching: from intractable to polynomial time. In: VLDB (2010)
17. Fan, W., Li, J., Ma, S., Wang, H., Wu, Y.: Graph homomorphism revisited for graph matching. In: VLDB (2010)
18. Gallagher, B.: Matching structure and semantics: a survey on graph-based pattern matching. In: AAAI FS (2006)
19. Guo, C., Lu, G., Li, D., Wu, H., Zhang, X., Shi, Y., Tian, C., Zhang, Y., Lu, S.: Bcube: a high performance, server-centric network architecture for modular data centers. In: SIGCOMM (2009)
20. Lischka, J., Karl, H.: A virtual network mapping algorithm based on subgraph isomorphism detection. In: SIGCOMM workshop VISA (2009)

21. Reinhardt, W.: Advance reservation of network resources for multimedia applications. In: IWACA (1994)
22. Ricci, R., Alfeld, C., Lepreau, J.: A solver for the network testbed mapping problem. SIGCOMM CCR **33**, 65–81 (2003)
23. Trelles, O., Prins, P., Snir, M., Jansen, R.C.: Big data, but are we ready? Nat. Rev. Genet. **12**(3), 224 (2011)
24. Xiong, P., Chi, Y., Zhu, S., Moon, H.J., Pu, C., Hacigümüs, H.: Intelligent management of virtualized resources for database systems in cloud environment. In: ICDE (2011)
25. Yu, M., Yi, Y., Rexford, J., Chiang, M.: Rethinking virtual network embedding: substrate support for path splitting and migration. SIGCOMM CCR **38**(2), 17–29 (2008)
26. Zong, B., Raghavendra, R., Srivatsa, M., Yan, X., Singh, A.K., Lee, K.: Cloud service placement via subgraph matching. In: ICDE (2014)

A Fast Approach for Detecting Overlapping Communities in Social Networks Based on Game Theory

Lihua Zhou[1], Peizhong Yang[1], Kevin Lü[2(✉)], Lizhen Wang[1], and Hongmei Chen[1]

[1] School of Information, Yunnan University, Kunming 650091, China
{lhzhou, lzwang, hmchen}@ynu.edu.cn, 285342456@qq.com
[2] Brunel University, Uxbridge UB8 3PH, UK
kevin.lu.brunel@gmail.com

Abstract. Community detection, a fundamental task in social network analysis, aims to identify groups of nodes in a network such that nodes within a group are much more connected to each other than to the rest of the network. The cooperative theory and non-cooperative game theory have been used separately for detecting communities. In this paper, we develop a new approach that utilizes both cooperative and non-cooperative game theory to detect communities. The individuals in a social network are modelled as playing cooperative game for achieving and improving group's utilities, meanwhile individuals also play the non-cooperative game for improving individual's utilities. By combining the cooperative and non-cooperative game theories, utilities of groups and individuals can be taken into account simultaneously, thus the communities detected can be more rational and the computational cost will be decreased. The experimental results on synthetic and real networks show that our algorithm can fast detect overlapping communities.

Keywords: Social network · Overlapping community detection · Cooperative game · Non-cooperative game

1 Introduction

In social network analysis, the task of community detection is to identify groups of nodes in a network such that nodes within a group are much more connected to each other than to the rest of the network [1, 2]. Detecting communities is important to understand the structural properties of social networks, and to improve user-oriented services such as identification of influential users and the setup of efficient recommender systems for targeted marketing. With online social networks become increasingly popular, community detection has received a great deal of attention [3–5].

In social network environments, behaviors of individuals are not entirely independent [6], co-operations co-exist with conflicts amongst individuals, and thus social networks can be analyzed based on the game theory. The game theory is a mathematic tool for studying the complex conflict and cooperation amongst rational agents. In general, the game theory can be divided into the non-cooperative and the cooperative

© Springer International Publishing Switzerland 2015
S. Maneth (Ed.): BICOD 2015, LNCS 9147, pp. 62–73, 2015.
DOI: 10.1007/978-3-319-20424-6_7

game theory. The non-cooperative game theory [7] studies the individual behaviors of agents, where each agent selects its strategy independently for improving its own utility. The cooperative game theory [8] studies the cooperative behaviors of groups of agents, where agents cooperate to each other for improving the group's utility and a group of agents is called a coalition.

The game theory, either cooperative or not, has been used separately to solve community detection problems. The non-cooperative game theory-based methods consider community formation as the result of the individual behaviors of selfish agents and the community structure as the equilibrium amongst individual agents, while the cooperative game theory-based methods consider community formation as the result of the group behaviors of rational agents and the community structure as the equilibrium amongst groups of rational agents. The cooperative game theory-based methods neglect individual utilities of agents while the non-cooperative game theory-based methods neglect utilities of groups. Thus, it is a challenging task to improve existing methods to obtain more rational and logical results.

In this study, we develop a new approach that utilizes both cooperative and non-cooperative game theory to detect communities. Firstly, individuals in a social network are regarded as rational agents who cooperate with other agents to form coalitions for achieving and improving group's utilities. Then, each individual is modelled as a selfish agent who selects coalitions to join or leave based on its own utility measurement. Each agent is allowed to select multiple coalitions, thus overlapping coalitions can be formed. Because the non-cooperative game is played on the basis of the result of the cooperative game rather than taking the initiative in which every agent has one community of its own, the number of agents that would change their community memberships to improve their utilities could decrease, thus the efficiency of the non-cooperative game will be improved. By combining the cooperative and non-cooperative game theory, utilities of groups and individuals can be taken into account simultaneously, thus the rational and accuracy of communities detected can be improved and the computational cost will be decreased.

The rest of this paper is organized as follows: Sect. 2 introduces related work and Sect. 3 introduces a game theory-based approach for community detection. The experimental results on the real networks and benchmark networks are presented in Sects. 4 and 5 summarizes this paper.

2 Related Work

To detect overlapping communities, Palla et al. [9] defined a k-clique-community as the union of all k-cliques that can be reached from each other through a series of adjacent k-cliques, however the size of the clique is required as an input that is usually unknown beforehand. Ahn et al. [10] considered a community to be a set of closely interrelated links. This algorithm suffers from more computation cost because the number of links is more than the number of nodes. Ball et al. [11] proposed a probabilistic model of link communities, but they do not offer criterion for determining the number of communities in a network.

Chen et al. [12] proposed a non-cooperative game theory-based framework for overlapping community detection. Alvari et al. [13] considered the formation of communities in social networks as an iterative game in a multiagent environment, in which each node is regarded as an agent trying to be in the communities with members such that they are structurally equivalent. Lung et al. [14] formulated the community detection problem from a game theory point of view and solved this problem by using an algorithm adapted for detecting Nash equilibrium of non-cooperative games. Hajibagheri et al. [15] used a framework based on the *information diffusion model* and the Shapley Value concept to address the community detection problem.

In our previous studies [16, 17], we proposed two coalitional game models for community detection. The first model [16] mainly focused on the structure information of a network and used the Shapley Value to evaluate each individual's contribution to the closeness of connection; while the second model [17] incorporated the structure information of a network and the attribute information of individuals, and used the Shapley Value to evaluate each individual's contribution to the closeness of connection and its preference to a specific topic. These two approaches do not able to identify overlapping communities.

3   A Game Theory-Based Approach for Community Detection

Consider $G = (V, E)$ be an undirected unweighted graph representing a social network with $n = |V|$ nodes and $m = |E|$ edges. Let A be an adjacency matrix of G with $A(x, y) = 1$ if $(x, y) \in E$ for any pair of nodes $x, y \in V$ and 0 otherwise. Let S_i denote a subset of V and S_i be a coalition, meanwhile let Γ denote a coalition structure (a *collection* of coalitions), i.e. $\Gamma = \{S_1, S_2, \ldots, S_k\}$.

Our approach consists of the *group game* and *the individual game*. The former is a cooperative game in which agents cooperate to each other for improving the utilities of coalitions, while the later is a non-cooperative game in which each agent chooses its strategy independently for improving its own utility. Agents first play group game to achieve equilibrium of coalitions in which no coalition can improve the group's utility by cooperating with others, and then they play the individual game to achieve equilibrium of agents in which no agent can improve its own utility by changing its strategy. The equilibrium of agents in the individual game is regarded as the community structure of a network. The framework of our study is shown in Fig. 1.

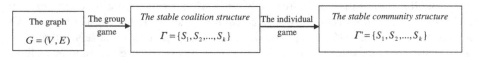

Fig. 1. The framework of our approach

3.1 Group Game

In the *group game*, individuals in a social network are modeled as rational agents trying to achieve and improve group's utilities by cooperating with other agents to form coalitions. Coalitions with fewer agents can merge into larger coalitions as long as the merge operation can contribute to improve the utilities of coalitions merged. The game starts from the nodes as separate coalitions (singletons), coalitions that can result the highest utility increment are iteratively merged into larger coalitions to improve groups' utilities until no such merge operation can be performed. It indicates that the game has achieved an *equilibrium state of coalitions*, in which no group of agents has an interest in performing a merge operation any further.

Definition 1. The *utility function of a coalition*. Let S_i be a coalition of $G = (V, E)$, $e(S_i)$ be the number of edges amongst nodes inside S_i and $d(x)$ be the degree of node x, then the utility function $v(S_i)$ of S_i is defined by the following Eq. (1):

$$v(S_i) = \frac{2e(S_i)}{\sum_{x \in S_i} d(x)} - \left(\frac{\sum_{x \in S_i} d(x)}{2m} \right)^2 \tag{1}$$

In fact, $v(S_i)$ is a modified version of the summand term of the Newman and Girvan's [1] modularity Q (that is defined as $Q = \sum_{c=1}^{n_c} \left(\frac{e(S_c)}{m} - \left(\frac{d(S_c)}{m} \right)^2 \right)$).

Definition 2. *Stable coalitions*. A coalition S_i is regarded as a *stable coalition* if S_i can not further improve its utility by merging with other coalitions, i.e. $\forall S_j \neq S_i$, $v(S_i + S_j) < v(S_i)$ and $\forall S_j \subseteq S_i, v(S_i) > v(S_j)$.

Definition 3. *The increment of utility of a coalition*. Let $S_{ij} = S_i + S_j$, a super coalition obtained by merging coalition S_i and S_j, then the increment of utility of coalition S_i with respect to S_{ij} is defined by $\Delta v(S_i, S_{ij}) = v(S_{ij}) - v(S_i)$.

There are two conditions must be satisfied for merging S_i and S_j, i.e. $e(S_i, S_j) \neq 0$ and $\Delta v(S_i, S_{ij}) > 0$ & $\Delta v(S_j, S_{ij}) > 0$. The former condition implies that two coalitions without an edge between them can not merge into a larger coalition. This is natural because this merge operation cannot contribute to improve the closeness of the connection. So, whether a coalition is merged with others can be decided by looking only at its neighbors (coalitions that have edges between them), without an exhaustive search over the entire network. The later condition implies that the utilities of S_i and S_j should be improved through the merge operation. The unilateral meet of two inequalities shows that two coalitions fail to reach an agreement to cooperate.

Definition 4. *Stable coalition structure*. A *collection* of coalitions $\Gamma = \{S_1, S_2, \ldots, S_k\}$ is regarded as a *stable coalition structure* if $\forall S_i \in \Gamma, \max(\max_{S_{ij}} \Delta v(S_i, S_{ij}), 0) = 0$ holds.

A *stable coalition structure* can be regarded as a kind of *equilibrium state of coalitions*, in which no group of agents has an interest in performing a merge operation any further. After the *group game* achieves *equilibrium state of coalitions*, the utility of each coalition can not be improved any further, but some agents may do not satisfy their individual utilities, so agents begin to play the *individual game* to improve their individual utilities.

3.2   Individual Game

In an *individual game*, each individual in a social network is modeled as a selfish agent, who selects independently coalitions from the *stable coalition structure* $\Gamma = \{S_1, S_2, \ldots, S_k\}$ to join or leave based on its own utility measurement. Each agent is allowed to select multiple coalitions to join or leave. A community structure can be interpreted as equilibrium of this *individual game*, in which no agent has an interest in changing its coalition memberships any further.

Definition 5. *The utility function of a node.* Let $x \in V$, $S_i \in \Gamma$, $d(x)$ be the degree of node x, then the utility function of node x with respect to S_i is defined by the following Eq. (2):

$$v_x(S_i) = \frac{e(x, S_i)}{d(x)} \qquad (2)$$

Where $e(x, S_i)$ denotes the the number of edges that link x to nodes of coalition S_i. The value of $v_x(S_i)$ is the ratio of edges between x and S_i over the degree of x, and it measures how close between x and S_i. $0 \le v_x(S_i) \le 1$. $v_x(S_i) = 1$ means all edges of x is connected to nodes of S_i, in this case, x will be an inner node of S_i after x joins S_i; $v_x(S_i) = 0$ means no one edge connects x to a node of S_i. The greater the value of $v_x(S_i)$ is, the closer the connection between x and S_i will be.

Definition 6. *Two operations: join and leave.* Let $x \in V$, $S_i \in \Gamma$. If $x \notin S_i$ & $v_x(S_i) \ge \omega$, then x joins S_i, $S_i = S_i + \{x\}$; If $x \in S_i$ & $v_x(S_i) < \varepsilon$, then x leaves S_i, $S_i = S_i - \{x\}$.

ω is the lower bound of the utility value of x who can join a new coalition, and ε is the upper bound of the utility value of x who can leave the coalition that it is in.

Definition 7. *The (ω, ε)-stable community structure.* A *collection* of coalitions $\Gamma = \{S_1, S_2, \ldots, S_k\}$ is regarded as a *stable community structure* if $\forall S_i \in \Gamma$, $\forall x \in S_i$, $v_x(S_i) \ge \omega$, and $\forall x \notin S_i$, $v_x(S_i) < \varepsilon$ holds.

A *stable community structure* can be regarded as a kind of *equilibrium state of agents*, in which no agent has an interest in changing its coalition memberships any further.

3.3   The Game Theory-Based Algorithm for Community Detection

The main steps of our game theory-based algorithm for community detection, referred as *CoCo-game* algorithm, are described as follows:

(1) Initialize each node to a singleton coalition and coalition structure as collection of singleton coalitions $\Gamma = \{\{1\},\{2\},...,\{n\}\}$

(2) Repeat (3) until the *stable coalition structure* is formed (no coalition can improve itself)

(3) $\forall S_i, S_j \in \Gamma$ & $e(S_i,S_j) \neq 0$, $S_{ij} = S_i + S_j$, if $\Delta v(S_i,S_{ij}) > 0$ & $\Delta v(S_j,S_{ij}) > 0$, then, $\Gamma = \Gamma + \{S_{ij}\} - \{S_i\} - \{S_j\}$

(4) Repeat (5) until the (ω,ε)-*stable coalition structure* is formed (no agent can improve itself)

(5) $\forall x \in V$, if $x \notin S_i$ & $v_x(S_i) \geq \omega$, then $S_i = S_i + \{x\}$; if $x \in S_i$ & $v_x(S_i) < \varepsilon$, then $S_i = S_i - \{x\}$

(6) Output the (ω,ε)-*stable community structure* $\Gamma = \{S_1, S_2,...,S_k\}$

4 Experiments

To evaluate our approach, we conduct experiments on two well-known real networks and the benchmark network of Lancichinetti & Fortunato [18]. We visualize the results of real networks and compute the *Normalized mutual information (NMI)* [19, 20] between the detected community structures and the underlying ground truth of benchmark networks as the evaluation metric. We also compare our results of the *group game* (Step(1)–Step(3) of the *CoCo-game* algorithm) and the *CoCo-game* with the results of *LocalEquilibrium* [12], an approach for detecting overlapping communities based on non-cooperative game theory.

4.1 Real Networks

The real networks used in this study are the *Zachary's network of Karate* [21] and the *Les Misèrables' network of characters* [22]. They are two well-known networks used to test community detection algorithms. The *Zachary's network of Karate* consists of 34 nodes and 79 edges that were set between individuals who were observed to interact outside the activities of the club, and the *Les Misèrables' network of characters* consists of 77 nodes and 508 edges that represent co-appearance of the corresponding characters in one or more scenes. In the *CoCo-game*, $\omega = 1/3$, $\varepsilon = 1/4$.

Figure 2 presents the result of the *Zachary's Karate network*, where (a) is the result of *LocaEquilibrium* [12], (b) is the result of the *group game* of this study, and (c) is the result of the *CoCo-game*. In this network, *LocaEquilibrium* detects 6 communities, the *group game* detects 3 communities, and the *CoCo-game* detects 4 communities. Compare (b) with (c), node 3 changes its memberships and this change initiate the result that the right community of (b) is split into two right communities of (c). Compare (a) with (c), we can see that the community structures detected by the *LocaEquilibrium* and the *CoCo-game* are refinements of the community structures discovered in the Newman and Girvan's study [1], in which the network are divided into two components, corresponding to the left overlapping communities and the two right communities in Fig. 2(c).

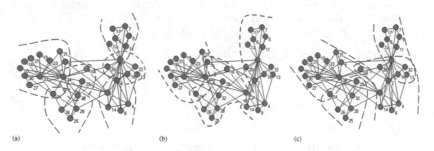

(a)   (b)   (c)

Fig. 2. The community structures of *the Zachary's karate network*. (a) The *LocalEquilibrium* [12]; (b) The *group game*; (c) The *CoCo-game*

Figure 3 presents the result of the *Les Misèrables' network of characters*, where (a) is the network structure, (b) is the result of the *LocaEquilibrium*, (c) is the result of the *group game*, and (d) is the result of the *CoCo-game*. In this network, the *LocaEquilibrium* detects 13 communities, the *group game* detects 6 communities, and the *CoCo-game* detects 5 communities. Compare (c) with (d), node 3, 4, 47, 48 change their

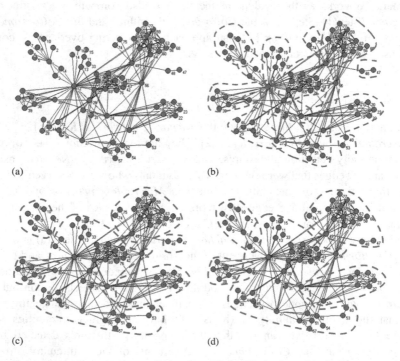

(a)   (b)

(c)   (d)

Fig. 3. The community structures of the *Les Misèrables' network of characters*. (a) The networks (b) The *LocalEquilibrium*; (c) The *group game*; (d) The *CoCo-game*

memberships. Compare (b) with (d), we can see that the middle community of (d) approximates the combination of communities containing node 12 in (b).

4.2 Benchmark Networks

We produce a series of benchmark networks by using the method of Lancichinetti & Fortunato [18]. The parameters used are listed as follows: the average degree $k = 20$, the maximum degree $\max k = 50$, the number of memberships of overlapping nodes $om = 2$, and the fractions of overlapping nodes range between 0 and 0.5; the number of nodes $N = 1000$ for Figs. 4 and 5 (a)–(d), $N = 5000$ for Figs. 4 and 5 (e)–(h); the mixing parameter $mu = 0.1$ for Figs. 4 and 5 (a), (c), (e), (g), and $mu = 0.3$ for Figs. 4 and 5 (b), (d), (f), (h); the minimum and maximum of the community sizes $\min c = 10$ and $\max c = 50$ for Figs. 4 and 5 (a), (b), (e), (f), while $\min c = 20$ and $\max c = 100$ for Figs. 4 and 5 (c), (d), (g), (h). In the *CoCo-game*, $\omega = 1/3$, $\varepsilon = 1/4$.

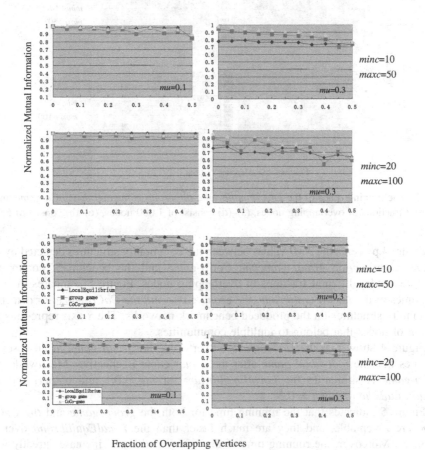

Fig. 4. The *NMI* values between the community structures detected by the *LocalEquilibrium/the group game/the CoCo-game* and the benchmark community structures under different fractions of overlapping nodes, (a)–(d) consist of 1,000 nodes, (e)–(h) consist of 5,000 nodes.

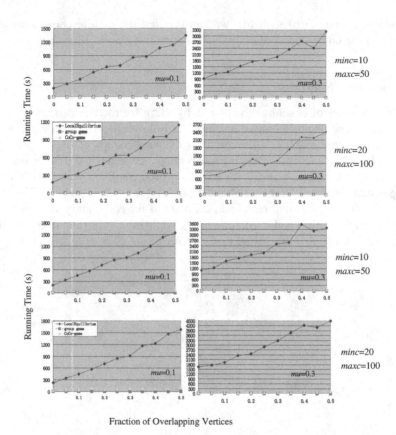

Fig. 5. The running times of the *LocalEquilibrium, the group game and the CoCo-game* under different fractions of overlapping nodes, (a)–(d) consist of 1,000 nodes, (e)–(h) consist of 5,000 nodes.

Figure 4 presents the *NMI* values between the community structures detected by the *LocalEquilibrium/the group game/the CoCo-game* and the benchmark community structures under different fractions of overlapping nodes. Figure 5 compares the running times of the *LocalEquilibrium*, the *group game and the CoCo-game* for detecting community structures on the produced benchmark networks. The *x*-axis represents the portion of nodes that belong to multiple communities.

Figure 4 show that the *CoCo-game* outperforms the *group game* in all cases. It indicates that the *individual game* after the *group game* is effective. Meanwhile, the *CoCo-game* is similar to the *LocalEquilibrium* for *mu* = 0.1 and outperforms the *LocalEquilibrium* for *mu* = 0.3.

Figure 5 indicates that the running time for both the *group game* and *the CoCo-game* are acceptable, and they are much faster than the *LocalEquilibrium* over all instances. Moreover, the running time of the *LocalEquilibrium* increases greatly with the number of nodes *N*, the portion of crossing edges *mu*, and the fraction of overlapping nodes. Meanwhile, the running times of both the *group game* and *the CoCo-game* are more stable than the *LocalEquilibrium*.

Figure 6 (a) and (b) present the *NMI* values between the community structures detected by the *CoCo-game* and the benchmark community structures under different ω and ε. The network used consists 1000 nodes in which 150 nodes belong to 2 communities, $mu = 0.3$, min$c = 20$, max$c = 100$. The *x*-axis represents the value of ω or ε. From Fig. 6, we can see that the value of *NMI* is affected by ω and ε. How to set automatically ω and ε is our future work.

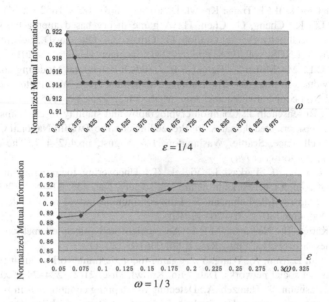

Fig. 6. The *NMI* values between the community structures detected by the *CoCo-game* and the benchmark community structures under different ω and ε.

5 Summary

In this paper, we develop a new approach that utilizes both cooperative and non-cooperative game theory to detect communities with improved accuracy. Because each agent is allowed to select multiple coalitions, the overlapping communities can be identified rationally. The experimental results demonstrated the features of our approach, they show that the joint use of cooperative and non-cooperative game theories to detect overlapping communities is effective and efficient.

Acknowledgement. The authors thank sincerely Mr. Wei Chen from Microsoft Research Asia for providing code on their work and helps. This work is supported by the National Natural Science Foundation of China under Grant No.61262069, No. 61472346, Program for Young and Middle-aged Teachers Grant, Yunnan University, and Program for Innovation Research Team in Yunnan University (Grant No. XT412011).

References

1. Newman, M.E.J., Girvan, M.: Finding and evaluating community structure in networks. Phys. Rev. E **69**, 026113 (2004)
2. Fortunato, S.: Community detection in graphs. Phys. Rep. **486**, 75–174 (2010)
3. Li, X.T., Ng, M.K., Ye, Y.M.: Multicomm: finding community structure in multi-dimensional networks. IEEE Trans. Knowl. Data Eng. **26**(4), 929–941 (2014)
4. Folino, F., Pizzuti, C.: An evolutionary multiobjective approach for community discovery in dynamic networks. IEEE Trans. Knowl. Data Eng. **26**(8), 1838–1852 (2014)
5. Zhou, L., Lü, K., Cheng, C., Chen, H.: A game theory based approach for community detection in social networks. In: Gottlob, G., Grasso, G., Olteanu, D., Schallhart, C. (eds.) BNCOD 2013. LNCS, vol. 7968, pp. 268–281. Springer, Heidelberg (2013)
6. Zacharias, G.L., MacMillan, J., Hemel, S.B.V. (eds.): Behavioral Modeling and Simulation: From Individuals to Societies. The National Academies Press, Washington (2008)
7. Nash, J.F.: Non-cooperative games. Ann. Math. **54**(2), 286–295 (1951)
8. Zlotkin, G., Rosenschein J.: Coalition cryptography and stability mechanisms for coalition formation in task oriented domains. In: Proceedings of The Twelfth National Conference on Artificial Intelligence, Seattle, Washington, 1-4 August, pp.432–437. The AAAI Press, Menlo Park, California (1994)
9. Palla, G., Derenyi, I., Farkas, I., Vicsek, T.: Uncovering the overlapping community structures of complex networks in nature and society. Nat. **435**, 814–818 (2005)
10. Ahn, Y.Y., Bagrow, J.P., Lehmann, S.: Link communities reveal multi-scale complexity in networks. Nat. **466**(7307), 761–764 (2010)
11. Ball, B., Karrer, B., Newman, M.E.J.: An efficient and principled method for detecting communities in networks. Phys. Rev. E **84**, 036103 (2011)
12. Chen, W., Liu, Z., Sun, X., Wang, Y.: A game-theoretic framework to identify overlapping communities in social networks. Data Min. Knowl. Disc. **21**(2), 224–240 (2010)
13. Alvari, H., Hashemi, S., Hamzeh, A.: Detecting overlapping communities in social networks by game theory and structural equivalence concept. In: Deng, H., Miao, D., Lei, J., Wang, F.L. (eds.) AICI 2011, Part II. LNCS, vol. 7003, pp. 620–630. Springer, Heidelberg (2011)
14. Lung, R.I., Gog, A., Chira, C.: A game theoretic approach to community detection in social networks. In: Pelta, D.A., Krasnogor, N., Dumitrescu, D., Chira, C., Lung, R. (eds.) NICSO 2011. SCI, vol. 387, pp. 121–131. Springer, Heidelberg (2011)
15. Hajibagheri, A., Alvari, H., Hamzeh, A., Hashemi, A.: Social networks community detection using the shapley value. In: 16th CSI International Symposium on Artificial Intelligence and Signal Processing (AISwww.lw20.comP), Shiraz, Iran, 2-3 May, pp. 222–227 (2012)
16. Zhou, L., Cheng, C., Lü, K., Chen, H.: Using coalitional games to detect communities in social networks. In: Wang, J., Xiong, H., Ishikawa, Y., Xu, J., Zhou, J. (eds.) WAIM 2013. LNCS, vol. 7923, pp. 326–331. Springer, Heidelberg (2013)
17. Zhou, L., Lü, K.: Detecting communities with different sizes for social network analysis. The Comput. J. Oxford University Press (2014). doi:10.1093/comjnl/bxu087
18. Lancichinetti, A., Fortunato, S.: Benchmarks for testing community detection algorithms on directed and weighted graphs with overlapping communities. Phys. Rev. E **80**(1), 16118 (2009)
19. Danon, L., Díaz-Guilera, A., Duch, J., Arenas, A.: Comparing community structure identification. J. Stat. Mech.: Theory Exp. **2005**(09), P09008 (2005)

20. Lancichinetti, A., Fortunato, S., Kertesz, J.: Detecting the overlapping and hierarchical community structure in complex networks. New J. Phys. **11**, 033015 (2009)
21. Zachary, W.W.: An information flow model for conflict and fission in small groups. J. Anthropol. Res. **33**, 452–473 (1977)
22. Knuth, D.E.: The Stanford GraphBase: A Platform for Combinatorial Computing. ACM Press, New York (1993)

Consistent RDF Updates
with Correct Dense *Deltas*

Sana Al Azwari and John N. Wilson[✉]

Department of Computer and Information Sciences,
University of Strathclyde, Glasgow, UK
{sana.al-azwari,john.n.wilson}@strath.ac.uk

Abstract. RDF is widely used in the Semantic Web for representing ontology data. Many real world RDF collections are large and contain complex graph relationships that represent knowledge in a particular domain. Such large RDF collections evolve in consequence of their representation of the changing world. Although this data may be distributed over the Internet, it needs to be managed and updated in the face of such evolutionary changes. In view of the size of typical collections, it is important to derive efficient ways of propagating updates to distributed data stores. The contribution of this paper is a detailed analysis of the performance of RDF change detection techniques. In addition the work describes a new approach to maintaining the consistency of RDF by using knowledge embedded in the structure to generate efficient update transactions. The evaluation of this approach indicates that it reduces the overall update size at the cost of increasing the processing time needed to generate the transactions.

1 Introduction

Resource Description Framework (RDF) is an annotation language that provides a graph-based representation of information about Web resources in the Semantic Web. Because RDF content (in triple form) is shared between different agents, a common interpretation of the terms used in annotations is required. This interpretation is typically provided by an ontology expressed as RDF Schema (RDFS) or Web Ontology Language (OWL). Both RDFS and OWL are expressed as RDF triples. The schema provides additional semantics for the basic RDF model. In any particular data collection, changes in the domain that are reflected by evolution of the ontology may require changes in the underlying RDF data. Due to the dynamic and evolving nature of typical Semantic Web structures, RDF data may change on a regular basis, producing successive versions that are available for publication and distribution [4]. In the context of such dynamic RDF data collections, which may be very large structures, it quickly becomes infeasible to store a historic sequence of updates in any accessible form as a consequence of the significant storage space needed. An alternative solution to propagation and storage of successively updated copies of a data collection is to compute the differences between these copies and use these as a means of transforming the

© Springer International Publishing Switzerland 2015
S. Maneth (Ed.): BICOD 2015, LNCS 9147, pp. 74–86, 2015.
DOI: 10.1007/978-3-319-20424-6_8

base data structure into subsequent versions. These differences (the *delta*) show triple content that has been changed between two RDF models and can be used to transform one RDF model into another. Rather than storing all versions of a data structure, it is only necessary to store one version and retain the capability of restoring any version of interest by executing the consecutive *deltas*.

The work presented in this paper addresses the problem of change detection in RDF knowledge bases. An important requirement of change detection tools is their ability to produce the smallest correct *delta* that will efficiently transform one RDF model to another. This is a particularly important problem when RDF collections are large and dynamic. In this context, propagation between server and client or between nodes in a peer-to-peer system becomes challenging as a consequence of the potentially excessive use of network bandwidth. In a scenario where RDF update is carried out by push-based processes, the update itself needs to be minimised to restrict network bandwidth costs. In addition, in pull-based scenarios, it is important to limit server processing so that updates can be generated with maximum efficiency. The contribution of this work is an approach for using the smallest *deltas* that will maintain the consistency of an RDF knowledge base together with an evaluation of the performance challenges of generating this structure.

2   Related Work

Managing the differences between RDF knowledge bases using *deltas* is an important task in the ontology evolution process. because they allow the synchronization of ontology changes [2], the update of ontologies to newer versions, and the reduction of storage overhead required to hold ontology versions [8]. Changes between ontologies can be detected using change detection tools that report changes in low-level (RDF) or high level (ontology) structures. High-level change detection techniques typically focus on exploiting semantic variation between ontologies. Example of these tools include SemVersion [9] and PromptDiff [6]. High-level changes may involve adding or generalising domains or renaming classes [7]. By contrast, low-level change detection techniques focus on reporting ontology changes in terms of simple change operations (i.e. add/delete triples). These tools differ in the level of semantic complexity represented by the ontology languages. Work in low-level change detection tools focuses on the exploitation of useful properties for producing *deltas* (e.g. the *delta* size and the level of execution semantics) that can be interpreted by both human and machine.

For example, Zeginis et al. [10] proposed three RDF/S differential *delta* functions associated with the inferred knowledge from RDFS knowledge bases: dense (ΔD); dense & closure (ΔDC) and explicit & dense (ΔED). These *deltas* vary in the application of inference to reduce their size and are explained in greater detail in Sect. 3. Results show that ΔD produced the smallest *delta* but was prone to ambiguity and may potentially produce inconsistently updated RDF knowledge bases. In this paper, we characterise ΔD_c, which is a correction method for ΔD

that supports consistency when updating an RDF knowledge base. We demonstrate the correctness of ΔD_c and evaluate ΔD_c, ΔED and ΔE in terms of *delta* size and the processing performance of producing the *deltas* using different sizes of synthetic datasets.

3   RDF Change Detection Techniques

RDF updates allow low-level triple operations for insertion and deletion that were formalised by Zeginis et al. [10]. In the context of the two example RDF models M and M' in Fig. 1, the naïve way of generating the *delta* involves computing the set-difference between the two versions using the explicit sets of triples forming these versions. The explicit *delta* (ΔE) contains a set of triples to be deleted from and inserted into M in order to transform it into M'.

M	M'
(Graduate subClassOf Person),	(Head_Teacher subClassOf Teacher),
(Student subClassOf Person),	(Teacher subClassOf Staff),
(Head_Teacher subClassOf Staff),	(Staff subClassOf Person),
(Teacher subClassOf Staff),	(Graduate subClassOf Student),
(Staff subClassOf Person),	(Student subClassOf Person),
(John type Student).	(Teacher subClassOf Person),
	(Head_Teacher subClassOf Person),
	(John type Person).

Fig. 1. Sample data structure before and after update

Definition 1 (Explicit *Delta*). *Given two RDF models M and M', let t denote a triple in these models, Del denote triple deletion which is calculated by $M - M'$, and Ins denote triple insertion which is calculated by $M' - M$. The explicit* delta *is defined as:*

$$\Delta E = \{Del(t) \mid t \in M - M'\} \cup \{Ins(t) \mid t \in M' - M\}$$

From the example in Fig. 1, the *delta* obtained by applying the above change detection function is shown in Fig. 2.

Executing these updates against M will correctly transform it to M'. However, this function handles only the syntactic level of RDF and does not exploit its semantics. In the latter context, executing some of the updates in ΔE is not necessary as they can still be inferred from other triples. For instance, we can observe from the example in Fig. 1 that deleting *(Graduate subClassOf Person)* from M, in order to transform it into M', is not necessary as this triple can still be inferred from the triples *(Graduate subClassOf Student)* and *(Student subClassOf Person)* in M'. Since this update is not necessary, it is useful to remove it from the *delta*. RDF data is rich in semantic content and exploiting this in the process of updating RDF models can minimize the *delta* size and therefore the storage space and the time to synchronize changes between models.

ΔE = {Del (Graduate subClassOf Person),
    Del (Head_Teacher subClassOf Staff),
    Del (John type Student)}
  ∪ {Ins (Head_Teacher subClassOf Teacher),
    Ins (Graduate subClassOf Student),
    Ins (Teacher subClassOf Person),
    Ins (Head_Teacher subClassOf Person),
    Ins (John type Person)}

ΔED = {Del (John type Student)}
  ∪ {Ins (Head_Teacher subClassOf Teacher),
    Ins (Graduate subClassOf Student),
    Ins (Teacher subClassOf Person),
    Ins (Head_Teacher subClassOf Person),
    Ins (John type Person)}

Fig. 2. The explicit *delta*   **Fig. 3.** The explicit dense *delta*

Unnecessary updates can be avoided by applying a differential function that supports reasoning over the closure of an RDF graph. In RDF inference, the closure can be calculated in order to infer some conclusions from explicit triples. This process is carried out by applying entailment rules against the RDF knowledge base. In this work, we consider the RDFS entailment rules provided by the RDFS semantics specification [3]. This specification contains 13 RDFS entailments rules, however only the rules that have an effect on minimizing the *delta* size are used in the current approach for change detection. These rules are shown in Table 1.

Table 1. Relevant rules

	If KB contains	Then add to KB
rdfs1	s rdf:type x *and* x rdfs:subClassOf y	s rdf:type y
rdfs2	x rdfs:subClassOf y *and* y rdfs:subClassOf z	x rdfs:subClassOf z
rdfs3	p rdfs:subPropertyOf q *and* q rdfs:subPropertyOf r	p rdfs:subPropertyOf r

Definition 2 (Closure). *Let t be a triple with subject, predicate, object (SPO). The closure of M is defined as M extended by those triples that can be inferred from the graph M. The closure of an RDF graph M is denoted by:*

$$C(M) = M \cup \{t \in (SPO) \mid M \models t\}$$

Example 1. Let $M = \{a\ subClassOf\ b, b\ subClassOf\ c\}$ then the closure of M will contain these triples and a further triple $\{a\ subClassOf\ c\}$.

The rules in Table 1 can be used in the explicit dense function (ΔED), which combines both explicit and inference approaches for computing the *delta*. The inserted set of triples is computed explicitly as in ΔE, while the delete set is computed based on inference using the rule set.

Definition 3 (Explicit Dense *Delta*). *Let M, M', Del(t), Ins(t) be as stated in Definition 1. Additionally let $C(M')$ denote the closure of M'. ΔED is defined as:*

$$\Delta ED = \{Del(t) \mid t \in M - C(M')\} \cup \{Ins(t) \mid t \in M' - M\}$$

Applying this function to the example in Fig. 1 produces the *delta* shown in Fig. 3. The inserts in this *delta* are achieved by explicitly calculating the set difference $M' - M$ to provide the set of triples that should be inserted to M in order to transform it into M'. On the other hand, the set of deleted triples is achieved by calculating the closure of M' using the RDFS entailment rules to infer new triples and add them to M'. From the example, the inferred triples in M' are:

(Teacher subClassOf Person)
(Head_Teacher subClassOf Person)
(Head_Teacher subClassOf Staff)
(Graduate subClassOf Student)

These inferred triples are then added to M' to calculate the set difference $M - C(M')$ which results in only one triple to delete: *(John type Student)*. The number of updates produced by this *delta* is smaller than the one produced by the ΔE as a result of the inference process.

The effect of the inference process in minimising ΔED was limited to applying the inference rules when computing the deleted set of triples only. Applying inference rules for computing the inserted triples may further reduce the number of updates. For example, inserting the three triples *(Teacher subClassOf Person)*, *(Head_Teacher subClassOf Person)* and *(John type Person)* into M may not be necessary because these triples implicitly exist in M and can be inferred in M using the RDFS entailment rules. In this example, applying *rdfs1* to M would infer *(John Type Person)* while the other two triples could be inferred using *rdfs2*. The application of inference over both the insert and delete sets produces the *dense delta* (ΔD).

Definition 4 (Dense Delta). *Let M, M', Del(t), Ins(t) be as stated in Definition 1. The dense delta is defined as:*

$$\Delta D = \{Del(t) \mid t \in M - C(M')\} \cup \{Ins(t) \mid t \in M' - C(M)\}$$

Figure 4(a) and (b) illustrate the distinction between ΔED and ΔD. In the former only the deletes that are not in $C(M')$ need to be carried out. In this case, $C(M)$ is not checked to see whether all of the planned inserts need to be applied. In the case of ΔD, deletes are handled in the same way as in ΔED however inserts are only applied if they are not in $C(M)$. This results in minimising both delete and insert operations.

From the example in Fig. 1, the updates generated by applying (ΔD) are shown in Fig. 5. ΔD is smaller than either ΔE or ΔED with only three updates to transform M to M'. However, in contrast to ΔE and ΔED, ΔD does not always provide the correct *delta* to carry out the transformation. In this case, applying ΔD to transform M into M' will transform M as shown in Fig. 7. This *delta* function does not correctly update M to M' because when applying the updates, *(John type Person)* is not inserted into M and cannot be inferred in M after the triple *(John type Student)* has been deleted.

Algorithm 1. Generation of the corrected dense *delta* ΔD_c

    Data: M, M'
    Result: ΔD_c
1 Del $= M - M'$;
2 Ins $= M' - M$;
3 **for** $a \in Del$ **do**
4   **if** *inferable(a, M')* **then**
5   remove a from Del;

6 **for** $b \in Ins$ **do**
7   **if** *(inferable(b, M)) and (all antecedents of b $\notin$ Del)* **then**
8   remove b from Ins;

9 $\Delta D_c = $ Del $\cup$ Ins;

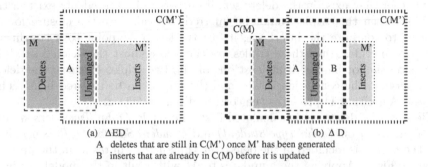

(a) ΔED

(b) ΔD

A deletes that are still in C(M') once M' has been generated
B inserts that are already in C(M) before it is updated

Fig. 4. The distinction between ΔED and ΔD.

$\Delta D = \{$Del (John type Student)$\}$
  $\cup \{$Ins (Head_Teacher subClassOf Teacher),
    Ins (Graduate subClassOf Student) $\}$

$\Delta D_c = \{$ Del (John type Student)$\}$
  $\cup \{$Ins (Head_Teacher subClassOf Teacher),
    Ins (Graduate subClassOf Student),
    Ins (John type Person)$\}$

Fig. 5. The dense *delta* (ΔD)

Fig. 6. The corrected dense *delta* ΔD_c

4   Checking the Dense *Delta*

The contribution of this work is a solution to the correctness of ΔD.

Definition 5 (Corrected dense *delta*). *Let ΔE, $C(M)$ and $C(M')$ be as defined previously and additionally let $s \to t$ indicate that s is an antecedent of t. The corrected dense delta ΔD_c is defined as*

$$\Delta D_c = \Delta E - (\{Del(t) \mid t \in C(M')\} \cup \{Ins(t) \mid t \in C(M) \wedge \{s \to t \mid s \notin Del(t)\}\})$$

Under the semantics of the subset of RDFS rules in Table 1 all *deltas* are unique with respect to the difference between $C(M)$ and $C(M')$. ΔD_c does not require M or M' to be closed and consequently it is not unique.

	M
Original triples	(Graduate subClassOf Person), (Student subClassOf Person), (Head_Teacher subClassOf Staff), (Teacher subClassOf Staff), (Staff subClassOf Person), ~~(John Type Student).~~
Inserted triples	(Head_Teacher subClassOf Teacher), (Graduate subClassOf Person).

	M
Original triples	(Graduate subClassOf Person), (Student subClassOf Person), (Head_Teacher subClassOf Staff), (Teacher subClassOf Staff), (Staff subClassOf Person), ~~(John Type Student).~~
Inserted triples	(Head_Teacher subClassOf Teacher), (Graduate subClassOf Person). (John Type Person)

Fig. 7. Incorrect updates   **Fig. 8.** Correct updates

The corrected dense *delta* is produced by checking triples in both the insert and delete sets of ΔE. Firstly, the delete set should be calculated before the insert set. Secondly, all antecedents for each inferred triple must be checked to see whether they exist in the delete set. If one or both antecedents exist in the delete set then this triple cannot be inferred. To calculate the closure for M in order to compute the insert set, if two triples in M point to a conclusion based on the rules, then these triples are checked against the deleted set. The conclusion cannot be true if at least one of the two triples exists in the delete set, otherwise, the conclusion is true and the triple can be inferred in M. This process (Algorithm 1) produces the corrected dense *delta* ΔD_c.

Because the delete set is calculated first, the triple *(John Type Person)* will not be inferred from *(John Type Student)* and *(Student SubclassOf Person)* given that the former is included in the delete set. The *delta* will result in the updates shown in Fig. 6. Applying these updates to M will result in the model in Fig. 8. This model is identical to M', indicating the correctness of ΔD_c. The number of updates after fixing the incorrectness problem is increased but it produces a correct *delta*. However, this number is smaller than the number of updates produced by ΔED or equal to it in the worst case. In such a worst case, none of the inserted triples in ΔD_c can be inferred in M because either there are no triples that can be inferred or at least one of the antecedents of every inferable triple is included in the delete set.

Both ΔED and ΔD_c functions discussed above apply *inference-then-difference* strategy. This implies that the full closure of the RDF models should be calculated and all the possible conclusions under the RDFS entailment rules are stored in these models. By contrast, a backward inference approach uses the *difference-then-inference* strategy. That is, instead of computing the entire closure of M', in the case of ΔED, this method calculates first the set-differences $M - M'$ and $M' - M$, and then checks every triple in $M - M'$ and removes it if it can be inferred in M'. The operation becomes:

$$\text{Remove } t \text{ from } (M - M') \text{ if } t \in C(M')$$

Instead of pre-computing the full closure in advance, this method infers only triples related to the result of $M - M'$. This would be expected to improve the time and space required in change detection by comparison with the forward inference approach.

In the example dataset shown in Fig. 1, to calculate ΔED using the backward inference strategy, the sets of inserted and deleted triples are calculated using set-difference operation in the same way as when calculating ΔE. After calculating the changes at the syntactic level, each triple in the delete set is checked to see if it can be inferred in M' using the RDFS entailment rules. For example, the triple *(Graduate subClassOf Person)* in $M - M'$ is checked to see if it can be derived in M'. Using the RDFS entailment rules this triple can be derived from the two triples *(Graduate subClassOf Student)* and *(Student subClassOf Person)*, therefore, this triple is removed from $M - M'$. Rather than checking all the triples in M', only the three triples in $M - M'$ are checked.

For applying the backward inference in ΔD_c, first the set of deleted triples in $M - M'$ is inferred as explained above, then the set of inserted triples in $M' - M$ is also checked to see if it can be derived in M. However, to guarantee the correctness of the *delta*, before removing the inferable triples from the *delta*, antecedents of each inferable triple in $M' - M$ are checked to see if at least one of them exists in $M - M'$. If this is the case, this triple cannot be removed from the *delta*. Algorithm 1 describes the generation of ΔD_c by backward inference.

Both forward inference and backward inference produce the same *delta*, but the latter applies the inference rules on only the necessary triples. However, although the backward inference method is applied to infer only relevant triples, applying the inference on some of these triples might be unnecessary allowing pruning to be applied before backward inference [4]. The general rule for pruning is that if the subject or object of a triple in $M - M'$ or $M' - M$ does not exist in M' or M, respectively, then this triple cannot be inferred, consequently the triple can be pruned before the inference process begins. Although pruning may reduce the workload for inferencing, it carries a potential performance penalty [1].

5   Results and Discussion

To evaluate the correction method described above in the context of ΔE and ΔED, the correctness, processing time and *delta* size of updates to enhanced RDF KBs of different sizes are assessed. The objective of this evaluation is to compare the different *delta* computation methods (i.e. ΔE, ΔED, ΔD_c) and approaches (i.e. forward inference (FI), backward inference (BI) and pruned backward inference (PBI)) by measuring and comparing their *delta* computation times over synthetic datasets and by validating their effect on the integrity of the resulting RDFS KBs.

The dataset contains both the Gene Ontology (GO) vocabulary and associations between GO terms and gene products including the Uniprot Taxonomy. This data set was chosen because it is frequently updated, with a new version being released every month. The dataset includes five versions selected to show a range of values over the period 2005 and 2014. Using this dataset, the oldest version (i.e. the 2005 version) was transformed to five versions released between 2006 and 2014. This gradually increases the *delta* size with a consequent effect on the performance of the different change detection methods. The real-world

Table 2. Triple counts used in evaluation.

Versions	M	ΔE	ΔED	ΔD_c	ΔD	Reduction strength[1]		
						ΔED	ΔD_c	ΔD
$(M - M1')$	121374	48136	47270	44270	44212	1.8%	8.0%	8.2%
$(M - M2')$	127374	126710	125228	119228	119098	1.2%	5.9%	6.0%
$(M - M3')$	139374	230372	227334	215334	214926	1.3%	6.5%	6.7%
$(M - M4')$	157374	343594	338663	317662	317109	1.4%	7.5%	7.7%
$(M - M5')$	169374	412233	406129	379129	378482	1.5%	8.0%	8.2%

Table 3. Change detection techniques.

Abbr.	delta
E	explicit
EDFI	explicit dense, forward inference
EDBI	explicit dense, backward inference
EDPBI	explicit dense, pruned,backward inf.
D_cFI	corrected dense,forward inference
D_cBI	corrected dense, backward inference
D_cPBI	corrected dense, pruned, backward inf.

data was enhanced by synthetic data prepared by incorporating 20 % additional triples representing *subClass*, *subProperty* and *type* properties. Synthetic data was added to ensure that subProperty rule was exercised and to arrange for the model to contain redundant triples (i.e. explicit data that can also be inferred from antecedents). The level of enhancement was chosen to secure a measurable effect without obscuring the structure of the original data.

Using the enhanced datasets, change detection techniques shown in Table 3 were implemented. A triple store was constructed in MySQL to handle the RDF collections and the *deltas*. Indexing was excluded to preserve the validity of the use-case. The Jena framework was used to read the RDF dataset into the triple store and to validate change detection techniques by comparing the updated RDF dataset with the target RDF dataset. All experiment were performed on Intel Xeon CPU X3470 @ 2.93 GHz - 1 cpu with 4 cores and hyperthreading, Ubuntu 12.04 LTS operating system and 16 GB memory. Garbage collection and JIT compilation were controlled.

Table 2 and Figs. 9, 10, 11 and 12 report the *delta* sizes and the *delta* computation times, respectively. From Table 1, the *deltas* produced by ΔE exceed those of ΔED and ΔD. These *deltas* are smaller than those produced by ΔE as a consequence of applying inference on the delete set of triples (ΔED) and ΔD_c further reduces the *deltas* as a result of inferring both the delete and insert set of triples when calculating the *deltas*. ΔD in turn may be smaller than ΔD_c but its application in the update process may lead to an inconsistent result as noted in Fig. 7.

In Fig. 9 it can be seen that of the *deltas* evaluated in these experiments, EDBI and the pruned version of the same approach can be generated with the lowest inference time. This is a consequence of both the efficiency of backward inference and the application of inference only to the delete set. At the other end of the spectrum, forward inference methods are slower, as a consequence of the time needed to produce the closure for both models. Forward inference is expensive but becomes useful where models are being queried. However since the focus of this work is updating models, backward inference is a more appropriate approach.

Pruning generally helps to further reduce the inference time however the process adds further expense. Figure 10 shows the reasoning time (i.e. the time taken up by both inferencing and pruning). This indicates that for the data

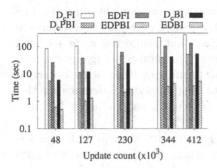

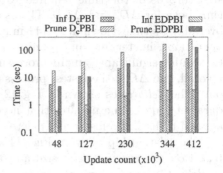

Fig. 9. Inference time

Fig. 10. Reasoning times

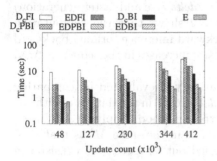

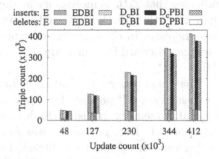

Fig. 11. *Delta* time

Fig. 12. *Delta* size

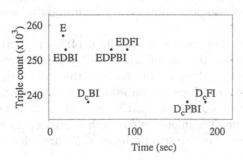

Fig. 13. Comparison of *delta* approaches.

structure used, the time required to carry out pruning exceeds the inference time both for ΔD_c and ΔED. This is consistent with previous findings [1]. The overall *delta* time shown in Fig. 11 indicates that taking account of set difference operations, inferencing and pruning, approaches that prune the *delta* set tend to require significantly more processing power than non-pruning approaches. Overall, the ΔE is the fastest process since no pruning or inferencing is carried out. The *delta* sizes shown in Fig. 12 indicate that applying inference on this data set reduces the updates that need to be executed, particularly when it is applied to both the insert and delete sets.

The relationship between Figs. 11 and 12 is summarised in Fig. 13, which is based on the average *delta* size and average generation time for all the data models. Figure 13 shows the interaction between the degree of inference (i.e. the delete set and/or the insert set or no inference at all) and the approach to inferencing (i.e. inferring all triples or only necessary triples) and their impact on the delta size and the delta computation time. It can be seen that ΔD_c has the smallest delta size compared to ΔED and ΔE. It can also be seen that the approach to inferencing affects the delta computation time. Figure 13 indicates that ΔB_c is more efficient (i.e. smaller *delta* size and faster generation) than the other methods tested. Overall, Fig. 12 shows that the computation time increases in the sequence of explicit, backward inference, pruned backward inference, forward inference whereas the *delta* size increases in the sequence ΔD_c, ΔED, ΔE.

The consistency of M' after *delta* application was evaluated by comparing the in-memory M' produced by applying the *delta* to M in the database with the original in-memory M' using the Jena isIsomorphic method. Applying ΔD_c using the approach described above was found to result in the same M' as that used to generate the *delta*. By contrast, tests carried out to assess the consistency of applying the uncorrected ΔD indicate that in all the models tested, this approach always failed to produce consistent updates.

The overall effect of these results is to indicate that ΔD_c provides a viable route to minimising the data that would need to be transferred from a server to a client in order to update copies of an RDF data store. Pruning may assist this process but comes at a cost of additional processing time, which may be unacceptable in a peer-to-peer context or where updates need to be generated on demand.

By contrast with inference strength[1] [10, p 14:20], reduction strength shown in Table 2 indicates when the size of ΔE, ΔED and ΔD_c are different i.e. when inference is capable of making a difference to the size of the *delta*. When the inference strength is zero, there are no inferences to be made and the model is closed. Under these circumstances, $|\Delta E| = |\Delta D_c|$. However, $|\Delta E|$ may still be equal to $|\Delta D_c|$ when the inference strength is greater than zero. This occurs when, for example, none of the triples in the *delta* are inferable in M.

---

[1] $Inference\ strength = \frac{|C(M)| - |M|}{|M|}$.

Example 2 Let $M = \{w \; subClassOf \; x, x \; subClassOf \; y, y \; subClassOf \; z\}$ and $M' = \{w \; subClassOf \; x, x \; subClassOf \; y, y \; subClassOf \; z, n \; subClassOf \; r\}$. Under these circumstances, $\Delta E = \{ins\{n \; subClassOf \; r\}\}$ and since this triple can not be inferred in M, $\Delta D_c = \{ins\{n \; subClassOf \; r\}\}$. Using the expression in footnote 2, the inference strength has a value of 1 but $|\Delta E| = |\Delta D_c|$ i.e. the inference strength is significantly different from zero but there are no inferred triples. This contrasts with the definition provided by [10, p14:20], which states that inference strength is proportional to the count of inferable triples. Alternatively, the reduction strength in this example is zero, thereby providing an effective guide to indicate when $|\Delta E| = |\Delta D_c|$, which is not clearly shown by the inference strength.

Both inference strength and reduction strength also give an indication of the work load of pruning. High values for these parameters indicate that a large number of triples can be inferred. However, adding such inferable triples provides a large collection of data that needs to be checked for possible pruning before inference can take place.

Example 3 Let $M = \{w \; subClassOf \; x, x \; subClassOf \; y, y \; subClassOf \; z\}$ and $M' = \{w \; subClassOf \; x, x \; subClassOf \; y, y \; subClassOf \; z, nsubClassOf \; r, w \; subClassOf \; z, w \; subClassOf \; y, x \; subClassOf \; z\}$. Here, $\Delta E = \{ins\{n \; subClassOf \; r\}, ins\{w \; subClassOf \; z\}, ins\{w \; subClassOf \; y\}, ins\{x \; subClassOf \; z\}\}$. Pruning this list will involve checking every entry to ensure that the subject or object does not occur in M in order to prune that triple from the list to be entered into the inference process. Of the four triples added in this example, all must be checked for pruning but only one triple ($ins\{n \; subClassOf \; r\}$) will be removed before the remaining three triples will enter the inference process.

In general terms, reduction strength appears to be a better indication of the differences between ΔE and ΔD_c than inference strength. Similar arguments apply to establishing the difference between ΔE and ΔED

6   Conclusion and Future Work

This paper describes a correction method for dense *deltas* that results in consistent update of RDF datasets. We have eliminated the need for conditions on the dataset by checking the antecedents of inferable triples in the insert set. If at least one such antecedent is found in the delete set then the inferable triple in the insert set cannot be removed from the *delta*. Otherwise, this triple can be safely removed from the *delta* to minimize its size.

A summary of our results is shown in Fig. 13, which characterises the interaction between the degree of inference (i.e. the delete set and/or the insert set or no inference at all) and the approach to inferencing (i.e. inferring all triples or only necessary triples) and their combined impact on the *delta* size and computation time. It can be seen that ΔD_c has the smallest delta size compared to ΔED and ΔE. It can also be seen that the approach to inferencing affects the delta computation time. Figure 13 indicates that backward inference is more efficient (i.e. smaller delta size and faster generation) than the other methods tested.

In this work we have investigated the effect of inference degree and inference approach on both the delta computation time and storage space over RDF datasets. Similar methods can be applied to ontologies that are represented in OWL 2. Here the RL rule set [5] is much richer than the rule set for RDFS with consequent potential for benefits to *delta* generation performance and size. Also, it is worth exploring different inference strengths to further evaluate the *delta* sizes and performance of the different approaches to producing these *deltas*. In particular while backward inference may be efficient, combining it with pruning may be expensive in terms of computation time where data is characterised by large inference strengths. Exploiting the inferred triples to infer new information may provide further improvements in update performance.

References

1. Al Azwari, S., Wilson, J.N.: The cost of reasoning with RDF updates. In: ICSC 2015, pp. 328–331. IEEE (2015)
2. Cloran, R., Irwin, B.: XML digital signature and RDF. In: Information Society South Africa (ISSA 2005), July 2005
3. Hayes, P., McBride, B.: RDF semantics. W3C recommendation. World Wide Web Consortium (2004)
4. Im, D.H., Lee, S.W., Kim, H.J.: Backward inference and pruning for RDF change detection using RDBMS. J. Info. Science **39**(2), 238–255 (2013)
5. Motik, B., Grau, B.C., Horrocks, I., Wu, Z., Fokoue, A., Lutz, C.: OWL 2 Web ontology language profiles, W3C Recommendation 11 December 2012 (2013)
6. Noy, N., Musen, M.: Promptdiff: a fixed-point algorithm for comparing ontology versions. AAAI/IAAI **2002**, 744–750 (2002)
7. Papavasileiou, V., Flouris, G., Fundulaki, I., Kotzinos, D., Christophides, V.: High-level change detection in RDF(S) KBs. ACM Trans. Database Syst. **38**, 1:1–1:42 (2013)
8. PaPavaSSiliou, S., PaPagianni, C., DiStefano, S.: M2M interactions paradigm via volunteer computing and mobile crowdsensing. In: Misic, V., Misic, J. (eds.) Machine-to-machine communications: architectures, technology, standards, and applications, pp. 295–309. CRC Press, Boca Raton (2014)
9. Völkel, M., Groza, T.: SemVersion: An RDF-based ontology versioning system. In: Nunes, M., Isaas, P., Martnez, I. (eds.) Proceedings of the IADIS International Conference on WWW/Internet, p. 44. IADIS (2006)
10. Zeginis, D., Tzitzikas, Y., Christophides, V.: On computing deltas of RDF/S knowledge bases. ACM Trans. Web (TWEB) **5**(3), 14 (2011)

Query-Oriented Summarization of RDF Graphs

Šejla Čebirić[1]([⊠]), François Goasdoué[1,2], and Ioana Manolescu[1]

[1] INRIA and U. Paris-Sud, Saclay, France
{sejla.cebiric,ioana.manolescu}@inria.fr
[2] U. Rennes 1, Lannion, France
fg@irisa.fr

Abstract. The Resource Description Framework (RDF) is the W3C's graph data model for Semantic Web applications. We study the problem of RDF graph summarization: given an input RDF graph G, find an RDF graph S_G which summarizes G as accurately as possible, while being possibly orders of magnitude smaller than the original graph. Our approach is *query-oriented*, i.e., querying a summary of a graph should reflect whether the query has some answers against this graph. The summaries are aimed as a help for query formulation and optimization. We introduce two summaries: a *baseline* which is compact and simple and satisfies certain accuracy and representativeness properties, but may oversimplify the RDF graph, and a *refined* one which trades some of these properties for more accuracy in representing the structure.

1 Introduction

The Resource Description Framework (RDF) is a graph-based data model promoted by the W3C as the standard for Semantic Web applications; SPARQL is the W3C's standard language for querying RDF data.

RDF graphs are often *large* and *varied*, produced in a variety of contexts, e.g., scientific applications, social or online media, government data etc. They are *heterogeneous*, i.e., resources described in an RDF graph may have very different sets of properties. An RDF resource may have: no types, one or several types (which may or may not be related to each other). *RDF Schema* (RDFS) information may optionally be attached to an RDF graph, to enhance the description of its resources. Such statements also entail that in an RDF graph, some data is **implicit**. According to the W3C RDF and SPARQL specification, **the semantics of an RDF graph comprises both its explicit and its implicit data**; in particular, SPARQL query answers must be computed *reflecting both its explicit and implicit data*, even if the latter is not physically stored.

In this work, we study the problem of *RDF graph summarization*, that is: given an input RDF graph G, find an RDF graph S_G which *summarizes* G *as accurately as possible, while being possibly orders of magnitude smaller* than the original graph. Such a summary can be used in a variety of contexts: to help an RDF application designer get acquainted with a new dataset, as a first-level user interface, or as a support for query optimization as traditionally the case in

© Springer International Publishing Switzerland 2015
S. Maneth (Ed.): BICOD 2015, LNCS 9147, pp. 87–91, 2015.
DOI: 10.1007/978-3-319-20424-6_9

semi-structured graph data management [3] etc. Our approach is *query-oriented*, i.e., querying a summary of a graph should reflect whether the query has some answers against this graph. The properties our summaries aim at are related to query processing, in particular enabling static analysis, query formulation and optimization (i.e., deciding if a query is empty or finding a simpler way to formulate a query). While semi-structured data summarization has been studied before, our work is the first focused on *partially explicit, partially implicit* RDF graphs. Our ongoing technical report [5] provides proofs for the results presented here and a discussion of related work.

2 RDF Graphs and Summary Requirements

RDF graphs and queries An *RDF graph* (or *graph*) is a set of *triples* of the form s p o, stating that the *subject* s has the *property* p, and the value of that property is the *object* o. Triples are formed using uniform resource identifiers (URIs), typed or untyped literals (constants), and *blank nodes* (unknown URIs or literals) corresponding to incomplete information. We use s, p, and o in triples as placeholders. Literals are shown as strings between quotes, e.g., *"string"*.

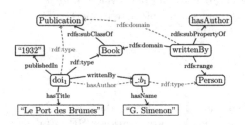

Fig. 1. Sample RDF graph

The RDF standard provides a set of built-in classes and properties in the rdf: and rdfs: pre-defined namespaces, e.g., triples of the form s rdf:type o specify the class(es) to which a resource belongs. *For brevity, we use* type *to denote* rdf:type. For example, the RDF graph G below describes a book, identified by doi_1: its author (a blank node $\_:b_1$ related to the author name), title and publication date.

$$G = \{doi_1 \text{ rdf:type Book}, doi_1 \text{ writtenBy } \_:b_1, doi_1 \text{ publishedIn "1932"}, \\ doi_1 \text{ hasTitle "Port des Brumes"}, \_:b_1 \text{ hasName "G. Simenon"}\}$$

RDF Schema triples allow enhancing the descriptions in RDF graphs by declaring *deductive constraints* between the graph classes and properties, namely: *subClassOf*, *subPropertyOf*, *domain* and *range*, where the latter two denote the first and second attribute of a property, respectively. Consequently, an RDF graph may have **implicit triples** even though they do not exist explicitly. For instance, assume the RDF graph G above is extended with the following constraints:

- books are publications: Book rdfs:subClassOf Publication
- writing something means being an author:
  writtenBy rdfs:subPropertyOf hasAuthor
- writtenBy is a relation between books and people:
  writtenBy rdfs:domain Book and writtenBy rdfs:range Person

The resulting graph is depicted in Fig. 1. Its implicit triples are those represented by dashed-line edges. Adding all the implicit triples to an RDF graph G leads to its *saturation* G^∞, which is the RDF graph stating the semantics of G.

In this work, we consider *conjunctive* SPARQL queries, a.k.a. Basic Graph Pattern (BGP) queries. The evaluation of a query q against an RDF graph G based on G's explicit triples may lead to an incomplete answer; the complete answer is obtained by evaluating q against G^∞. e.g., consider:

$q(x_3)$:- x_1 hasAuthor x_2, x_2 hasName x_3, x_1 hasTitle "Le Port des Brumes"

Its answer against the graph in Fig. 1 is $q(G^\infty) = \{\langle$"G. Simenon"$\rangle\}$. Note that evaluating q against G leads to an empty answer.

| **Summary Requirements** | We assume that *the summary* S_G *of an RDF graph*

G *is an RDF graph itself.* Further, we require summaries to satisfy the following conditions: (i) The saturation of the summary of an RDF graph G must be the same as the summary of its saturation G^∞, since the semantics of an RDF graph is its saturation; (ii) The summary should be (if possible, much) smaller than the RDF graph; (iii) The summary should be *representative*: queries with results on G should also have results on the summary; (iv) The summary should be *accurate*: queries with results on the summary should reflect that such data existed indeed in the graph. To formalize these, let Q be a SPARQL dialect.

Definition 1. *(Query-Based Representativeness)* S_G *is Q-representative of G if and only if for any query $q \in Q$ such that $q(G^\infty) \neq \emptyset$, we have $q(S_G^\infty) \neq \emptyset$.*

Note that *several graphs may have the same summary*, since a summary loses *some* of the information from the original graph. If two RDF graphs differ only with respect to such information, they have the same summary. We term *inverse set* of S_G, the set of all RDF graphs whose summary is S_G. This leads to the accuracy criterion, with respect to *any graph a summary may correspond to*:

Definition 2. *(Query-Based Accuracy) Let S_G be a summary, and $\mathcal{G}$ the inverse set of S_G. The summary S_G is Q-accurate if for any query $q \in Q$ such that $q(S_G^\infty) \neq \emptyset$, there exists $G \in \mathcal{G}$ such that $q(G^\infty) \neq \emptyset$.*

For compactness, the (voluminous) set of literals, along with subject and object URIs for non-type triples from G should not appear in the summary. However, given that property URIs are often specified in SPARQL queries [1], and that typically there are far less distinct property URIs than the subject or object URIs [4], property URIs should be preserved by the summary. This leads us to considering the following SPARQL dialect:

Definition 3. *(RBGP queries) A relational basic graph pattern query (RBGP) is a conjunctive SPARQL query whose body has: (i) URIs in all the property positions, (ii) a URI in the object position of every* type *triple, and (iii) variables in any other positions.*

We define *RBGP representativeness* and *RBGP accuracy* by instantiating Q in Definition 1 and Definition 2, respectively, to RBGP queries.

3   RDF Summaries

We assume a function newURI() returning a fresh URI on each call. We call *data property* any property p in G different from type. Further, for any data property p, the *property source of* p, denoted $S(p)$, is a URI set using newURI(), and similarly, the *property target of* p, denoted $T(p)$, is a URI set using newURI().

We introduce our summaries below; examples are delegated to [5] and can also be found at https://team.inria.fr/oak/projects/rdfsummary/.

Definition 4. *(Baseline Summary) Given an RDF graph* G, *the baseline summary of* G *is an RDF graph* B_G *such that:*

Schema B_G *has the same schema triples as* G.

DNT *(Data triples of* B_G *whose property is not* type*) Let* p, p_1, p_2 *be some data properties from* G.

    DNT1 *The triple* $S(p)$ p $T(p)$ *belongs to* B_G*;*

    DNT2 *if* s p_1 o_1, s p_2 $o_2 \in$ G, *then* $S(p_1) = S(p_2)$*;*

    DNT3 *if* s_1 p_1 o, s_2 p_2 o $\in$ G, *then* $T(p_1) = T(p_2)$*;*

    DNT4 *if* s p_1 o_1, o_1 p_2 $o_2 \in$ G, *then* $T(p_1) = S(p_2)$*;*

DT *(Data triples of* B_G *whose property is* type*)*

    DT1 *If* s p o, s type c *are in* G, *then* $S(p)$ type c *is in* B_G*;*

    DT2 *if* s p o, o type c *are in* G, *then* $T(p)$ type c *is in* B_G*;*

    DT3 *Let* n_{all} *be set to* newURI()*. If* s type c $\in$ G, *and* $\not\exists$s p o $\in$ G, *then* n_{all} type c $\in B_G$.

Refined Summary The baseline summary may unify property source and target URIs quite aggressively. For instance, if a *store* and a *person* both have a *zipcode*, they will lead to the same baseline URI, even though they are very different things. To mitigate this issue, we designed a second flavor of summary of an RDF graph G, termed *refined* and denoted R_G. For space reasons, the definition is delegated to [5]. Intuitively, the difference between the baseline and the refined summary is that the latter fuses data property source and/or target URIs *only if one resource in* G *that leads to their unification has no type at all.*

Summary Properties Both summaries meet our requirements (*i*), (*iii*) and (*iv*) as follows. We say two summary graphs are *equivalent*, denoted $\equiv$, iff they are identical up to a bijection between their sets of URIs. The summaries *commute with saturation*, i.e., $(S_G)^\infty \equiv S_{G^\infty}$, and are RBGP accurate. The B_G is fully RBGP representative, and the R_G is representative of *RBGPs having no more than one* type *triple with the same subject*. This follows from a *graph homomorphism* from G^∞ to $(S_G)^\infty$ [5]. Observe that S_G is not a core of G, since we cannot guarantee a homomorphism from S_G to G (S_G may comprise false positives).

The size of the baseline summary is bounded by the size of G's schema plus the number of data properties and class assertions from G. It can be built in $O(|G|^2)$ time. Computing the refined summary has $O(|G|^5)$ complexity, requiring an efficient underlying system e.g., based on triple partitioning and indexing or a distributed processing platform such as [2]. An upper bound for its size is the number of classes in G × the number of distinct data properties in G.

Acknowledgments. This work has been partially funded by the projects Datalyse "Investissement d'Avenir" and ODIN "DGA RAPID".

References

1. Arias, M., Fernández, J.D., Martínez-Prieto, M.A., de la Fuente, P.: An empirical study of real-world SPARQL queries (2011). CoRR, abs/1103.5043
2. Goasdoué, F., Kaoudi, Z., Manolescu, I., Quiané-Ruiz, J.-A., Zampetakis, S.: CliqueSquare: flat plans for massively parallel RDF queries. In: ICDE (2015)
3. Goldman, R., Widom, J.: Dataguides: Enabling query formulation and optimization in semistructured databases. In: VLDB (1997)
4. Statistics on The Billion Triple Challenge Dataset (2010). http://gromgull.net/blog/2010/09/btc2010-basic-stats
5. Technical report (2015)

Data Exploration

ReX: Extrapolating Relational Data in a Representative Way

Teodora Sandra Buda[1]($\boxtimes$), Thomas Cerqueus[2], John Murphy[1], and Morten Kristiansen[3]

[1] Lero, Performance Engineering Lab, School of Computer Science and Informatics, University College Dublin, Dublin, Ireland
`teodora.buda@ucdconnect.ie`, `j.murphy@ucd.ie`
[2] Université de Lyon, CNRS, INSA-Lyon, LIRIS, UMR5205, 69621 Lyon, France
`thomas.cerqueus@insa-lyon.fr`
[3] IBM Collaboration Solutions, IBM Software Group, Dublin, Ireland
`morten_kristiansen@ie.ibm.com`

Abstract. Generating synthetic data is useful in multiple application areas (e.g., database testing, software testing). Nevertheless, existing synthetic data generators generally lack the necessary mechanism to produce realistic data, unless a complex set of inputs are given from the user, such as the characteristics of the desired data. An automated and efficient technique is needed for generating realistic data. In this paper, we propose ReX, a novel extrapolation system targeting relational databases that aims to produce a representative extrapolated database given an original one and a natural scaling rate. Furthermore, we evaluate our system in comparison with an existing realistic scaling method, UpSizeR, by measuring the representativeness of the extrapolated database to the original one, the accuracy for approximate query answering, the database size, and their performance. Results show that our solution significantly outperforms the compared method for all considered dimensions.

Keywords: Representative extrapolation · Scaling problem · Synthetic data generation · Relational database

1 Introduction

Generating synthetic data is convenient in multiple application areas (e.g., software validation, data masking, database testing). Synthetic data is generally used when real data is not available, when it cannot be published publicly or when larger amounts of data are needed. Therefore, it represents an artificial enabler for any analysis that requires data. When using synthetic data, a necessary evaluation is how representative it is in comparison to real-life data.

Extrapolating the data from an existing relational database is a potential solution to overcome the lack of realism of the synthetic data. There are two directions that can be explored for scaling data: (i) to a particular size, or (ii) to a particular time in the future. The first is useful in multiple application areas

© Springer International Publishing Switzerland 2015
S. Maneth (Ed.): BICOD 2015, LNCS 9147, pp. 95–107, 2015.
DOI: 10.1007/978-3-319-20424-6_10

where the size of the generated database matters, such as scalability testing. The second direction could be addressed by applying machine learning techniques to predict how data will evolve using accurate historical data. In this paper, we explore the first path, which represents a starting point for studying the evolution of a database. Maintaining the distributions present in the original database contributes to the realism of the generated data. The representativeness dimension is crucial as the results of the analysis to be applied on the representative extrapolated database are expected to be similar to the ones from the original database (e.g., in approximate query answering). This path has been explored before. In [19], the authors introduce the scaling problem as follows:

Scaling Problem. *Given a relational database D and a scaling factor s, generate a database D′ that is similar to D but s times its size.*

The authors propose a novel tool, namely UpSizeR, which aims to solve the scaling problem in an innovative way, using mining algorithms such as clustering to ensure that the representativeness is maintained. The method requires complex inputs from the user (e.g., the probability perturbation exponent). Most of the existing synthetic database generators require complex inputs from the user in order to generate realistic data [1,3,11]. However, complex inputs require expert knowledge, and thus may lead to poor accuracy in the results.

In this paper, we propose an automated representative extrapolation technique, ReX, that addresses the scaling problem above. Similarly to [4] and [19], we define a representative database as a database where the distributions of the relationships between the tables are preserved from the original database. As foreign keys are enforced links between tables, they represent invaluable inputs to depict the relationships between data in a relational database. This represents a first step towards achieving a representative extrapolated database. We devise two techniques for handling non-key attributes. To illustrate ReX's applicability in a real scenario, we perform approximate query answering evaluation. We compare ReX to UpSizeR [19] and show that our solution outperforms UpSizeR in terms of representativeness, query answering, database size, and execution time.

The remainder of this paper is organized as follows: Sect. 2 introduces the potential solutions to the scaling problem. Section 3 presents the representative extrapolation system, ReX. Section 4 presents the evaluation of ReX. Section 5 presents the related work. Finally, Sect. 6 concludes the paper.

2   Potential Scaling Strategies

In this section we investigate the potential directions in which relational data should grow such that it is representative of the original database.

Notations. We denote by FK_i^j the set of attributes of table t_i that reference table t_j. We denote this relationship by $t_i \rightarrow t_j$ and say that t_i and t_j are associated tables. This notation is used for constructing the graph structure of a database where an edge represents a relationship and a node represents

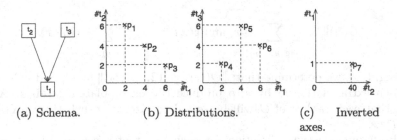

| | (a) Schema. | (b) Distributions. | (c)   Inverted axes. |

Fig. 1. Example graph schema and distributions.

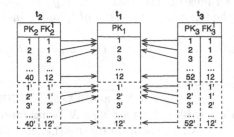

Fig. 2. Extrapolation solution, with $s = 2$.

Table 1. $f_i(x)$ example.

Pos	$k : (k1, k2)$	$f_0(x)$	$f_1(x)$
1	8, "a"	1, "1"	6, "6"
2	15, "b"	2, "2"	7, "7"
3	13, "c"	3, "3"	8, "8"
4	1, "g"	4, "4"	9, "9"
5	3, "e"	5, "5"	10, "10"

a table. Moreover, we refer to parents of t as the set of tables that reference t: $parents(t) = \{t_i \in T : t_i \to t\}$. In Fig. 1(a), $parents(t_1) = \{t_2, t_3\}$. Similarly, we refer to children of table t by: $children(t) = \{t_i \in T : t \to t_i\}$. For instance, $children(t_2) = \{t_1\}$. A table with no children is called a *leaf* table (e.g., t_1). In order to determine the growth direction of a database O, we represent the relationships between each pair of tables, $\forall t_i, t_j \in T$, $t_j \to t_i$, through a scatter plot denoted by $sp_{t_i}^{t_j}$, where t_i appears on the x-axis and t_j on the y-axis. Let us consider the case study presented in Fig. 1. Figure 1(a) presents the graph-structured schema of the database O. Figure 1(b) portrays the generated scatter plots $sp_{t_1}^{t_2}$ between t_1 and t_2, and $sp_{t_1}^{t_3}$ between t_1 and t_3. A point at a coordinate (x, y) of a scatter plot $sp_{t_i}^{t_j}$ expresses that x tuples of t_i are individually referenced by y distinct tuples of t_j, and that $y \cdot x$ tuples of t_j reference x tuples of t_i. For instance, point $p_1(2, 6)$ in $sp_{t_1}^{t_2}$ indicates that two tuples of table t_1 are each individually referenced by six tuples of table t_2 (i.e., $6 \cdot 2 = 12$ tuples of t_2 reference 2 tuples of t_1). When the axes are inverted, $sp_{t_j}^{t_i}$, since $t_j \to t_i$, a point $p(x, y)$ of $sp_{t_j}^{t_i}$ expresses the x tuples of t_j reference y distinct tuples of t_i. In this case, $sp_{t_j}^{t_i}$ consists of a single point, $p(\|t_j\|, 1)$, as each tuple of t_j has a single foreign key value referencing t_i. For instance in Fig. 1(c), the scatter plot $sp_{t_2}^{t_1}$ indicates that $\|t_2\|$ tuples of t_2 are referencing a single tuple of t_1, as each tuple of t_2 contains a single reference to t_1. Through a scatter plot $sp_{t_i}^{t_j}$ we can compute the number of tuples of t_i and t_j from O, $\|O(t_i)\|$ and $\|O(t_j)\|$, with:

$$\|O(t_i)\| = \sum_{\forall p(x,y)\in sp_{t_i}^{t_j}} x, \text{ and } \|O(t_j)\| = \sum_{\forall p(x,y)\in sp_{t_i}^{t_j}} (y\cdot x)$$

From Fig. 1(b), we determine that: $\|O(t_1)\| = 12$, $\|O(t_2)\| = 40$, and $\|O(t_3)\| = 52$. When extrapolating O by s to produce the extrapolated database X, we expect that each table t of O will be scaled in size by s such that: $\|X(t)\| = s\cdot\|O(t)\|$.

A **horizontal** growth direction for each point of a scatter plot produces the optimal results in terms of database size. Considering a horizontal growth direction, each point p of $sp_{t_i}^{t_j}$ scales s times on the x-axis: $\forall p(x,y)$ becomes $p'(x',y)$, where $x' = s\cdot x$. This leads to the following properties of t_i and t_j in X:

$$\|X(t_i)\| = \sum_{\forall p(x',y)\in sp_{t_i}^{t_j}} (s\cdot x) = s\cdot\|O(t_i)\|, \|X(t_j)\| = \sum_{\forall p(x',y)\in sp_{t_i}^{t_j}} (y\cdot(s\cdot x)) = s\cdot\|O(t_j)\|$$

Through horizontal scaling: $\|X(t_1)\| = 24$, $\|X(t_2)\| = 80$, and $\|X(t_3)\| = 104$. These are the desired expected sizes of the tables. This leads to X being representative of O (i.e., as each point is scaled by s), and of accurate size (i.e., as each table is scaled by s). Therefore, the extrapolation solution must create for each of the x identifiers of t_i, pk_i, exactly s-1 new identifiers, pk_i', and for each of the $x\cdot y$ key values of t_j, (pk_j, fk_j), exactly s-1 new key values of t_j, (pk_j', fk_j'), each individually referencing one of the s-1 new identifiers created for t_i, $fk_j' = pk_i'$. This is exemplified in Fig. 2, where $t_i = t_1$, and $parents(t_i) = \{t_2, t_3\}$.

3   ReX: Extrapolation System

In this paper, we propose a system called ReX[1] that aims to produce a representative extrapolated database X, given a scaling rate, $s \in \mathbb{N}$, and a relational database O. The objective is to maintain the distributions between the consecutive linked tables and the referential integrity of the data. We assume that there are no cycles of dependencies and that foreign keys only reference primary keys.

ReXproduces the extrapolated database in a single pass over the entire original database and thus reduces the complexity of a two-step algorithm that would compute the expected scaled distribution and generate data accordingly through horizontal scaling to ensure representativeness.

Natural Scale Discussion. When the scaling rate is a real number (i.e., $s \notin \mathbb{N}$), the floating part requires the generation of tuples for only a fraction of each table from O. Thus, the method must decide for which partial number of tuples of t_j it should create new tuples. As this represents a different problem by itself [4,8], in this paper we consider only natural scaling rates. Moreover, the scenario of naturally scaling databases is commonly applicable to enterprises where it is rarely needed to extrapolate to a fraction rather than a natural number.

---

[1] Representative eXtrapolation System, https://github.com/tbuda/ReX.

The maximum error brought by approximating the real scaling rate to a natural number is 33.33 %, and occurs for $s = 1.5$ (i.e., caused by X containing 33.33 % less or more tuples than desired). The impact of the floating part decreases as s increases (e.g., when $s = 10.5$ the error caused by approximating is is reduced to 4.8 %). Another solution is using a sampling method for the remaining fractional number. However, both solutions would introduce errors in the results, and in this paper we are interested in evaluating the extrapolation technique.

3.1 Key Attributes Generation

The keys generation function targets both primary and foreign keys of a table. We denote the function by $f_i : \mathbb{D}_k \rightarrow \mathbb{D}_k$, where $\mathbb{D}_k$ is the domain of the key k, and i is the iteration number, $i \in [0, s)$. The function is required to satisfy the following properties: (i) injectivity: $\forall i, j \in \mathbb{N}, \forall x_1, x_2 \in \mathbb{D}_k, x_1 \neq x_2 \Rightarrow f_i(x_1) \neq f_j(x_2)$, (ii) uniqueness between iterations: $\forall\, i, j \in \mathbb{N}, i \neq j, \forall x \in \mathbb{D}_k$, $f_i(x) \neq f_j(x)$. ReXuses a positive arithmetic progression with a common difference of 1 (i.e., 1,2,3,...). The function receives as input a value x and the iteration number $i \in [0, s)$, and outputs a new value converted to $\mathbb{D}_k$: $f_i(x) = cast(p(x) + i \cdot \|t\|)_{\mathbb{D}_k}$, where x is a value of the key k, primary in table t, and $p(x)$ represents the position of the tuple identified by x in $O(t)$. The *cast* function converts the natural number produced by the arithmetic progression to the domain of the key. An example of $f_i(x)$ is presented in Table 1 where $T = \{t\}$, $\|O(t)\| = 5$, $\|PK_t\| = 2$, *integer* and *varchar*, and $s = 2$. When a key is composed of multiple attributes, the function is applied on each attribute, using the first position for each value across their occurrences to ensure referential integrity. Moreover, for the same key value and position, the function generates the same output. This ensures that the referential integrity is not breached as the newly generated foreign key values will reference the new primary key values.

3.2 Non-key Attributes Generation

ReXcan perform the following operations: (1) generate **new** values for the non-key attributes either by: (i) generating synthetic values using the generation function proposed, or (ii) using a dictionary with sample values for each type of attribute, or (2) manipulate the **existing** values for the non-key attributes either by: (i) selecting a random value from the original database, (ii) selecting a random value from the original database such that the frequency count of the non-key attribute is maintained, or (iii) maintaining their original values. In this paper, we present results of ReXimplemented using (2.ii) denoted further by ReX$_{\mathrm{rfc}}$, and (2.iii) denoted by ReX$_{\mathrm{main}}$, as these ensure that the value range constraints are not breached and that the approximate query evaluation will not be affected by the synthetic values. The first solution, ReX$_{\mathrm{rfc}}$, increases the diversity of the data produced by generating random content from O, and might cover certain scenarios that the second solution would miss. Such a scenario is for instance the sudden growth of female computer scientists. This could be vital for instance in software testing, as a random selection of non-key attributes' values could cover more test cases than the original ones. Moreover, we expect that maintaining the frequency count of the non-key attributes ensures that queries that compute an aggregate of a non-key attribute scale according to s with no errors (e.g., the maximum age entry in a *Person* table). Furthermore, the second solution, ReX$_{main}$, ensures that the X preserves intra-tuple correlations (e.g., between the age and marital status attributes of a *Person* table), intra-table correlations at an attribute level (e.g., between the age of a *Person* table and its balance in an *Account* table) and frequency count of non-key values.

3.3 Approach

ReXselects the leaf tables as starting tables. The algorithm maintains the position of each primary key value when populating a table using a hash table. Thus, by starting with the leaf tables, the method avoids potentially time consuming queries for determining the position of a foreign key value in its original referenced table, and retrieves is from the hash table previously constructed. Moreover, through this bottom-up approach, X is produced through a single pass over each table of O. Phase one of the algorithm consists of generating the new key and non-key attributes' values for the leaf tables. The method retrieves the records of the leaf table from O and enforces a horizontal growth direction by generating s new tuples for each tuple of a table from O. Regarding key values, ReXwill call the generation function $f_i(x)$, described in Sect. 3.1. Regarding non-key values, ReX$_{main}$ maintains their values from the original tuple. ReX$_{rfc}$ randomly selects a value from $O(t_i)$, while maintaing its frequency count. This is achieved through the SQL query on O: `SELECT` nk `FROM` t_i `ORDER BY RAND()`. In order to maintain the frequency count, ReX$_{rfc}$ runs the query s times and iterates through the result set returned, ensuring that each value has been used s times for producing X. Phase two consists of identifying the next table to be filled. The algorithm recursively fills the parents of the already populated tables until the entire database is processed. To avoid size overhead or referential breaches due to processing a table multiple times (e.g., due to diamond patterns [8]), a table can only be populated once its children have been populated.

4   Evaluation

In this section, we compare our extrapolation system ReXto the UpSizeR approach [19]. Both methods aim to construct an extrapolated database, X, representative of the original database, O, that maintains the referential integrity of the data.

UpSizeR Overview. UpSizeR represents a representative scaling method that addresses the scaling problem. Its objective is to generate synthetic data with similar distributions of the relationships between the tables of the database (i.e., between primary and foreign key pairs) to the ones from the original database [19]. For this purpose, the approach computes the relationship degree (i.e., cardinality constraint) of each existing key of each table in the original database and generates synthetic data accordingly.

Table 2. Queries used for approximate query evaluation.

G_1	F_1: SELECT AVG('Order' .amount) FROM 'Order' ⋈Account⋈Disposition⋈Card WHERE Card.type='classic'; F_4: SELECT SUM(Trans.balance) FROM Trans⋈Account⋈Disposition ⋈Card WHERE Card.type='junior';
G_2	F_2: SELECT Card.card_id FROM Card ⋈Disposition WHERE Disposition.type='OWNER'; F_3: SELECT Loan.loan_id FROM Loan ⋈Account⋈Disposition WHERE Disposition.type='DISPONENT'; F_5: SELECT Client.client_id FROM Client⋈Disposition ⋈Account WHERE Account.frequency='POPLATEK MESICNE';
G_3	F_6: SELECT AVG($IQ.N$) FROM (SELECT district_id, COUNT(account_id) as N FROM Account GROUP BY district_id) AS IQ; H_6: SELECT AVG($IQ.N$) FROM (SELECT l_orderkey, COUNT(l_id) as N FROM Lineitem GROUP BY l_orderkey) AS IQ;
G_4	F_7: SELECT AVG(avg-salary) FROM District;

In the case of a table with multiple foreign key constraints, the method uses a clustering algorithm for generating a joint degree distribution of the table. However, the mechanisms employed by UpSizeR can lead to time-consuming operations and require complex parameters as inputs from the user, which can lead to inaccurate results.

Environment and Methodology. ReXwas developed using Java 1.6. ReXand UpSizeR were applied on MySQL 5.5.35 databases. They were deployed on a machine consisting of 2 Intel Xeon E5-2430 CPUs of 2.20 GHz and 6 cores each, 64 GB RAM, and 2 TB Serial ATA Drive with 7,200 rpm, running 64-bit Ubuntu 12.04. The MySQL server was run with default status variables. We used the centralized version of UpSizeR available online[2]. We assume that the user has no prior knowledge of the database to be extrapolated and keep the default parameters' values. This coincides with the evaluation strategy the authors presented in [19]. Moreover, we show in Sect. 4.1 that the default parameters provide a near optimal configuration for the database considered.

Database. We used the Financial database[3] from the PKDD'99 Challenge Discovery in order to evaluate ReXand UpSizeR in a real environment. It contains typical bank data, such as clients information, their accounts, and loans. It contains 8 tables, and a total of 1,079,680 tuples. The sizes of the tables range from 77 (*District*) to 1,056,320 tuples (*Trans*). The Financial database schema is depicted in [4]. The starting table identified by ReXis the *District* table.

---

[2] comp.nus.edu.sg/~upsizer/#download.

[3] lisp.vse.cz/pkdd99/Challenge/berka.htm.

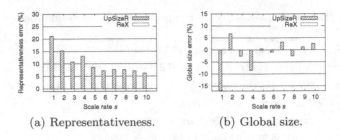

(a) Representativeness.   (b) Global size.

Fig. 3. Representativeness and database size errors.

Moreover, we performed similar experiments using the TPC-H[4] database, and UpSizeR showed lower errors for the criteria considered. Similar observations were drawn regarding ReX's performance compared to UpSizeR's.

Metrics. Both ReXand UpSizeR aim to scale the distributions of the relationships between tables by s (i.e., through primary and foreign keys). In [4] we proposed a sampling method that aimed to scale the same distributions by a sampling factor. We use the average **representativeness** error metric defined in [4], replacing the sampling rate with the scaling rate. Moreover, we use the **global size** error metric defined in [4] to evaluate the size of X related to O. We measure the **query relative** error of the extrapolated database X for evaluating the query answering on X compared to O. The metric is described in detail in [5]. In this evaluation, we consider: (G_1) queries that compute an aggregate value on a non-key attribute with a `WHERE` clause on a non-key attribute (e.g., average account balance for a male client), (G_2) queries that compute an aggregate value on a key attribute with a `WHERE` clause on a non-key attribute (e.g., average number of cards for a female client), (G_3) queries that compute an aggregate value on a key attribute (e.g., average number of cards per account), and (G_4) queries that compute an aggregate value on a non-key attribute. G_3 queries investigate whether the distributions between the tables have been preserved from a query answering perspective. Moreover, G_4 queries investigate if the frequency count preservation of non-key attributes increases the accuracy of queries targeting the attributes. Table 2 presents the queries used in this evaluation. Finally, we evaluate the methods' performance by measuring their **execution time**. This represents the run time (i.e., the pre-processing phases, such as the graph construction or diamond patterns discovery, together with the extrapolation time).

4.1   Results and Observations

In this section, we discuss the results of the evaluation of ReXand UpSizeR.

Representativeness. Fig. 3(a) presents the results of UpSizeR and ReX (i.e., ReX_main and ReX_rfc) in terms of representativeness of the relationships between

---

4 tpc.org/tpch.

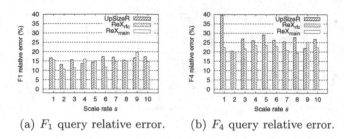

(a) F_1 query relative error.   (b) F_4 query relative error.

Fig. 4. G_1 query relative error on Financial.

consecutively linked tables of the Financial database. We observe that UpSizeR produces an extrapolated database with the representativeness error varying between 21.2 % and 6.5 %, and an average of 10.5 %. We observe that ReX maintains 0 % error with regards to representativeness. This is because both ReX$_{main}$ and ReX$_{rfc}$ enforce a horizontal scaling which leads to generating for each (pk, fk) pair of each table exactly s new pairs, described in Sect. 2.

Database Size. Fig. 3(b) presents the results of UpSizeR and ReX (i.e., ReX$_{main}$ and ReX$_{rfc}$) in terms of expected database size. We observe that UpSizeR's global size error varies between -16.9 % and 2.7 % error, with an absolute average of 4.6 % on the Financial database. Moreover, we observe that ReX maintain 0 % error in terms of global size errors due to horizontal scaling of each relationship, which determines scaling each table by s.

Query Answering. We observe in Fig. 4 that UpSizeR and ReX$_{rfc}$ show similar query answering errors on the Financial database. UpSizeR shows slightly worse results than ReX$_{rfc}$, with a peak error of 39.7 %, occurring for F_4 when s equals 1. This is because both methods do not aim at preserving intra table correlations at a non-key attribute level, and as such, their answers are influenced firstly by their non-key attribute generation strategy and secondly by how well they preserve the representativeness of the relationships across tables. The query answering errors are expected to decrease in the case of G_2 type queries, as a single non-key attribute is involved in the WHERE clause of the queries. Therefore, we observe in Figs. 5, 6 and 7 improved results of ReX$_{rfc}$ over UpSizeR due to its precision in preserving both representativeness of the key attributes relationships and frequency count of the non-key attributes. ReX$_{rfc}$ shows close to 0 % error for F_5 query. We observe from Figs. 4, 5, 6 and 7 that ReX$_{main}$ maintains 0 % query relative error in terms of G_1 and G_2 queries due to horizontal scaling and maintaining the original values of the non-key attributes. Moreover, we observe a similar trend between Figs. 8 and 3(a), for the F_6 query answering and the representativeness error for UpSizeR. We notice that ReX maintains 0 % error for the G_3 query answering, due to horizontal scaling. Moreover, we observe in Fig. 9 that UpSizeR shows little errors, confirming that the method considers preserving the frequency count when generating non-key attributes. We observe

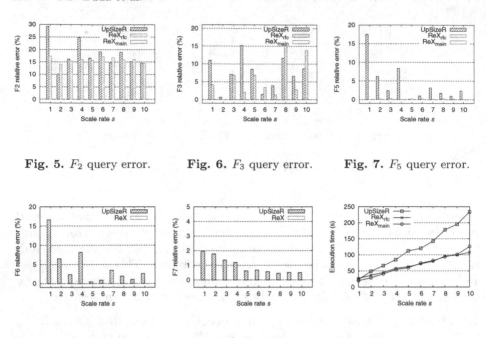

Fig. 5. F_2 query error.   **Fig. 6.** F_3 query error.   **Fig. 7.** F_5 query error.

Fig. 8. G_3 query error.   **Fig. 9.** G_4 query error.   **Fig. 10.** Execution time.

that ReX maintain 0 % error for the G_4 query answering, due to them preserving the frequency count of the non-key attributes.

Execution Time. Figure 10 presents the methods' execution time on the Financial database. We notice that ReX is up to 2 times faster than UpSizeR. When applied on a larger database, such as a 1 GB TPC-H database, we observed more significant differences between the methods' performance. In particular, ReX performed between 3 and 8.5 times faster with an average of 23 m difference between UpSizeR and ReX's execution run time.

Additional Discussion. When using a system with complex inputs, the challenge stands in determining the optimal parameters on the target database. We investigate the impact of the *number of clusters* expected, k (used in the generation of the joint degree distribution) and the *probability perturbation exponent*, p (used in the generation of the joint probability matrix) on UpSizeR, as they represent key inputs for UpSizeR's generation process. We considered the following set of values for k and p: {3,5,25,50,100,500,2500,5000}, and {-15,-10,-7,-5,-3, -1,0,10}, respectively. Increasing k to 5,000 raised the run time of UpSizeR to 16.4 h, compared to 12 s when k is 3 by default. Running UpSizeR with p equal to −25 and −50 did not scale and after 10 days their execution was stopped. Identical results were found for p equal to 10, 50, and 500. The query relative error of F_7 is 1.8 %, regardless of k and p. Similar conclusions were drawn for

$s = \{2, 5, 8\}$ and when jointly varying k and p. Results suggest that the modification of the parameters brings little benefits for all dimensions considered. In contrast, we observe that UpSizeR's parameters have a significant impact mainly on the query answering accuracy. Small variations of the parameters resulted in high errors in query answering. This suggests that a trial and error approach might not lead to any benefits, even after a large amount of time is invested.

5   Related Work

Significant efforts have been made to improve the realism of synthetic data generators. We acknowledge them below, based on their application area.

General Methods. Many commercial applications generate synthetic databases that respect the given schema constraints and use real sources as input for several attributes (e.g., names, age)[5]. Furthermore, the academic community have proposed many general-purpose synthetic data generators [9,11,12]. MUDD [17] is another parallel data generator that uses real data for the attributes' domain. In [3], the authors propose a *Data Generation Language* to specify and generate databases that can respect inter and intra table correlations. However, the user must learn the specification language and input the distributions.

Software Testing. Existing methods for populating testing environments usually generate synthetic data values or use some type of random distribution to select data from the production environment to be included in the resulting database [14,18]. AGENDA [7] is a synthetic data generator based on a-priori knowledge about the original database (e.g., test case expected behavior). Furthermore, in [6] the authors describe a new approach for generating data for specific queries received as input. QAGen [2], MyBenchmark [13], and Data-Synth [1] similarly generate query-aware test databases through cardinality constraints. However, they require complex inputs (e.g., distribution of an attribute, queries), which can be error-prone, as they might exclude vital test cases.

Data Mining. In [15], the authors propose a synthetic data generator for data clustering and outlier analysis, based on the parameters given as input (e.g., number of clusters expected, size, shape). In [16], the authors propose a synthetic data generator that receives as input a set of maximal frequent itemset distributions and generate itemset collections that satisfy these input distributions. Other tools that can be used in this field are WEKA [10], GraphGen[6], IBM QUEST[7]. For instance, GraphGen generates synthetic graph data for frequent subgraph mining. However, the approaches require input parameters and generally produce synthetic data targeting a data mining algorithm.

---

[5] sqledit.com/dg, spawner.sourceforge.net, dgmaster.sourceforge.net, generatedata.com.

[6] cse.ust.hk/graphgen.

[7] ibmquestdatagen.sourceforge.net.

6 Conclusion and Future Work

In this paper, we proposed ReX, a novel automated and efficient system to representatively extrapolate a relational database, given an existing database and a natural scaling rate. The objective is to preserve the distributions of the relationships between tables and the referential integrity of the data. We presented two variations of ReX: (i) ReX$_{main}$, which maintains the original non-key attributes' values of the generated tuples, and (ii) ReX$_{rfc}$ which randomly selects values for the non-key attributes from the original database such that their frequency count is preserved. We compared our technique with a representative scaling technique, UpSizeR, and showed that ReX significantly outperforms UpSizeR in representativeness and database size. Moreover, ReX is up to 2 times faster than UpSizeR. Results show that ReX is highly suitable for approximate query answering, which leads to various application scenarios, such as scalability testing. Finally, results suggest that UpSizeR is sensitive to the variation of the parameters, and a time consuming trial and error approach might not lead to significant benefits.

As future work, we plan to extend our system such that real scaling rates are accepted. A potential solution is to combine ReXwith a sampling technique in order to handle real scaling rates [4,8]. Furthermore, we plan to investigate a solution to extrapolate a database to a particular time in future by adapting the existing approach. This represents an interesting future direction, as it raises the challenge of studying an evolving dataset. Moreover, we plan to apply ReXon an existing testing environment from our industrial partner, IBM, and use the extrapolated database for testing the scalability of the system under test.

Acknowledgments. This work was supported, in part, by Science Foundation Ireland grant 10/CE/I1855 to Lero - the Irish Software Engineering Research Centre (www.lero.ie). The authors also acknowledge Dr. Nicola Stokes' feedback.

References

1. Arasu, A., Kaushik, R. Li, J.: Data generation using declarative constraints. In: SIGMOD, pp. 685–696 (2011)
2. Binnig, C., Kossmann, D., Lo, E., Özsu, M.T.: Qagen: Generating query-aware test databases. In: SIGMOD, pp. 341–352 (2007)
3. Bruno, N., Chaudhuri, S.: Flexible database generators. In: VLDB, pp. 1097–1107 (2005)
4. Buda, T.S., Cerqueus, T., Murphy, J., Kristiansen, M.: CoDS: a representative sampling method for relational databases. In: Decker, H., Lhotská, L., Link, S., Basl, J., Tjoa, A.M. (eds.) DEXA 2013, Part I. LNCS, vol. 8055, pp. 342–356. Springer, Heidelberg (2013)
5. Buda, T.S., Cerqueus, T., Murphy, J., Kristiansen, M.: VFDS: Very fast database sampling system. In: IEEE IRI, pp. 153–160 (2013)
6. Chays, D., Shahid, J., Frankl, P.G.: Query-based test generation for database applications. In: DBTest, pp. 1–6 (2008)
7. Deng, Y., Frankl, P., Chays, D.: Testing database transactions with agenda. In: ICSE, pp. 78–87 (2005)

 8. Gemulla, R., Rösch, P., Lehner, W.: Linked bernoulli synopses: sampling along foreign keys. In: Ludäscher, B., Mamoulis, N. (eds.) SSDBM 2008. LNCS, vol. 5069, pp. 6–23. Springer, Heidelberg (2008)
 9. Gray, J., Sundaresan, P., Englert, S., Baclawski, K., Weinberger, P.J.: Quickly generating billion-record synthetic databases. SIGMOD Rec. **23**(2), 243–252 (1994)
10. Hall, M., Frank, E., Holmes, G., Pfahringer, B., Reutemann, P., Witten, I.H.: The weka data mining software: an update. SIGKDD **11**(1), 10–18 (2009)
11. Hoag, J.E., Thompson, C.W.: A parallel general-purpose synthetic data generator. SIGMOD Rec. **36**(1), 19–24 (2007)
12. Houkjær, K., Torp, K., Wind, R.: Simple and realistic data generation. In: VLDB, pp. 1243–1246 (2006)
13. Lo, E., Cheng, N., Hon, W.-K.: Generating databases for query workloads. PVLDB **3**(1–2), 848–859 (2010)
14. Olston, C., Chopra, S., Srivastava, U.: Generating example data for dataflow programs. In: SIGMOD, pp. 245–256 (2009)
15. Pei, Y., Zaane, O.: A synthetic data generator for clustering and outlier analysis. Technical report (2006)
16. Ramesh, G., Zaki, M.J., Maniatty, W.A.: Distribution-based synthetic database generation techniques for itemset mining. In: IDEAS, pp. 307–316 (2005)
17. Stephens, J.M. Poess, M.: MUDD: a multidimensional data generator. In: WOSP, pp. 104–109 (2004)
18. Taneja, K., Zhang, Y., Xie, T.: MODA: Automated test generation for database applications via mock objects. In: ASE, pp. 289–292 (2010)
19. Tay, Y., Dai, B.T., Wang, D.T., Sun, E.Y., Lin, Y., Lin, Y.: UpSizeR: synthetically scaling an empirical relational database. Inf. Syst. **38**(8), 1168–1183 (2013)

Evaluation Measures for Event Detection Techniques on Twitter Data Streams

Andreas Weiler[✉], Michael Grossniklaus, and Marc H. Scholl

Department of Computer and Information Science, University of Konstanz,
P.O. Box 188, 78457 Konstanz, Germany
{andreas.weiler,michael.grossniklaus,marc.scholl}@uni-konstanz.de

Abstract. Twitter's popularity as a source of up-to-date news and information is constantly increasing. In response to this trend, numerous event detection techniques have been proposed to cope with the rate and volume of social media data streams. Although most of these works conduct some evaluation of the proposed technique, a comparative study is often omitted. In this paper, we present a series of measures that we designed to support the quantitative and qualitative comparison of event detection techniques. In order to demonstrate the effectiveness of these measures, we apply them to state-of-the-art event detection techniques as well as baseline approaches using real-world Twitter streaming data.

1 Introduction

Microblogging is a form of social media that enables users to broadcast short messages, links, and audiovisual content to a network of *followers* as well as to their own public timeline. In the case of Twitter, the most popular and fastest-growing microblogging service, these so-called *tweets* can contain up to 140 characters. Twitter's 288 million monthly active users produce a total of over 500 million tweets per day[1]. As a consequence, several proposals have been made to leverage Twitter as a source of up-to-date news and information, *e.g.*, to respond to natural disasters [13], to track epidemics [7], or to follow political elections [17].

A number of techniques have been designed and developed to detect such events in the Twitter social media data stream. Typically, they adopt the definition of an *event* introduced by research on Topic Detection and Tracking (TDT), *i.e.*, a real-world occurrence that takes place in a certain geographical location and over a certain time period [2]. The main focus of these event detection techniques lies in addressing the specific requirements introduced by Twitter data, such as the brevity of tweets together with the fact that they contain a substantial amount of spam, typos, slang, *etc*. Although most proposals provide some qualitative evidence to motivate the benefits of the technique, few perform a quantitative evaluation or compare their results to competing approaches.

We argue that this lack of comparative evaluation is explained by the fact that measuring the quantitative and qualitative performance of event detection

---

[1] https://about.twitter.com/company/.

S. Maneth (Ed.): BICOD 2015, LNCS 9147, pp. 108–119, 2015.
DOI: 10.1007/978-3-319-20424-6_11

techniques for Twitter data is itself a challenging research question. Crafting a gold standard manually in order to use textbook precision and recall measures is painstakingly slow and does therefore not scale to the volumes of data generated by Twitter users. In order to address this requirement, we build on our previous work in this field [15] and, in this paper, propose several scalable measures that can be automatically applied to the results of current and future event detection techniques. The specific contributions of this paper are as follows.

1. Definition of evaluation measures to automatically evaluate the precision and recall of event detection techniques for Twitter (Sect. 3).
2. Realization of several state-of-the-art event detection techniques as query plans for a data stream management (Sect. 4).
3. Detailed study using real-life Twitter data that demonstrates the ability of our measures to evaluate the different techniques (Sect. 5).

As our evaluation approach is platform-based and modular, it will also enable further systematic performance studies of future event detection techniques.

2   Background

Several event detection techniques for Twitter data streams have recently been proposed. Farzindar and Khreich [8] survey sixteen techniques and conclude that most approaches are evaluated by self-defined measures with manually labeled reference data sets. Also, almost none of the reviewed techniques are compared to competing approaches. In the following, we summarize what evaluations have been performed by the authors of the most-cited approaches and what corpora are currently available for evaluation purposes. Our findings show that neither the works discussed below nor the sixteen in the above-mentioned survey provide a general solution that can be used to evaluate approaches comparatively.

2.1   Evaluation of Event Detection Approaches

enBlogue [3] identifies unusual shifts in the co-occurrence of tag pairs and reports these shifts as events, which are rated in terms of quality in a user study. *Twitter-Monitor*[9] detects "bursty" keywords and then groups them into trends, which are visualized in order for users to decide whether a trend is interesting or not. Cordeiro [6] proposes the use of continuous wavelet analysis to detect event peaks in a signal based on hashtags frequency and summarizes the detected events into topic clusters with latent dirichlet allocation (LDA [5]). The technique is evaluated using a visualization of the results obtained from an eight day dataset with 13.6 million tweets. All of these manual evaluations are, however, not general in the sense that they do not scale and might suffer from human error or bias. Weng *et al.* [17] present a technique that uses term frequencies of individual terms as a signal for discrete wavelet analysis to detect event terms. Then, graph partitioning is used to group similar terms into events. The approach is evaluated using a custom ground truth that is built using LDA on a dataset containing of 4,331,937 tweets collected from Singapore-based users. After cleaning and filtering, a total of 8,140 unique words are retained per month of Twitter data. Detected events are compared to this ground truth on a daily basis. The result of this evaluation is that detected events are plausible, but also that there are several days with no events detected. Since event detection is often time-critical and events should be reported in (near) real-time, this coarse evaluation technique is not suited for general evaluations.

2.2 Available Corpora for Evaluation

In our work, we propose to address the problem of comparing various event detection techniques by defining general evaluation measures. In contrast to our approach, which does not rely on an existing reference data set, other works focus on the creation of evaluation corpora for Twitter-related analysis techniques.

For example, McCreadie et al. [10] created a set of approximately 16 million tweets for a two-week period. The proposed corpus contains an average of 50,000 tweets per hour, which is almost equal to the number of tweets per minute in our 10 % stream. Since no language filtering is performed, which can be estimated to retain approximately 30 % (see Fig. 2) of these tweets, only about 4,800,000 tweets are in English. Furthermore, their list of 49 reference topics for the two-weeks period is very limited and no description is given how these topics were created. Finally, this corpus focusses on ad-hoc retrieval tasks and is, therefore, not suited for the large-scale evaluation of event detection approaches. Becker et al. [4] created a Twitter corpus, that consists of over 2,600,000 Twitter message posted during February 2010. Since they only used their own approach to detect events, the corpus is strongly biased to their technique and not suited for general evaluation purposes. Furthermore, no list of reference events is provided and the data set is restricted to tweets from users located in New York City. Petrović et al. [12] presented a corpus of 50 million tweets, created from a manual analysis of the Twitter data stream between July 2011 and mid-September 2011, which led to the definition of 27 events for the whole time-frame. This very low number of "hits" makes it difficult to compare different event detection methods, if techniques used are very different. McMinn et al. [11] propose a methodology to create a corpus for evaluating event detection approaches. They used existing event detection techniques [1,12] together with Wikipedia to build a set of candidate events and associated tweets. The final corpus covers four weeks with about 120 million tweets and more than 500 events. However, since events are given in prose, they cannot be compared automatically to results of event detection techniques. It is important to note that all of these corpora only consist of tweet identifiers. To use them, the tweets themselves have to be crawled, which can be time-consuming and error-prone as some tweets might not exist anymore.

3   Measures

In order to address the lack of a common evaluation method for event detection in Twitter data streams, we propose a number of measures. Our goal is to define

measures that can easily be used by other researchers and that do not depre-
cate over time as most reference corpora do. While all of our measures support
relative comparisons, we do not claim that they can be used to draw absolute
conclusions. A single event detection technique can, therefore, only be evaluated
"against itself", *e.g.*, with respect to different parameter settings or to confirm
that improvements to the technique yield better results. For a set of techniques,
the measures can be used to rank them with respect to different criteria. In this
paper, we focus on the second application.

Run-Time Performance. We measure run-time performance as the number of
tweets that an approach processes per second. This measure is important to judge
the feasibility of a technique. Most event detection techniques can be configured
based on numerous parameter that influence both the processing speed and result
quality. In combination with other measures, the run-time performance measure
can, therefore, also be used to study the trade-off between these two objectives.

Duplicate Event Detection Rate (*DEDR*). This measure captures the percentage of duplicate events detected by an approach. The implementations of
state-of-the-art event detection techniques used in this paper avoid the reporting
of duplicate events within their processing time-frame, *e.g.*, a one-hour window.
Nevertheless, important or long-lasting events can reoccur across several time-
frames and, therefore, expecting a 0 % rate of duplicate events is not reasonable.

Precision. Our precision measure is composed of two components. First, we
query Google using the five event terms and a specific date range as search query
input. Doing so, we are able to verify if the detected event has been described
by an important article returned by Google for the corresponding time frame.
As important articles we define search results that are from one of the top 15
news websites such as CNN, CBSNews, USAToday, BBC, and Reuters. For the
second part of our precision measure, we query the archive of the New York
Times[2] with the five event terms as well as the specific date range. Since the
number of hits (h), which are in the range between 0 and 10 both for Google
(h^{G}) or New York Times (h^{NYT}), is an indicator of how important a reported
event is, we calculate the final precision score for all results (N) by weighting
the single results as

$$\frac{1}{N} \sum_{i=0}^{N} \left(\frac{1}{2} h_i^{\mathrm{G}} + \frac{1}{2} h_i^{\mathrm{NYT}} \right).$$

Recall. We propose to calculate recall by crawling the world news headlines on
the Reuters website[3] for the days corresponding to the analysis. Each headline
is represented as a list of terms T^{hl}. With this measure we intend to reflect the
percentage of detected events with respect to important news appearing on a
real-world news archive. To weigh the single results, we check for each term in
a news headline, which reported event, represented as a list of terms T^{e}, has

---

[2] http://query.nytimes.com/search/sitesearch/.
[3] http://www.reuters.com/news/archive/worldNews?date=02112015/.

the maximal similarity value (max_sim). Since we exclude matches on one term only, this similarity value can either be two, three, four, or five terms. With this weighting, we calculate the final recall score for all headlines (N) as

$$\frac{1}{N} \sum_{i=0}^{N} \frac{1}{2} \text{max\_sim}(T_i^{\text{hl}}, T^{\text{e}}).$$

4   Event Detection Approaches

In order to realize streaming implementations of state-of-the-art event detection techniques for Twitter, we use Niagarino[4], a data stream management system developed and maintained by our research group. The main purpose of Niagarino is to serve as an easy-to-use and extensible research platform for streaming applications such as the ones presented in the paper. Based on its operator-based processing pipeline our implementations are modular and can be easily configured. For example, we can configure the approaches to report the same number of events, which are represented as one main event term together with four associated event description terms. Using a common implementation platform also has the advantage that run-time performance results can be compared fairly.

For the evaluation of our measures we take nine different approaches into account. Figure 1 shows the Niagarino-based implementations of these approaches. Additionally, the pre-processing pipeline, which is used by all approaches, is shown on the left. The pre-processing removes all non-English tweets and retweets. Then, it tokenizes and unnests the terms of the remaining tweets. It also discards terms that can be classified as stop-words or as noise (*e.g.*, too short, invalid characters, *etc.*). Finally, a tumbling window of size s_{input} is continuously applied and its contents are forwarded to the subsequent operators.

At the bottom of Fig. 1, the query plans for *LDA, TopN, LastN, RandomEvents (RE)*, and *FullRandom (FR)* are shown. Since these approaches are not specifically tailored to the task of event detection, we use them as baseline approaches in order to confirm that the proposed measures are discriminating. *LDA* [5] uses the probabilities of terms in documents and groups those terms together that have the highest probability of belonging together. We realized LDA in Niagarino based on its user-defined function operator. Since LDA is normally used for topic modeling, we equate a topic to an event. The parameters that can be set for this approach include the number of topics, the number of terms per topic, and the number of iterations of the probability modeling. As there are a lot of repeating terms in tweets and also per time window, we expect that this technique is not suitable for event detection and therefore classify it as a baseline method. The other four baseline techniques use a grouping operator followed by a selection operator. *FR* constructs "events" by randomly selecting five terms from all distinct terms in a time window. *RE* selects the main event term in the same way as *FR*, but uses the four most co-occurring terms of the

---

[4] http://www.informatik.uni-konstanz.de/grossniklaus/software/niagarino/.

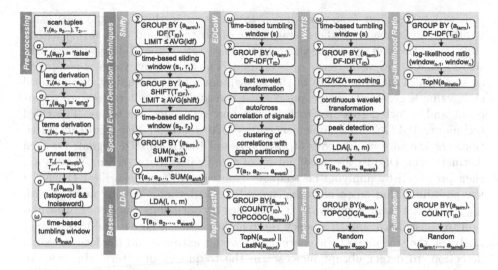

Fig. 1. Niagarino query plans of the studied event detection techniques.

event term as the associated event description terms. Both of these approaches report N events per time window. The next two approaches, *TopN* and *LastN* are based on the IDF score of single terms among all distinct terms in the time window. While *TopN* selects the N most frequent terms, *LastN* selects the N terms with the lowest frequency. Both of them report the selected event terms together with the four most co-occurring terms.

In addition to these baseline approaches, we implemented several techniques that have been proposed to detect events in Twitter data streams. The corresponding Niagarino query plans are shown at the top of Fig. 1. The first technique, *LLH*, is a reimplementation of Weiler *et al.* [16], which is realized as a *log-likelihood ratio* user-defined function that is applied to the grouped set of terms of a time window. In contrast to the original technique that detected events for pre-defined geographical areas, we adjusted the approach to calculate the log-likelihood measure for the frequency of all distinct terms in the current time window against their frequency in the past time windows. Events are reported by selecting the top N terms with the highest log-likelihood ratio together with the corresponding top four most co-occurring terms. Since, these are the terms with the highest abnormal behavior in their current frequency with respect to their historical frequency, we define these terms to be events. The second technique, *Shifty*, is a reimplementation of Weiler *et al.* [14]. In contrast to the original paper, which additionally analysis bigrams, we now only use single terms in the analysis. The technique calculates a measure that is based on the shift of IDF values of single terms in pairs of successive sliding windows of a pre-defined size s_{input}. First, the IDF value of each term in a single window is continuously computed and compared to the average IDF value of all terms within that window. Terms with an IDF value above the average are filtered out. The next step builds a window with size s_1 that slides with range r_1 in order to calculate the shift from one window to the next. In this step, the shift value is again checked against the average shift of all terms and only terms with a shift above the average are retained. In the last step, a new sliding window with size s_2 that slides with range r_2 is created. The total shift value is computed as the sum of all shift values of the sub-windows of this window. If this total shift value is greater than the pre-defined threshold Ω, the term is detected as event and reported together with its top four co-occurrence terms. The third technique, *WATIS*, is an implementation of Cordeiro [6]. The algorithm partitions the stream into intervals of s seconds and builds DF-IDF signals for each distinct term. Due to the noisy nature of the Twitter data stream, signals are then processed by applying an adaptive Kolmogorov-Zurbenko filter (KZA), a low-pass filter that smoothens the signal by calculating a moving average with i_{kza} iterations over N intervals. It then uses a continuous wavelet transformation to construct a time/frequency representation of the signal and two wavelet analyses, the tree map of the continuous wavelet extrema and the local maxima detection, to detect abrupt increases in the frequency of a term. In order to enrich events with more information, the previously mentioned LDA algorithm (with i_{LDA} iterations) is used to model one topic consisting of five terms. After the LDA phase the event is reported. Finally, the fourth technique, *EDCoW*, is an implementation of Weng *et al.* [17]. The first step of the algorithm is to partition the stream into intervals of s seconds and to build DF-IDF signals for each distinct term in the interval. These signals are further analyzed using a discrete wavelet analysis that builds a second signal for the individual terms. Each data point of this second signal summarizes a sequence of values from the first signal with length Δ. The next step then filters out trivial terms by checking the corresponding signal auto-correlations against a threshold γ. The remaining terms are then clustered to form events with a modularity-based graph partitioning technique. Insignificant events are filtered out using a threshold parameter ϵ. Since this approach detects events with a minimum of two terms, we introduced an additional enrichment step that adds the top co-occurring terms to obtain events with at least five terms. Since the original paper fails to mention the type of wavelet that was used, we experimented with several types. The results reported in this paper are based on the *Discrete Meyer* wavelet.

5   Evaluation

In order to demonstrate that the measures proposed in this paper are discriminating, we run experiments against three different real-world Twitter stream datasets (consisting of five days each) that we collected. The three datasets respectively contain the days of February 1 to 6, 11 to 16, and 21 to 26, 2015 (EST). By using the *Gardenhose* access of the Twitter streaming API, we are able to obtain a randomly sampled 10 % stream of all public tweets. The collection contains an average of 2.2 million tweets per hour and almost 50 million tweets per day. We pre-filtered the dataset for tweets with English language content by using a pre-existing Java library[5]. After this step, the dataset

---

[5] https://code.google.com/p/language-detection/.

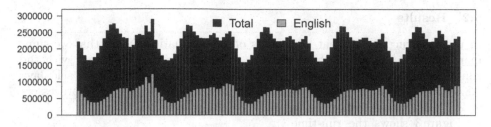

Fig. 2. Average hourly total and English tweets for all three datasets.

contains an average of 660,000 tweets per hour and 16 million tweets per day. Figure 2 shows the distribution of the total and the English number of tweets per hour for each day as an average of all three datasets.

5.1 Experimental Setup

The event detection techniques that we use for our evaluation have all been defined with slightly different use cases in mind. In order to fairly compare them, we defined a common task that all of the techniques can accomplish. As we are interested in (near) real-time event detection, we set the length of the time-window used for event reporting to one hour. This means that after each hour of processing the techniques need to report the results obtained so far. Note that within the time window of one hour no duplicate events are possible for any technique. As the number of events reported by the different techniques may vary significantly (depending on the parameter settings), we adjusted the parameters of each technique to report a number of events in a certain range. For techniques, for which the number of detected events is based on a single parameter N, we set this parameter to obtain 15 events per hour, which results in 1800 events per dataset. Note that some techniques report a few events with less than five terms, which are discarded. We compensated for this behavior by adjusting the parameters of such event detection techniques accordingly. Table 1 summarizes the parameter settings used. Note, however, that these settings are purely required to obtain comparable output and might not correspond to the optimal settings for each techniques. Also, it is unlikely that events are uniformly distributed over the hours of a day. Using these setting, we obtain 1,745 events for *Shifty*, 1,520 for *WATIS*, and 2,020 for *EDCoW*.

Table 1. Parameter settings for Shifty, WATIS, and EDCoW.

Approach	Parameters
Shifty	$s_{input} = 1\,\text{min}$, $s_1 = 2\,\text{min}$, $r_1 = 1\,\text{min}$, $s_2 = 4\,\text{min}$, $r_2 = 1\,\text{min}$, $\Omega = 30$
WATIS	$s = 85\,\text{s}$, $N = 5$ intervals, $i_{kza} = 5$, $i_{lda} = 500$
EDCoW	$s = 10\,\text{s}$, $N = 32$ intervals, $\gamma = 1$, $\epsilon = 0.2$

5.2   Results

In the following, we present the results of our evaluation. Note, that we summarized the results of both datasets as an average. First, we start with the run-time performance. Run-time performance was measured using Oracle Java 1.8.0_25 (64 bit) on server-grade hardware with 2 Intel Xeon E5345s processors at 2.33 GHz with 4 cores each and 24 GB of main memory.

Figure 3 shows the run-time performance results for all techniques measured in terms of average throughput (tweets/ second) for all three datasets. The baseline techniques, except for LDA, as well as the *LLH* technique achieve the highest throughput with around 12,000 tweets/second. The rate of our *Shifty* technique is lower at around 8,000 tweets/second. How-

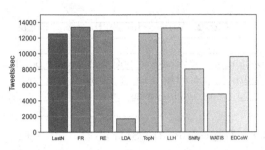

Fig. 3. Run-time performance.

ever, it should be noted that *Shifty* is the only online technique that processes the input incrementally. Therefore, *Shifty*'s performance does not depend on changes to the reporting schedule that we used (after each hour), which will affect the throughput of all other approaches. In contrast to *WATIS*, *EDCoW* scores very well. Since *WATIS* uses *LDA* at the end of processing to create the final events, this result is not surprising. As we see, applying *LDA* with 500 iterations is the slowest approach with around 1,700 tweets/second. If we take into account the 50 million tweets per day (~ 580 per second) of the 10 % stream, we can observe that all techniques could process this stream in (near) real-time and are therefore feasible. However, if these techniques were applied to the full 100 % stream ($\sim 5,800$ tweets per second), *WATIS* and *LDA* would not be feasible. Based on these observations, we conclude that our measure for run-time performance is discriminating and can be used to judge the feasibility of approaches.

In contrast to run-time performance, the remaining three measures assess the task-based performance, *i.e.*, the quality of an event detection technique. To further evaluate our measures, we also include the results of applying them to the so-called *Trending Topics (TT)* of Twitter in the following discussion. We collected the top 15 trending topics and enriched them by querying the Twitter API for the most current tweets belonging to each topic. The enrichment process also tokenizes and cleans the obtained tweets, and summarizes the five most co-occurring terms to a final event. Hereby, we also get 1,800 events per dataset. We begin by presenting the results obtained from our *DEDR* measure. For each technique, we calculate the percentage of events, which are classified as duplicates. As this classification is configurable, we present results obtained by requiring that one, two, three, four, or all five event terms need to be equal (*DEDR1*, ..., *DEDR5*). Figure 4 plots the average results of the duplicate event detection rate for all datasets. We can observe that all techniques report a very high number

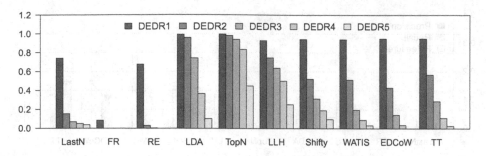

Fig. 4. Average duplicate event detection rate.

of duplicates for *DEDR1*. Since the terms of *FR* and *RE* are randomly chosen, they generally report a lower number of duplicates. From the event detection techniques, the results for *Shifty*, *WATIS*, and *EDCoW* closely resemble the results of applying our *DEDR* measure to *TT*, whereas the all other approaches have significantly different profiles. We therefore argue that *DEDR* is a useful measure to characterize event detection techniques.

For the evaluation of our precision and recall measures, we only use events that were not filtered out by *DEDR3*, *i.e.*, all events with three or more common terms are removed from the result set and only the remaining non-duplicate events are further analyzed. Note that this results in an implicit inclusion of the *DEDR* measure in our precision and recall measures. Figure 5 shows the average precision, recall, and F-measure over all three data sets for all techniques. Based on these measure, we observe that all of the dedicated event detection techniques clearly outperform the baseline approaches. This finding confirms the validity of the precision and recall measure proposed in this paper. We conclude our evaluation by discussing the results shown in Fig. 5 in more detail. First, we note that the scores are generally very low. However, since we are only interested in relative comparisons, this is not a problem. Among the baseline approaches, both *LDA* and *RE* score comparable to dedicated event detection techniques with respect to specific measures. The precision of *LDA* is higher than the one of *LLH* and *Shifty*, *RE* scores well in terms of recall. In both cases, this result can be explained with the way these approaches work. Also, it demonstrates the importance of studying both precision and recall, which we support with our F-measure. The best approaches according to our measures are the advanced *WATIS* and *EDCoW* techniques, which are also the most cited event detection techniques. Since *EDCoW* produces the most events of all techniques, its parameters could also be adjusted to increase its precision score. Also, the basic enrichment process that we implemented for *EDCoW* could be improved. For example, *WATIS* uses *LDA* for the same purpose and scores very well in terms of recall. Our own techniques, *LLH* and *Shifty*, do not perform as well as the two advanced techniques. However, we note that *Shifty* is the only online event reporting technique and therefore only uses very short time intervals (of four minutes in this case) instead of a full hour to classify terms as events.

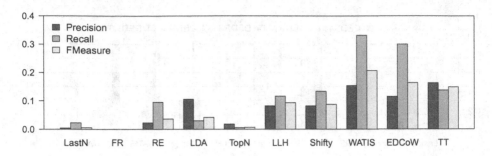

Fig. 5. Precision, Recall, and F-Measure of all techniques.

Additionally, we do not use bigrams in this paper as opposed to the original *Shifty* algorithm. *LLH* was originally designed to use both the spatial and the time dimension to detect unusual rates of terms in pre-defined geographical areas over time. In this paper, we only use the time dimension, which has weakened the performance of the approach. Finally, our measures assign high precision and recall scores to the Twitter Trending Topics (*TT*). However, in contrast to our results, *TT* is based on the full 100 % stream.

6   Conclusions

In this paper, we have addressed the lack of quantitative and comparative evaluation of event detection techniques by proposing a number of measures, both for run-time and task-based performance. In contrast to previous evaluation methods, all our measures can be automatically applied to evaluate large results sets without the requirement of an existing gold standard. In order to demonstrate the validity of our proposed measures, we have studied them based on several baseline approaches and state-of-the-art event detection techniques. We have shown that our measures are able to discriminate between different techniques and support relative comparisons.

As future work, we plan to further confirm the findings presented in this paper by implementing additional event detection techniques, such as *enBlogue* [3], in our evaluation framework. Based on these fully validated measures, we will tune the parameters of each technique, which will enable us to draw absolute conclusions about their performance.

Acknowledgement. We would like to thank our students Christina Papavasileiou and Harry Schilling for their contributions to the implementations of *WATIS* and *EDCoW*.

References

1. Aggarwal, C.C., Subbian, K.: Event detection in social streams. In: Proceedings of the SIAM International Conference on Data Mining (SDM), pp. 624–635 (2012)

2. Allan, J.: Topic Detection and Tracking: Event-based Information Organization. Kluwer Academic Publishers, The Netherlands (2002)
3. Alvanaki, F., Michel, S., Ramamritham, K., Weikum, G.: See what's enBlogue: real-time emergent topic identification in social media. In: Proceedings of the International Conference on Extending Database Technology (EDBT), pp. 336–347 (2012)
4. Becker, H., Naaman, M., Gravano, L.: Beyond trending topics: real-world event identification on twitter. In: Proceedings of the International Conference on Weblogs and Social Media (ICWSM), pp. 438–441 (2011)
5. Blei, D.M., Ng, A.Y., Jordan, M.I.: Latent dirichlet allocation. J. Mach. Learn. Res. **3**, 993–1022 (2003)
6. Cordeiro, M.: Twitter event detection: combining wavelet analysis and topic inference summarization. In: Proceedings of the Doctoral Symposium on Informatics Engineering (DSIE) (2012)
7. Culotta, A.: Towards detecting influenza epidemics by analyzing twitter messages. In: Proceedings of the Workshop on Social Media Analytics (SOMA), pp. 115–122 (2010)
8. Farzindar, A., Khreich, W.: A survey of techniques for event detection in twitter. Comput. Intell. **31**(1), 132–164 (2015)
9. Mathioudakis, M., Koudas, N.: TwitterMonitor: trend detection over the twitter stream. In: Proceedings of the International Conference on Management of Data (SIGMOD), pp. 1155–1158 (2010)
10. McCreadie, R., Soboroff, I., Lin, J., Macdonald, C., Ounis, I., McCullough, D.: On building a reusable twitter corpus. In: Proceedings of the International Conference on Research and Development in Information Retrieval (SIGIR), pp. 1113–1114 (2012)
11. McMinn, A.J., Moshfeghi, Y., Jose, J.M.: Building a large-scale corpus for evaluating event detection on twitter. In: Proceedings of the International Conference on Information and Knowledge Management (CIKM), pp. 409–418 (2013)
12. Petrović, S., Osborne, M., Lavrenko, V.: Using paraphrases for improving first story detection in news and twitter. In: Proceedings of the Conference of the North American Chapter of the Association for Computational Linguistics: Human Language Technologies (NAACL HLT), pp. 338–346 (2012)
13. Sakaki, T., Okazaki, M., Matsuo, Y.: Earthquake shakes twitter users: real-time event detection by social sensors. In: Proceedings of the International Conference on World Wide Web (WWW), pp. 851–860 (2010)
14. Weiler, A., Grossniklaus, M., Scholl, M.H.: Event identification and tracking in social media streaming data. In: Proceedings of the EDBT Workshop on Multimodal Social Data Management (MSDM), pp. 282–287 (2014)
15. Weiler, A., Grossniklaus, M., Scholl, M.H.: Run-time and task-based performance of event detection techniques for twitter. In: Zdravkovic, J., Kirikova, M., Johannesson, P. (eds.) CAiSE 2015. LNCS, vol. 9097, pp. 35–49. Springer, Heidelberg (2015)
16. Weiler, A., Scholl, M.H., Wanner, F., Rohrdantz, C.: Event identification for local areas using social media streaming data. In: Proceedings of the SIGMOD Workshop on Databases and Social Networks (DBSocial), pp. 1–6 (2013)
17. Weng, J., Lee, B.S.: Event detection in twitter. In: Proceedings of the International Conference on Weblogs and Social Media (ICWSM), pp. 401–408 (2011)

A Framework for Selecting Deep Learning Hyper-parameters

Jim O' Donoghue$^{(\boxtimes)}$ and Mark Roantree

Insight Centre for Data Analytics, School of Computing, DCU,
Collins Ave., Dublin 9, Ireland
jodonoghue@computing.dcu.ie

Abstract. Recent research has found that deep learning architectures show significant improvements over traditional shallow algorithms when mining high dimensional datasets. When the choice of algorithm employed, hyper-parameter setting, number of hidden layers and nodes within a layer are combined, the identification of an optimal configuration can be a lengthy process. Our work provides a framework for building deep learning architectures via a stepwise approach, together with an evaluation methodology to quickly identify poorly performing architectural configurations. Using a dataset with high dimensionality, we illustrate how different architectures perform and how one algorithm configuration can provide input for fine-tuning more complex models.

1 Introduction and Motivation

The research presented here was carried out as part of the FP7 In-Mindd project [10,19] where researchers use the Maastricht Ageing Study (MAAS) dataset [9,16,22] to understand the determinants of cognitive ageing from behavioural characteristics and other biometrics. The MAAS dataset recorded a high number of features regarding the lifestyle and behaviour of almost 2,000 participants over a 12-year period. The challenge with this dataset is to determine those features which provide the best predictive capabilities for a particular outcome. Unlike health base studies where data is automatically generated using electronic sensors [8,20], data in MAAS is not easily mined. Machine learning takes two broad strategies: the more common *shallow* approach and the more complex *deep learning* (DL) approach. Where multiple issues - like high-dimensionality or sparsity - arise within the dataset, the use of many shallow algorithms in series is generally required. Shallow refers to the *depth* of algorithm architecture and *depth* refers to the number of layers of learning function operations [4], where anything less than 3 layers is considered *shallow*. *Deep* architectures are algorithms where multiple layers of hidden, usually latent variables are learned through many layers of non-linear operations [4], usually in the context of artificial neural networks (ANNs).

Research funded by In-MINDD, an EU FP7 project, Grant Agreement Number 304979.

S. Maneth (Ed.): BICOD 2015, LNCS 9147, pp. 120–132, 2015.
DOI: 10.1007/978-3-319-20424-6_12

Furthermore, these DL architectures have in the past, proved very successful in learning models from high-dimensional datasets [14, 21].

DL architectures have been shown to perform well in learning feature representations but require the optimisation of many hyper-parameters[1] which is a difficult process. In this work, we have developed a framework which can test combinations of features and hyper-parameters in different deep learning configurations. Our goal is to find the Deep Learning architectural configuration most applicable to prediction in the MAAS clinical study for dementia.

Contribution. Deep architectures have primarily been used in image, audio and video domains where feature sets are often large and complex. Our contribution is to develop an easily-configurable machine to facilitate the generic implementation of algorithms with interchangeable activation functions. As a result, we can easily run and evaluate many experiments with deep or shallow learners in a variety of configurations. Essentially, we provide a framework for the selection of an initial hyper-parameter configuration in a deep learning algorithm.

Paper Structure. The paper is structure as follows: in Sect. 2, we present a detailed description of the Configurable Deep Network (CDN) which underpins our framework; Sects. 3 and 4, describe our evaluation approach and setup together with results and analysis; in Sect. 5, we discuss related research; and finally in Sect. 6, we present our conclusions.

2   CDN - The Configurable Deep Network Architecture

Most classification algorithms have a similar procedure for training. First, **initialisation** occurs. This instantiates the model parameters (known as θ, a combination of the weights and biases for the entire model) which allow for prediction and this process gives a starting point from which these parameters can then be tuned. A **hypothesis function $h_\theta(x)$** is then employed through which the data, bounded by the model parameters goes, in order to predict an outcome, which in our case is "forgetful? (yes/no)". The **cost $J(\theta)$** of these initial parameters is then calculated with a function that measures the information lost between the *predicted* outcome (result of hypothesis function) and the *actual* outcome. A predictive *model* is learned by minimising the cost calculated by this function.

Gradient descent is one method to optimise the cost function and it proceeds as follows: compute the *gradient* (or partial derivative) of the cost function with respect to the model parameters, giving the slope denoted by $\frac{\delta}{\delta\theta}J(\theta)$; then *update* the model parameters by taking the value found for the slope, multiplied by a term called the learning rate (determines how far down the slope the update will take the model parameters) and subtract the result from the previous parameters; and finally, repeat these steps until the model converges on the lowest possible *cost* for the data. Stochastic Gradient Descent (SGD) calculates the cost on an individual sample in the dataset and subsequently updates the parameters. Mini-batch Stochastic Gradient Descent (MSGD) instead calculates the

---

[1] Parameters not learned by the algorithm but instead passed as input.

cost on a subset of the dataset and then updates the parameters. This process allows us to achieve a *predictive model* for: "forgetful? (yes/no)" in MAAS.

2.1   Framework Overview

There are three high-level constructs in our architecture: *nodes* which contain and execute the activation functions, *layers* which contain the nodes and handle connections between layers and *machines* which contain the logic for the over-arching algorithm. Each node in the bottom *visible input* layer reflects a feature in the dataset and for supervised models (predicts an outcome given an input) there is a visible *output* layer at the top of each configuration which performs classification. In unsupervised models (learns a model without a class label) as well for the internal layers (where applicable) in supervised models there is a *hidden* layer or layers, where the feature representation is learned.

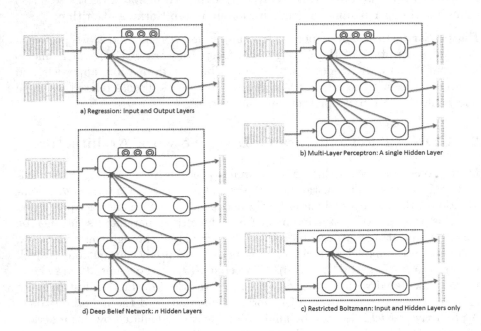

Fig. 1. Machine configurations within the framework

Our architecture is implemented in Python and built upon Theano [2,7] - a library for building and compiling symbolic mathematics expressions and GPU computation. The functions below are implemented for every algorithm.

- `initialise`: instantiates model parameters (weights and biases), configures layers and nodes, and associates hyper-parameters with the architecture.
- `buildhypothesis`: dependent on the classification type it builds a symbolic expression for the hypothesis function, giving the prediction $h_\theta(x_i) = \hat{y}_i$ for the sample x_i.

- `buildcost`: based on the classification type it creates symbolic expressions for: the cost $J(\theta)$ with regularisation[2] (if applicable) and prediction error.
- `buildmodel`: computes the gradient of the cost function with respect to the model parameters and uses this gradient to build a symbolic expression to update the parameters. It compiles these symbolic expressions into functions to train and (if applicable) pre-train the model.
- `train`: optimises the cost function. Can be supervised (with respect to a class label) or unsupervised (no class label) depending on the algorithm. For the DBN it performs unsupervised pre-training and supervised fine-tuning (explained further in Sect. 2.5).
- `predict`: uses the hypothesis function and model learned to predict an outcome, or reconstruct the data dependent on the algorithm.

The following four machines: Regression, Multi-Layer Perceptron (MLP), Restricted Boltzman Machine (RBM) and Deep Belief Network (DBN) are currently implemented in our architecture and displayed in Fig. 1. As our focus is not an in-depth discussion of the technical detail of these algorithms but their application to high dimensional clinical data and determining a DBNs best hyper-parameters via a step-wise optimisation of its constituent algorithms, we refer the reader to [4] for detailed technical information.

2.2 Regression

Three types of regression are currently implemented in our architecture: **Linear**, **Logistic** and **Softmax regression**. As our experiments only evaluate softmax regression, it will form the focus of our discussion. Softmax regression is a non-linear multi-class classification algorithm which uses the softmax function for the hypothesis and the negative log likelihood function for the cost. It is used where class membership is mutually exclusive (sample can only belong to one class) to generate a probability of class membership from $1, \ldots, K$ where K is the number of classes. In our architecture we train softmax regression with stochastic gradient descent.

2.3 Multi-layer Perceptron

An MLP is a simple form of one hidden layer neural network, where latent and abstract features are learned in the hidden layer. As with the other machines in our architecture and for artificial neural networks (ANN) in general, each node in a hidden layer $L^{(i)}$ is connected to every node in layer $L^{(i-1)}$ and every node in $L^{(i+1)}$. Each node $n_1^{(i)}$ to $n_n^{(i)}$ in layer $L^{(i)}$ contains a non-linear activation function, which calculates a node's activation energy. This value is propagated through the layers via the connections, a subset of which are shown in Fig. 1. This process is called feed-forward propagation and is the hypothesis function for all shallow and deep *feed-forward* neural networks.

---

[2] ensures features with large data values does not overly impact the model.

Our MLP was trained with SGD and back-propagation. It is similar to training a regression model and uses the same cost function except the parameters in each layer must be updated with respect to the cost of the output.

2.4   Restricted Boltzmann Machine

An RBM is an *energy-based*, two-layer neural network. An RBM's aim is to learn a model which occupies a low energy state over its visible and hidden layers for likely configurations of the data. The energy paradigm is an idea taken from particle physics and associates a scalar energy value (real-number) for every configuration of the variables in a dataset. Highly likely configurations of the data occupy low energy states, synonymous to low energy configurations of particles being most probable [4]. Training achieves this by maximising the probability of the training data in the hidden and visible layers by learning their joint probability distribution. This process gives a way of learning the abstract features that aid in prediction in MAAS. The RBM was trained with contrastive divergence [13] and MSGD.

2.5   Deep Belief Network

A Deep Belief Network is a deep ANN, meaning it can be successfully trained with more than one hidden layer and differs from RBMs and MLPs as such. Each subsequent layer learns a more abstract feature representation and increases the models predictive power. DBNs are generative models characterised by unsupervised pre-training and supervised fine-tuning. Unsupervised pre-training updates the weights in a greedy layer-wise fashion, where two layers at a time are trained as an RBM, where the hidden layer of one acts as the visible layer in the next. Supervised fine-tuning then adjusts these parameters with respect to an outcome via back-propagation, in much the same way as an MLP. Again, like an MLP it makes predictions via feed-forward propagation. Here we pre-trained the DBN with MSGD and fine-tuned with SGD.

3   Experimental Set-Up and Design

3.1   Dataset Preparation and Preprocessing

The MAAS dataset [16] is a longitudinal clinical trial which recorded biometric data on middle-aged individuals at 3 year intervals over 12 years. There are 3441 unique records and 1835 unique features spread throughout 86 'tests' or study subsections. To remove the temporal nature of the data, only baseline data was analysed. To remove test level sparsity, a subset of the dataset was selected and the remaining sparsity was removed through deletion or mean imputation. The data was scaled to unit variance and categorised to one-hot encoded vectors so that it could be input into our DBN and RBM. The continuous data had 523 instances and 337 features, whereas the one-hot encoded categorical data had 523 instances and 3567 features.

3.2   Experimental Procedure and Parameter Initialisation

The optimum parameters for each machine were located via a process called grid search which tests a range of values to find wherein the optimum lies. Regression was used to determine the learning rate, regularisation term and fine-tune steps for the RBM, MLP and DBN; and the RBM and MLP were used to determine the number of nodes in the first and second hidden layers of the DBN respectively.

The range searched for regularisation and learning rate was from 0.001 to 1, roughly divided into 10 gradations. Three values for steps of GD were tested: 100; 1000; and 10000 as we estimated any larger values would lead to over-fitting (not generalising well to new data) given the sample-size. All possible combinations were tested for both continuous *and* categorical data, giving 246 in total.

The number of hidden nodes tested for both the RBM and MLP were 10, 30, 337, 900, 1300 and 2000. There were 337 features before categorisation therefore, any more than 2000 hidden nodes was deemed unnecessary. Each configuration was run twice (for categorical and continuous) in the MLP but 5 times each in the RBM (only categorical) as there were 5 epoch values (1, 5, 10, 15 and 20) being tested. Any more than 20 would have over-fit the data.

Bias terms were initialised to zero for all models. From Glorot et. al [12], the MLP, RBM, and DBN weights were randomly initialised between the bounds: $[-4 \sqrt{\frac{6}{fan_{in}+fan_{out}}}, 4 \sqrt{\frac{6}{fan_{in}+fan_{out}}}]$, whereas for regression the weights were randomly initialised without bounds. fan_{in} is the number of inputs to and fan_{out} is the number of outputs from a node.

All experiments were run on a Dell Optiplex 790 running 64-bit Windows 7 Home Premium SP1 with an Intel Core i7-2600 quad-core 3.40 GHz CPU and 16.0 GB of RAM. The code was developed in Python using the Enthought Canopy (1.4.1.1975) distribution of 64-bit Python 2.7.6 and developed in PyCharm 3.4.1 IDE, making use of the NumPy 1.8.1-1 and Theano 0.6.0.

4   Experimental Results and Analysis

4.1   Evaluation Metrics

- **Ex.:** Experiment number - a particular hyper-parameter configuration. Each number is an index into a list of the hyper-parameters being tested.
- **I. Cost** Initial cost - negative log likelihood (NLL) cost of untrained model on training data
- **T. Cost:** Training cost - NLL cost of trained model on training data
- **V. Cost:** Validation cost - NLL cost of trained model on validation data
- **Tst. Cost:** Test cost - NLL cost of trained model on the test set
- **Error:** Prediction error achieved on the test set: $1 - \left(\frac{true\_pos+true\_neg}{num\_predictions}\right)$
- **Alpha:** Learning rate, a coefficient for the model parameter updates which decides how big of a step to take in gradient descent.
- **Lambda:** Regularisation parameter, determines how much to penalise large data values

- **Steps:** Number of steps of stochastic gradient descent taken
- **Data:** Format of the data - cont. (continuous) or cat. (categorical one-hot encoded)
- **Epochs:** Iterations through the dataset, 1 epoch = 1 complete iteration
- **Nodes:** Number of nodes in each layer, visible-hidden$_1$-...-hidden$_n$(-output)

4.2 Regression: Search for DBN Learning Rate and Regularisation Term

Table 1 shows the results and hyper-parameter configurations for the ten best performing models in a series of grid-search experiments for regression. The models are ranked by the lowest negative log-likelihood found on the training data out of the 246 experiments performed.

Table 1. Regression learning rate, regularisation and steps grid search

Ex	I. Cost	T. cost	V. cost	Error	Alpha	Lambda	Steps	Data
8-0-0	13.188452	0.001	45.818	0.258	0.9	0.001	100	cat
8-1-0	**4.925**	**0.002**	**7.725**	**0.305**	**0.9**	**0.003**	**100**	**cat.**
8-2-0	7.608	0.00334	22.615	0.225	0.9	0.009	100	cat
7-0-1	21.066	0.003	6.449	0.391	0.3	0.001	1000	cat
8-1-1	9.718	0.004	35.637	0.238	0.9	0.003	1000	cat
8-0-1	9.200	0.003919	15.913	0.305	0.9	0.001	1000	cat
4-0-2	12.103	0.004	14.097	0.298	0.03	0.001	10000	cat
4-0-2	16.553	0.004	16.351	0.338	0.03	0.001	10000	cont
7-0-1	**6.193**	**0.004**	**8.180**	**0.298**	**0.3**	**0.001**	**1000**	cont
5-0-2	11.149	0.005	9.223	0.291	0.09	0.001	10000	cat

Experiments 8-1-0 and 7-0-1 achieved the best results for the categorical and continuous data respectively. 8-1-0 achieved a low training cost of 0.002, a validation cost of 7.725 and a test cost of 0.305. 7-0-1 achieved a slightly poorer result of 0.004, 8.180 and 2.816 for the same measures. Both experiments achieved the *second lowest* cost on the training data, but performed significantly better on the validation data, meaning these hyper-parameters generalised better. Models learned were not optimal, but given the amount of data available they were adequate as over 69 % of the instances were correctly classified for the categorical data and just over 70 % for the continuous data.

Although the categorical data achieved a lower cost, the continuous data made better predictions. This suggests categorising the data helped remove noise but along with this the transformation eliminated some information relevant to modelling. Interestingly the best performing learning rate (alpha) is much higher for the categorical than the continuous data and ten times less iterations of gradient descent (GD) were required. Therefore gradient descent was far steeper for the categorical data as it converged and gave us the best parameters much faster than with the continuous, showing that one-hot encoded data can be modelled easier, building a predictive model in far less time.

4.3 RBM: To Select Optimum Node Count in First Hidden Layer of DBN

Table 2 shows the 10 highest scoring RBM model configurations out of 35 runs, ranked by the best reconstruction cost (closest to 0) achieved on training data.

Table 2. RBM layer 2 hidden nodes grid search

Ex	T. cost	V. Cost	Alpha	Epochs	Nodes
2-0	-68.719	-22.112	0.9	1	3567-100
1-0	**-73.357**	**-19.580**	**0.9**	**1**	**3567-30**
3-0	-75.110	-22.009	0.9	1	3567-337
0-0	-77.774	-20.665	0.9	1	3567-10
4-0	-98.590	-20.914	0.9	1	3567-900
5-0	-107.553	-20.575	0.9	1	3567-1300
6-0	-141.144	-22.532	0.9	1	3567-2000
2-1	-241.274	-18.547	0.9	5	3567-100
1-1	-241.527	-18.823	0.9	5	3567-30
3-1	-246.462	-18.575	0.9	5	3567-337

The result of the best performing RBM configuration can be seen in bold in Table 2. It has 30 hidden nodes and went through 1 epoch of training. A node configuration of 100 units in the hidden layer achieved the best reconstruction cost of -68.719 on the training data, compared to the configuration with 30 hidden nodes which scored -73.357. The 30 hidden node configuration was determined to be the better architecture as it performed only slightly worse on the training data but it scored -19.580 on the validation set, performing better than every other configuration in the top 5 which measured in the 20's. Therefore, the 30 hidden unit configuration generalises better to unseen data.

The reconstruction cost achieved on the training data by Ex. 3-1 is far worse at -435.809, but the validation score is better at -17.977 due to the higher number of epochs. As the model iterates through the training data, more and more abstract features are learned so the model makes a better estimate at reconstructing unseen data. We want to learn the features that perform comparable on the training data as well as unseen data, therefore one training epoch gave the best performance.

4.4   MLP: To Select Optimum Node Count in Final Hidden Layer of DBN

Table 3 shows the top 10 scoring experiments out of the 14 performed. Here, experiments 2 and 10 gave the best results achieving training, validation and test negative log likelihood costs of 0.17, 2.107, 0.76 and 0.842, 11.664, 0.974 respectively.

Table 3. MLP layer 3 hidden nodes grid search

Ex	I. Cost	T. cost	V. Cost	Error	Data	Alpha	Lambda	Steps	Nodes
2	**2.389**	**0.17**	**2.107**	**0.232**	**cont.**	**0.3**	**0.001**	**1000**	**337-10-2**
4	5.319	0.231	4.609	0.225	cont	0.3	0.001	1000	337-30-2
6	13.466	0.332	12.436	0.225	cont	0.3	0.001	1000	337-100-2
8	33.467	0.456	30.394	0.238	cont	0.3	0.001	1000	337-337-2
1	**11.247**	**0.842**	**11.664**	**0.291**	**cat.**	**0.9**	**0.003**	**100**	**3567-10-2**
10	64.252	0.929	62.453	0.232	cont	0.3	0.001	1000	337-900-2
12	73.305	1.426	78.562	0.212	cont	0.3	0.001	1000	337-1300-2
3	30.256	1.473	35.802	0.318	cat	0.9	0.003	100	3567-30-2
14	121.088	2.211	113.605	0.219	cont	0.3	0.001	1000	337-2000-2
5	99.757	2.549	134.606	0.616	cat	0.9	0.003	100	3567-100-2

From the above table it can be shown that ten hidden nodes - which is the smallest possible number of hidden nodes - gave the best results for both the categorical and continuous data. Further to this, the MLP improves upon the model found with regression for both data-types as the best performing MLP model was 76.8 % accurate in its predictions for the continuous test data and 70.9 % for the categorical.

As a better predictive model was found through the MLP when we compare to regression, it would suggest that abstract features were learned in the hidden layer. Further to this, as the smallest available hidden node value performed best we conclude that the number of features particularly relevant to the outcome we are modelling are relatively low. It can again be seen from the results that that the continuous data lends itself to more powerful models in comparison to the categorical data and this can be put down to information being lost during transformation.

4.5   DBN: Comparing Configurations

Table 4 compares the results of the model learned with the hyper-parameters found through grid-search in earlier experiments (Ex. 6 - parameters in bold from previous experiments) with a randomly selected configuration (Ex. 1 - estimated to be a logical starting point) which was then tuned (Ex. 3, 4, 5) and two other configurations (Ex. 7, 8) which were an attempt to improve upon the results of Ex. 6.

Tuning here refers to adjusting the hyper-parameters to find a better model. The heuristic used was to start the learning rate and training steps low and gradually increase one while observing if either the cost achieved or the accuracy improves. If the measures improve up to a point before deteriorating it can be seen that the global optimum has been overshot.

Table 4. Comparing DBN configurations

Exp	I. Cost	T. cost	V. Cost	Error	Alpha	Lambda	Steps	Nodes
1	2.582	0.680	2.950	0.536	0.001	0.003	3000	3567-337-200-2000-10-2
2	1.653	0.434	1.383	0.272	0.001	0.003	3000	3567-3567-200-10-2
3	3.837	0.541	4.435	0.305	0.01	0.003	3000	3567-3567-200-10-2
4	0.694	0.693	0.695	0.616	0.9	0.003	3000	3567-3567-200-10-2
5	0.916	**0.344**	1.042	0.272	0.01	0.003	1000	3567-3567-200-10-2
6	**2.818**	**0.632**	**0.858**	**0.265**	**0.9**	**0.003**	**100**	**3567-30-10-2**
7	9.236	0.451	6.378	**0.238**	0.9	0.003	100	3567-337-10-2
8	0.748	0.579	0.624	0.245	0.9	0.003	100	3567-337-100-10-2

Ex. 6 achieved the third best error rate on the test data. It immediately improved on 0.272 which was the lowest error rate achieved by picking a random initial configuration and tuning using technique outlined above. In fact, 0.272 was the best test error achievable without hyper-parameters found from previous experiments. Tuning improved the model up to a point (Ex. 2) before it degraded (Ex. 3, 4) and then again achieved previous levels of accuracy (Ex. 5).

When choosing the estimated best starting point for the comparison configuration it was thought that more hidden layers would better model the data. The opposite was found when 2 hidden layers performed best. Interestingly, when a number of nodes the same as the number of features for the continuous data were inserted for the first hidden layer (Ex. 7) it improved on the test error from in Ex. 6. Our analysis is that an abstract feature representation similar to that of the original continuous data was learned in the first hidden layer.

0.238 - the lowest test error achieved (Ex. 7), improved upon on the error for the best categorical data model found with the MLP and approaches our previous best *continuous data* model score of 0.232 with the MLP. We concluded that this was due to the DBN learning a better feature representation in its hidden layers. This shows that a DBN with multiple-layers has great potential in learning a feature representation from text based datasets, given that this model was learned on only a small subset of the MAAS dataset and deep architectures have been shown to far outperform shallow models given enough data [24].

Therefore, it can be seen that performing a grid search on: the regression layer to find the learning rate and regularisation term; the RBM to find the number of nodes in the first hidden layer; and the MLP to find the number of nodes in the last hidden layer gave us a methodology for selecting a good starting point from which to determine the best hyper-parameter configuration for our deep network, at least in the case of a DBN.

5   Related Research

In [6], the authors introduce a random search method to find the best hyper-parameter configuration for a DL architecture and compares their results to previous work [17] which - like our own - uses a multi-resolution grid-search coupled with a manual optimisation intervention element. In [6], they also carry out a series of simulation experiments where random search is compared to both grid-search and low discrepancy sequential methods. Their main contribution is a large series of non-simulated experiments which search for the best hyper-parameters for a one-layer neural network and Deep Belief Network. These are carried out on eight datasets in order to recreate and compare their experimental results with those obtained in [17].

Random search is found to outperform grid search on all datasets in a one-layer neural network, but for the DBN experiments, random and grid search perform comparably on four datasets with grid search outperforming on three datasets and random search finding the best model on the fourth dataset. In [6], the authors offer many reasons as to why random search is a better option but most hinge on the fact that they show that the hyper-parameter search space, although high-dimensional, has a low effective dimensionality. This means that although there are many parameters to tune, only a particular subset of these have a great effect on training the model and this subset is different for every dataset (also shown in the paper). This property leads to random search being more effective as it leaves fewer gaps in the search space and it does not require as many iterations in order to find the optimum hyper-parameter configuration. We chose grid and manual search for these exploratory experiments as it was shown to perform comparably to random search for a DBN. Both [6] and [17] chose to globally optimise the parameters of the entire DBN at once rather than incrementally tune its constituent parts. In other words, they do not optimise each model first where the results of the last set of experiments feed into the next. Contrary to an adaptive approach, which *is* the focus of our experiments and methodology.

A second major issue is the analysis of high-dimensional data and feature selection [4,5,15] which has been extensively explored in a healthcare context [1,3,11]. In [11] and [1], both groups describe a methodology where features are selected in a two-step manually intensive fashion in order to learn predictive models. In these two approaches for selecting a feature representation in the health domain, shallow algorithms are utilised and high dimensional data is not encountered, where in one instance only nine features were modelled [11]. Furthermore, sometimes relevant features were completely eliminated which impacted on the performance of the model [1].

Finally, in the medical context, DBNs have been used for medical text classification [24], as well as to aid in medical decision making with electronic health recordds [18], but never for the analysis of clinical trial data. Neither [24] or [18] provide a methodology on how to choose the initial hyper-parameter configuration of a deep learning architecture. Furthermore, they use third party implementations of a DBN which do not allow for the extension with further algorithms, activation functions or hyper-parameter configurations. In [24], the authors utilise a single hidden layer in their DBN, which arguably is not a deep architecture, although they do employ a unsupervised pre-training step.

6 Conclusions and Future Work

Long term clinical studies present a number of key issues for data miners, of which high dimensionality, the identification of the principal features for prediction and distinguishing the optimal hyper-parameter configuration are most prevalent. To address these issues, we developed a strategy which uses a configurable deep network to facilitate many combinations of attributes and multiple layers of attribute manipulation using regression, MLP, RBM and DBN models. Our framework demonstrated the ability to improve upon a randomly selected and tuned DBN configuration, as well the ability to configure many experimental runs in order to test hyper-parameter configurations found with grid-search. Furthermore, the MLP and DBN showed an ability to learn a feature representation in the hidden layers as an increased predictive accuracy was found compared to regression alone.

We are now extending our CDN to make use of: more accurate imputations via hidden layer sampling; Gaussian hidden units for continuous data (avoiding one-hot encoding); random search for hyper-parameter optimisation; and dropconnect for improved accuracy [23].

References

1. Arauzo-Azofra, A., Aznarte, J.L., Bentez, J.M.: Empirical study of feature selection methods based on individual feature evaluation for classification problems. Expert Syst. Appl. **38**(7), 8170–8177 (2011)
2. Bastien, F., Lamblin, P., Pascanu, R., Bergstra, J., Ian Goodfellow, J., Bergeron, A., Bouchard, N., Bengio, Y.: Theano: new features and speed improvements. In: Deep Learning and Unsupervised Feature Learning NIPS 2012 Workshop (2012)
3. Bellazzi, R., Zupan, B.: Predictive data mining in clinical medicine: current issues and guidelines. Int. J. Med. Inform. **77**(2), 81–97 (2008)
4. Bengio, Y.: Learning deep architectures for AI. Found. Trends Mach. Learn. **2**(1), 1–127 (2009)
5. Bengio, Y., Courville, A., Vincent, P.: Representation learning: a review and new perspectives. IEEE Trans. Pattern Anal. Mach. Intell. **35**(8), 1798–1828 (2013)
6. Bergstra, J., Bengio, Y.: Random search for hyper-parameter optimization. J. Mach. Learn. Res. **13**, 281–305 (2012)
7. Bergstra, J., Breuleux, O., Bastien, F., Lamblin, P., Pascanu, R., Desjardins, G., Turian, J., Warde-Farley, D., Bengio, Y.: Theano: a CPU and GPU math expression compiler. In: Proceedings of the Python for Scientific Computing Conference (SciPy), June 2010. Oral Presentation
8. Camous, F., McCann, D., Roantree, M.: Capturing personal health data from wearable sensors. In: International Symposium on Applications and the Internet, SAINT 2008, pp. 153–156. IEEE (2008)

9. Deckers, K., Boxtel, M.P.J., Schiepers, O.J.G., Vugt, M., Sánchez, J.L.M., Anstey, K.J., Brayne, C., Dartigues, J.-F., Engedal, K., Kivipelto, M., et al.: Target risk factors for dementia prevention: a systematic review and delphi consensus study on the evidence from observational studies. Int. J.Geriatr. Psychiatry **30**(3), 234–246 (2014)

10. Donnelly, N., Irving, K., Roantree, M.: Cooperation across multiple healthcare clinics on the cloud. In: Magoutis, K., Pietzuch, P. (eds.) DAIS 2014. LNCS, vol. 8460, pp. 82–88. Springer, Heidelberg (2014)

11. Fakhraei, S., Soltanian-Zadeh, H., Fotouhi, F., Elisevich, K.: Confidence in medical decision making: application in temporal lobe epilepsy data mining. In: Proceedings of the 2011 Workshop on Data Mining for Medicine and Healthcare, pp. 60–63. ACM (2011)

12. Glorot, X., Bengio, Y.: Understanding the difficulty of training deep feedforward neural networks. In: International Conference on Artificial Intelligence and Statistics, pp. 249–256 (2010)

13. Hinton, G.: A practical guide to training restricted boltzmann machines. Momentum **9**(1), 926 (2010)

14. Hinton, G.E., Osindero, S., Teh, Y.-W.: A fast learning algorithm for deep belief nets. Neural Comput. **18**(7), 1527–1554 (2006)

15. Humphrey, E.J., Bello, J.P., LeCun, Y.: Feature learning and deep architectures: new directions for music informatics. J. Intell. Inf. Syst. **41**(3), 461–481 (2013)

16. van Boxtel, M.P.J., Ponds, R.H.W.M., Jolles, J., Houx, P.J.: The Maastricht Aging Study: Determinants of Cognitive Aging. Neuropsych Publishers, Maastricht (1995)

17. Larochelle, H., Erhan, D., Courville, A., Bergstra, J., Bengio, Y.: An empirical evaluation of deep architectures on problems with many factors of variation. In: Proceedings of the 24th International Conference on Machine Learning, ICML 2007, pp. 473–480. ACM, New York, NY, USA (2007)

18. Liang, Z., Zhang, G., Huang, J.X., Hu, Q.V.: Deep learning for healthcare decision making with EMRs. In: 2014 IEEE International Conference on Bioinformatics and Biomedicine (BIBM), pp. 556–559. IEEE (2014)

19. Roantree, M., O'Donoghue, J., O'Kelly, N., Pierce, M., Irving, K., Van Boxtel, M., Köhler, S.: Mapping longitudinal studies to risk factors in an ontology for dementia. Health Inf. J., pp. 1–13 (2015)

20. Roantree, M., Shi, J., Cappellari, P., O'Connor, M.F., Whelan, M., Moyna, N.: Data transformation and query management in personal health sensor networks. J. Netw. Comput. Appl. **35**(4), 1191–1202 (2012). Intelligent Algorithms for Data-Centric Sensor Networks

21. Salakhutdinov, R., Hinton, G.E.: Deep boltzmann machines. In: International Conference on Artificial Intelligence and Statistics, pp. 448–455 (2009)

22. van Boxtel, M.P., Buntinx, F., Houx, P.J., Metsemakers, J.F., Knottnerus, A., Jolles, J.: The relation between morbidity and cognitive performance in a normal aging population. J. Gerontol. Ser. A Biol. Sci. Med. Sci. **53**(2), 147–154 (1998)

23. Wan, L., Zeiler, M., Zhang, S., Cun, Y.L., Fergus, R.: Regularization of neural networks using dropconnect. In: Proceedings of the 30th International Conference on Machine Learning, ICML-2013, pp. 1058–1066 (2013)

24. Jimeno Yepes, A., MacKinlay, A., Bedo, J., Garnavi, R., Chen, Q.: Deep belief networks and biomedical text categorisation. In: Australasian Language Technology Association Workshop, p. 123 (2014)

Using Virtual Meeting Structure to Support Summarisation

Antonios G. Nanos[✉], Anne E. James, Rahat Iqbal, and
Yih-ling Hedley

Distributed Systems and Modelling Group, Faculty of Engineering
and Computing, Coventry University, Coventry CV1 5FB, UK
{nanos,a.james,r.iqbal,y.hedley}@coventry.ac.uk

Abstract. Archiving meeting transcripts in databases is not always efficient. Users need to be able to catch up with past meetings quickly, and therefore it is non-productive to read the full meeting transcript from scratch. A summarisation of the meeting transcript is preferable but the lack of meeting structure may lead to missing information. Therefore, we have introduced a virtual meeting system that is characterised by features that provide the meeting session with structure and a summarisation system that applies a TextRank approach on the structured meeting transcripts. The agenda with timed items guides the conversation. Thus the item delineation and title can be considered as the key characteristics of a valuable summary. Results show that combining an extraction summarisation technique with meeting structure leads to a relevant summary.

Keywords: Virtual meeting · Data model · Automatic summarisation

1 Introduction

A virtual meeting system has been developed, called V-Room [1], which makes use of agendas with timed items and meeting roles, leading to improved topic guidance and subsequent summarisation. The roles currently fall into four categories: the chair; the facilitator; item leaders; and participants. Roles can always be interpreted in different ways in order to suit different meeting protocols. For instance in the educational domain case described in this paper, the chairman is the module leader, the facilitator is the assistant lecturer and students are the participants. Item leaders can be any of the participants depending on their interest in the item discussed. The agenda, items and roles are set up as part of a pre-meeting process. This paper illustrates how the use of such a model of meeting structure can drive automated summarisation of virtual meeting content.

The paper is organised as follows. Section 2 briefly describes some related literature. Section 3 describes our summarisation approach. Some experimental results are provided in Sect. 4, while Sect. 5 provides a brief conclusion and directions for future work.

S. Maneth (Ed.): BICOD 2015, LNCS 9147, pp. 133–136, 2015.
DOI: 10.1007/978-3-319-20424-6_13

2 Related Work

Extensive work has been carried out in automatic summarisation [2, 3]. The approach adopted in V-ROOM is textual sentence extraction with meta-information added to provide the context of the discussion. Since both context and content is provided we consider our summarisation to be indicative and informative. The term indicative is used to describe summaries that give heading information such as topics of discussion and the term informative is used to describe summarisations that include the content of the discussion rather than just the topic headings.

One of the techniques we have used for sentence extraction is TextRank, an unsupervised method. TextRank is a graph-based algorithm [4] for ranking sentences within a text. It achieves this by building a graph where a unit of text is represented by a vertex and a link between two units of text is represented by an edge. A link may be formed between two text units if the same word or phrase is used in both text units. Links between natural language text units may be multiple (more than one word or phrase connection occurs) or partial (part of a phrase connects but not the whole phrase). For this reason edges are assigned weights.

A novelty of our work is the exploration of the application of summarisation techniques such as TextRank to the area of virtual meetings and combining such techniques with the use of an underlying data model which holds the structure of the meeting and the roles of participants.

3 Our Summarisation Approach

The approach is based on an underlying data model representing structural aspects of the meeting. An extract from the data model schema is shown below. The use of item titles and other structural aspects can aid summarisation and automated minutes generation.

chat (time, meeting_id, username, message,)
user (user_id, username, password, last_ login).
item (item_id, item_title, meeting_id, item_endtime, status, leader).
meeting (meeting_id, meeting_title, starttime, endtime, chair, facilitator, status).

The messages are collected, analysed and the most important sentences are used for the summary. A pre-processing stage ensures basic punctuation of the input text and a post-processing stage adds meta-data to create the meeting context which helps to convey further meaning to the summarisation (see Fig. 1). The item title is used in order to locate and isolate sentences connected to it and then the TextRank algorithm is used in order to return the sentences that score higher in the marking. All of the sentences receive a score but the summary is based on the top sentences, returned in chronological order.

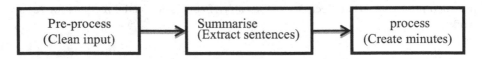

Fig. 1. Stages in the Summarisation Process

The summary can only be extracted when the meeting has been finished, otherwise the results will not be accurate. One of the biggest challenges is to match the item with the corresponding text on the database [5]. Let us assume that this step has been completed successfully. Within the summarisation component, the text is split into sentences. Then a sparse matrix of token counts is created based on the size of the vocabulary that has been identified by analysing the data. The matrix shows frequency of words across sentences. The matrix is normalised by associating weights to words depending on their importance. Then a similarity matrix is created across the sentences and an associated weighted graph is created. From the graph, we extract the sentences that are connected to the title based on the expectation that those sentences are more likely to be the heart of the conversation. Then the TextRank algorithm is applied in order to give a score to each of them with the assumption that top sentences are the most highly connected sentences and hence most representative of the conversation. Finally, the top sentences are returned in chronological order to maintain the flow of discussion.

4   Experimental Results

The evaluation of the summarisation system took place by examining the summarisation methods on a meeting transcript that we collected from a virtual meeting between 2 members of academic staff and 9 students. We tested the system on various meeting items using TextRank with and without reference to item title (we call these methods TR-IT and TR-NIT respectively). The results of the test of the item entitled "Types of Testing" is presented in Table 1. Originally the text conversation consisted of 36 sentences and the summary configuration was set to reduce to 6 sentences. We tested summarisation on various items and on the whole meeting without reference to item delineation or item title.

Table 1. Extractions from summary minutes after post-processing

TextRank without Item Title (TR-NIT)	TextRank with item title (TR-IT)
Types of Testing The following comments were made: 'For V-room I think usability testing would be most important.' 'Yes, black box will be but what kind?' 'Yes black box or even grey box as we will have access to both the code and system right?' 'I have found out about white box and black box testing.' 'I also think usability testing would be good as we are trying to develop this system so by using, testing and finding improvement we can develop VROOM acceptance testing.' 'Black box is best for this so yes.'	Types of Testing The following comments were made: 'For V-room I think usability testing would be most important.' 'I have found out about white box and black box testing.' "Black is when the internal structure and design of a software is not known and white is when it is known."'I also think usability testing would be good as we are trying to develop this system so by using, testing and finding improvement we can develop vroom acceptance testing.' 'Grey box testing is another one involves having knowledge of internal data structures and algorithms for purposes of designing tests.'

We found that delineation into items before applying TextRank led to better summaries. Both summaries shown in Table 1 are indicative and informative according to the definition given in Sect. 2. The TR-IT summary is perhaps more informative regarding the breadth of discussion but the TR-NIT gives a better indication of the emerging decision. For other items we found that TR-IT produced more clearly enhanced summaries. Our findings led to the recommendation that structural features could be used to enhance summaries. We noted that if a brief description of the item's purpose had been given as part of the agenda setting, further useful indicative context could have been provided and this would enhance the summaries.

5 Conclusion and Future Work

Our initial findings show that capturing and representing meeting structure can improve the quality of automated summaries of virtual meetings. Further evaluation is needed however. TextRank is not the only algorithm that can be used to find the best sentences for extraction. A future direction of exploration will be utilising the roles of the participants within the meeting to influence sentence extraction. We also note that additional meta-information could provide useful context. Our future work will explore these avenues.

References

1. Thompson, P., James, A., Nanos, A.: V-ROOM: virtual meeting system trial. In: 17th IEEE International Conference on Computer Supported Cooperative Work in Design, pp. 563–569. IEEE press, Washington (2013)
2. Jones, K.S.: Introduction to Text Summarisation. In: Mani, I., Maybury, M. (eds.) Advances in Automated Text Summarization. The MIT Press, Cambridge (1998)
3. Hovy, E., Lin, C., Y.: Automated text summarization and the SUMMARIST system. In: Proceedings of a Workshop held at Baltimore, Association for Computational Linguistics, pp. 197–214, Stroudsburg (1998)
4. Rada, M., Tarau, P., TextRank: bringing order into texts. In: Proceedings of the Conference on Empirical Methods in Natural Language Processing, Association for Computational Linguistics, pp. 404–411. , Stroudsburg (2004)
5. James, A., Nanos, A., Thompson, P.: V-ROOM: A virtual meeting system with intelligent structured summarisation. Enterprise Information Systems, doi:10.1080/17517575.2015. 1019571

NoSQL and Distributed Processing

NotaQL Is Not a Query Language! It's for Data Transformation on Wide-Column Stores

Johannes Schildgen[✉] and Stefan Deßloch

University of Kaiserslautern, Kaiserslautern, Germany
{schildgen,dessloch}@cs.uni-kl.de

Abstract. It is simple to query a relational database because all columns of the tables are known and the language SQL is easily applicable. In NoSQL, there usually is no fixed schema and no query language. In this article, we present NotaQL, a data-transformation language for wide-column stores. NotaQL is easy to use and powerful. Many MapReduce algorithms like filtering, grouping, aggregation and even breadth-first-search, PageRank and other graph and text algorithms can be expressed in two or three short lines of code.

Keywords: NoSQL · Transformation · Language · Wide-column stores

1 Motivation

When we take a look at NoSQL databases[1], they differ from classical relational databases in terms of scalability, their data model and query method. The simplest form of such a database is a key-value store: One can simply write and read values using a key-based access. In this paper, we concentrate on wide-column stores. Such a store consists of tables that have one row-id column and one or more column

ROW_ID	information			children	
Peter	born 1967	cmpny IBM	salary €50000	Susi €5	John €10
Kate	born 1968	cmpny IBM	salary €60000	Susi €20	John €0
Susi	born 1989	school Eton			
John	born 1991	school Eton			

Fig. 1. Person table with a children graph and amounts of pocket money

families. Basically, each column family can be seen as a separate key-value store where column names function as keys. The three most popular wide-column stores are Google's Big Table [2], its open-source implementation Apache HBase[2], and Cassandra[3]. Figure 1 shows an example table with two column families.

At first sight, the table looks similar to a relational table. This is because both consist of columns and these columns hold atomic values. In relational

---

[1] http://nosql-database.org.
[2] http://hbase.apache.org.
[3] http://cassandra.apache.org.

© Springer International Publishing Switzerland 2015
S. Maneth (Ed.): BICOD 2015, LNCS 9147, pp. 139–151, 2015.
DOI: 10.1007/978-3-319-20424-6_14

databases, however, the database schema is static, i.e., all columns of a table are known, before values are inserted or modified. In contrast, in a wide-column store, at each insertion, one is able to set and create arbitrary columns. In other words, the database schema does not exist, or is dynamically evolving. The first column family *information* contains attributes of people. Note that different rows can have different columns which are not predefined at table-creation time. The second column family *children* models a graph structure. The names in the columns are references to row-ids of children and the values are the amounts of pocket money the children get from their parents. We will later use this table as an example for all of our NotaQL transformations. Web graphs are very akin to this example: The first column family comprises information about a web site, while the second contains links to other web sites.

If the table in Fig. 1 was stored in HBase, one could use a *Get* operation in the *HBase Shell* or the Java API to fetch a row with all its columns by its row-id. In HBase, there always is an index on the row-id. Other secondary indexes are not supported. To execute more complex queries, programmers can utilize a framework that allows access via an SQL-like query language. The most prominent system for that is Hive [21]; others are presented in the next section.

As an alternative, one may consider generating redundant data which then can be accessed via simple *Get* operations. This approach shows similarities with materialized views in traditional relational DBMS [7]. In [13], ideas are presented to do selections, joins, groupings and sorts by defining transformations over the data. The authors advocate that one does not need a query language like SQL when the data is stored in the way it is needed at query time. If finding all people with a specific year of birth is a frequent query, the application which modifies data should maintain a second table whose row-id is a year of birth and columns are foreign keys to the original row-id in the main table. As a drawback, applications have to be modified carefully to maintain all the tables, so every change in the base data immediately leads to many changes in different tables. In [5], similar approaches are presented to maintain secondary indexes on HBase, either with a dual-write strategy or by letting a MapReduce [3] job periodically update an index table.

In this paper, we present NotaQL, a data-transformation language for wide-column stores. Like SQL, it is easy to learn and powerful. NotaQL is made for schema-flexible databases, there is a support for horizontal aggregations, and metadata can be transformed to data and vice versa. Complex transformations with filters, groupings and aggregations, as well as graph and text algorithms can be expressed with minimal effort. The materialized output of a transformation can be efficiently read by applications with the simple Get API.

In the following section, we present some related work. In Sect. 3, NotaQL is introduced as a data-transformation language. We present a MapReduce-based transformation platform in Sect. 4 and the last section concludes the article.

2   Related Work

Transformations and queries on NoSQL, relational and graph databases can be done by using different frameworks and languages. With Clio [8], one can perform a schema mapping from different source schemata into a target schema using a graphical interface. Clio creates views in a semi-automatic way which can be used to access data from all sources. This virtual integration differs from our approach because NotaQL creates materialized views. Clio can only map metadata to metadata and data to data. There is no possibility to translate attribute names into values and vice versa. In [1], a copy-and-paste model is presented to load data from different sources into a curated database. Curated databases are similar to data warehouses, but here it is allowed to modify data in the target system. A tree-based model is used to support operations from SQL and XQuery as well as copying whole subtrees. The language presented in that paper also contains provenance functions to find out by which transaction a node was created, modified or copied. Although the language is very powerful, it does not support aggregations, unions and duplicate elimination because in these cases, the origin of a value is not uniquely defined.

There are many approaches to query wide-column stores using SQL, e.g. Hive, Phoenix[4] or Presto[5]. On the one hand, one does not need to learn a new query language and applications which are based on relational databases can be reused without many modifications. On the other hand, SQL is not well-suited for wide-column stores, so the expressiveness is limited. Figure 16 at the end of this paper shows the weak points of SQL: Transformations between metadata and data, horizontal aggregations and much more can not be expressed with an SQL query. Furthermore, many frameworks do not support the schema flexibility of HBase. Before an HBase table can be queried by *Hive*, one has to create a new Hive table and define how its columns are mapped to an existing HBase table[6]. With *Phoenix*, an HBase table can be queried with SQL after defining the columns and their types of a table with a **CREATE TABLE** command. *Presto* is an SQL query engine by Facebook. The presto coordinator creates an execution plan for a given query and a scheduler distributes the tasks to the nodes that are close to the data. Usually, Presto directly accesses data that is stored in the Hadoop distributed file system but connectors for other systems, e.g. HBase, exist as well. The strength of Presto is a nearly full ANSI-SQL support—including joins and window functions—and its ten times higher speed than Hive and MapReduce. But again, only relational queries on relational tables with static schemas are possible.

The HBase Query Language by Jaspersoft[7] can be used to support more complex queries on an HBase table. It is better suited for wide-column stores than SQL, but not easy to use. One has to define a query as a JSON document that can be very long, even for simple queries. The syntax of our language NotaQL is inspired by *Sawzall* [19], a programming language used by Google to define log processing tasks instead of manually writing a MapReduce job. The input of a Sawzall script is one single line of input (e.g. a log record) and the

---

[4] http://phoenix.apache.org.
[5] http://prestodb.io.
[6] https://cwiki.apache.org/confluence/display/Hive/HBaseIntegration.
[7] https://community.jaspersoft.com/wiki/jaspersoft-hbase-query-language.

output are insertions into virtual tables. A Sawzall script runs as a MapReduce job and the input and output is not an HBase table but a CSV file. The language *Pig Latin* [17] provides relational-algebra-like operators to load, filter and group data. Pig programs can be interconnected with a workflow manager like Nova [16]. Google BigQuery [20] is the publicly-available version of Dremel [14]. One can import and analyze data that is stored in the Google Cloud Storage using SQL. As the data is stored in a column-oriented manner, it can be filtered and aggregated very fast. In the paper, it is recommended to use BigQuery in combination with MapReduce. First, MapReduce can join and pre-process data, then this data can be analyzed using BigQuery. As NotaQL transformations are based on MapReduce, one can replace the complex MapReduce transformations by NotaQL scripts and combine them with fast query languages like BigQuery, Phoenix, or HBase QL.

Graph-Processing Frameworks. The language Green-Marl [9] is used to describe graph-analysis algorithms. Green-Marl programs are compiled into multi-threaded and highly efficient C++ code. In contrast to NotaQL, Green-Marl was not designed for graph transformations but to calculate a scalar value (e.g. diameter) of the graph, to add a property to every node (e.g. PageRank, see Sect. 3.3), or to select a subgraph of interest. Pregel [12] is a system to develop iterative graph algorithms by exchanging messages between nodes. Every node can send messages to its neighbors and change its properties and its state depending on incoming messages. When there is no incoming message, a node becomes inactive. When all nodes are inactive, the algorithm terminates. In PowerGraph [6], instead of sending messages, every node computes a MapReduce job for all its incoming edges (Gather phase) and computes a new value for a node attribute (Apply phase). In the end, for each edge, a predicate is evaluated (Scatter phase). If it is false for every incoming edge of a node, the node becomes inactive and it will be skipped in the next Gather-Apply-Scatter (GAS) round. Pregel and PowerGraph are not well-suited for graph construction and transformation. GraphX [23] is an extension of Spark [24] and it solves this problem by introducing a Resiliant Distributed Graph (RDG) interface for graph construction, filters, transformations, mappings, updates and aggregations. GraphX algorithms are seven times slower than PowerGraph jobs but eight times faster than native Hadoop jobs because they use a tabular representation of the graph and a vertex-cut partitioning over many worker nodes. As the GraphX interface is not easy to use, it is recommended to develop one's own API based on that interface. Pregel and PowerGraph can be reimplemented using GraphX in twenty lines of code. The NotaQL language is more user-friendly. We are planning to use the GraphX interface to develop a NotaQL-based API. This makes graph processing not only fast but also easy to develop. With Naiad [15], one can define a computation as a dataflow graph. A vertex can send messages to other vertexes for the next iteration which is executed in an incremental fashion. Like GraphX, it is recommended not to use Naiad directly but to build libraries for higher languages on top of it.

3   Transformations on Wide-Column Stores

In this section, we present the NotaQL language to define transformations. The first examples can be solved with SQL as well, but later in this article, there are graph algorithms and others which are not expressible in SQL.

3.1   Mapping of Input Cells to Output Cells

As we learned in the motivation section, each row in a wide-column store has a unique row-id. In the following examples, we access columns independent of their column family. If a table consists of multiple column families, their names can be used as a prefix, e.g. `information : born` instead of `born`. Each row can have an arbitrary number of columns and the column names are unique within one row. The combination of row-id and column name (`_r`, `_c`) is called a *cell*. Each cell has one atomic value, so the triple (`_r`, `_c`, `_v`) represents one cell together with its value, for example (`Peter, born, 1967`)[8].

The basic idea of NotaQL is to define mappings between input and output cells, or—more precisely—to specify how to construct output cells based on the input. These mappings are executed in three steps: (1) Selection on the input table; (2) For each row, split it into cells and perform a cell mapping; (3) Aggregate all values for the same output cell using an aggregate function.

Figure 2 shows the identity mapping where each cell is simply copied. Here, no row selection and no aggregation function is used.

When this transformation is executed, a snapshot of the input table is analyzed row by row. In every row, for each of its cells an output cell will be produced with exactly the same row-id, column name and value. So the result of this transformation looks just like the input. An equivalent SQL query would be: `INSERT INTO out (SELECT * FROM in)`. It

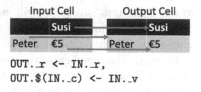

```
OUT._r <- IN._r,
OUT.$(IN._c) <- IN._v
```

Fig. 2. Table copy with NotaQL

copies a full table. HBase comes with a backup tool *CopyTable*[9] to solve this problem.

When not all columns should be copied, but only the `salary` and `born` columns, the second line in the table-copy example can be replaced by `OUT.salary <- IN.salary, OUT.born <- IN.born`.

Figure 3 shows the NotaQL syntax in BNF. We will see that most algorithms can be specified in one block containing one row and one cell specification. We illustrate the syntax further in the following subsections. In general, a NotaQL script can consist of many blocks to perform multiple cell mappings in one transformation.

---

[8] These triples are known as entity-attribute-value or object-attribute-value. They are very flexible regarding the number of attributes of each entity.

[9] http://blog.cloudera.com/blog/2012/06/online-hbase-backups-with-copytable-2/.

⟨NotaQL⟩ ⊨ [IN-FILTER: ⟨predicate⟩,]⟨rowspec⟩, ⟨cellspec⟩(, ⟨cellspec⟩) * [;]
⟨rowspec⟩ ⊨ OUT._r <- ⟨vdata⟩
⟨cellspec⟩ ⊨ OUT.(⟨colname⟩ | $(⟨input⟩)) <- (⟨vdata⟩ | ⟨aggfun⟩(⟨vdata⟩))
  ⟨input⟩ ⊨ (IN._r | IN.[⟨colfamily⟩ :](_c | _v) | IN.⟨colname⟩)[?(⟨predicate⟩)]
  ⟨vdata⟩ ⊨ ⟨input⟩ | ⟨const⟩ | ⟨vdata⟩(+ | − | * | /)⟨vdata⟩
  ⟨aggfun⟩ ⊨ COUNT | SUM | MIN | MAX | AVG
  ⟨const⟩ ⊨ '(A . . . Z | a . . . z | 0 . . . 9) + ' | (0 . . . 9) +
⟨colname⟩ ⊨ [⟨colfamily⟩ :](A . . . Z | a . . . z | 0 . . . 9) +
⟨colfamily⟩ ⊨ (A . . . Z | a . . . z | 0 . . . 9) +
⟨predicate⟩ ⊨ (⟨colname⟩ | @ | col_count([⟨colfamily⟩])) [⟨op⟩](⟨colname⟩ | ⟨const⟩]
    | (NOT | !)⟨predicate⟩ | ⟨predicate⟩(AND | OR)⟨predicate⟩
  ⟨op⟩ ⊨ = | ! = | < | <= | > | >=

Fig. 3. NotaQL language definition (simplified)

3.2 Predicates

There are two kinds of predicates in NotaQL: a *row predicate* which acts as an input-row filter to perform a row selection and a *cell predicate* which selects specific cells in a row. The row predicate is an optional filter definition placed at the beginning of a NotaQL script using an IN-FILTER clause. If such a predicate is set, every row in the input table which does not satisfy it will be skipped. That means, before a mapping is performed,

```
IN-FILTER: born>1950,
OUT._r <- IN._r,
OUT.salary <- IN.salary
```

Fig. 4. Row predicate

```
OUT._r <- IN._r,
OUT.$(IN._c?(@='€5')) <- IN._v
```

Fig. 5. Cell predicate

a whole row is handled as if it would not exist when the predicate is evaluated as false. In this predicate, comparison and logical operators as well as column names and constants can be used.

The transformation in Fig. 4 is executed as follows: Only rows that contain a column **born** with a value greater than 1950 are selected. The rest of the rows are skipped. In the remaining rows, only the column **salary** is read and returned. The result is one table with only one column **salary** and between zero and n rows, where **n** is the number of rows in the base table. The transformation is equivalent to the SQL query SELECT salary FROM in WHERE born>1950. Some more examples for row predicates:

- (born>1950 AND born<1960) OR cpny='IBM' OR col_count()>5,
- school respectively !school— checks column existence / absence in a row.

When cells should be filtered within one row without knowing their names, a *cell predicate* can be used. It starts with a ? and can be placed after an IN._c or IN._v. The transformation in Fig. 5 only copies columns with a value equal to €5, independent of their names. The question mark indicates the begin of a predicate so that cells are skipped which do not satisfy it. The @ symbol is used to refer to the current cell's value. A cell predicate can also be used to drop columns, e.g. OUT.$(IN._c?(!name)) <- IN._v.

SQL does not support predicates for column existence or absence. Furthermore, it is not possible to drop columns or check values of columns independent from their names. For wide-column stores these predicates are necessary because of their schema flexibility.

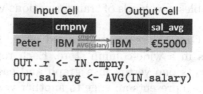

```
OUT._r <- IN.cmpny,
OUT.sal_avg <- AVG(IN.salary)
```

Fig. 6. Aggregation: AVG

The logical execution of a NotaQL transformation starts with splitting each input row into its cells. After a cell mapping is performed, new row-ids together with columns of an output row are collected. If there is more than one value for the same row-id/column pair, an implicit grouping is performed and the user has to define how the final value is aggregated based on the single values.

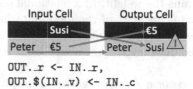

```
OUT._r <- IN._r,
OUT.$(IN._v) <- IN._c
```

Fig. 7. Corrupt NotaQL script

A popular example query is calculating the average salary values per company. In SQL, this is done by grouping and aggregation. Here, a row-id in the output table should be a company name which is stored as a value in the column cmpny. So, the

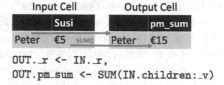

```
OUT._r <- IN._r,
OUT.pm_sum <- SUM(IN.children:_v)
```

Fig. 8. Aggregation: SUM

first NotaQL mapping is OUT._r <- IN.cmpny,. The output column name is set to 'sal_avg'. For setting the value of the output cell, the salary has to be read and summed up (see Fig. 6).

In the very first example which copies a table, the output mapping is uniquely defined in the sense that there is a single value for each row-id/column pair. This can be easily proven: As each input cell (_r,_c) is unique, each output cell (_r,_c) is unique, too. Figure 7 shows a transformation where the uniqueness is not given because different input cells can have equal values. Whenever a transformation can produce multiple values for the very same cell (OUT._r, _c), an aggregation function must be used. The output table of the query in Fig. 8 has the same number of rows as the input table, but each row only consists of one column (pm_sum) with the sum of all column values. These *horizontal aggregations* are not possible in SQL.

3.3 Graph-Processing Applications

The queries from the previous subsections are typical log-processing queries with projection, selection, grouping, and aggregation. These operations are well known from the relational algebra and from SQL and have been generalized further in NotaQL for wide-column stores. But NotaQL supports more complex computations as well. In this section, we show that graph-processing algorithms like PageRank and breadth-first search can be implemented in NotaQL. This illustrates the power of the simple NotaQL language and demonstrates that it enables new kinds of transformations which are not possible with classical query languages yet.

Graphs are often modeled as adjacency lists in a wide-column store. Each row represents one vertex in a graph and each column represents an edge to another vertex. If the edges are weighted, the value of a column contains the weight. In a relational database, columns are part of the meta-data level of a table. In a wide-column store, they are part of the data level. This is why SQL is not well-suited for graph algorithms.

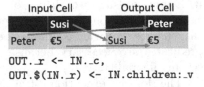

```
OUT._r <- IN._c,
OUT.$(IN._r) <- IN.children:_v
```

Fig. 9. Reversing a graph

Reversing a Graph. A simple graph algorithm that reverses the directions of edges in a graph can be defined by simply taking the first example *Table Copy* and swapping IN._r and IN._c (see Fig. 9). When this script is executed on our example table, it will produce a new table where for every person their parents can be found. On a web-link graph, this script produces an inverted graph, i.e. a list of web sites together with their incoming links. The given script can be extended to manipulate the graph structure. In the transformation in Fig. 10, row and cell predicates are used to remove vertices (people with less than two children) and edges (to children receiving €10 or less).

PageRank. The PageRank algorithm is an iterative algorithm to rank a vertex in a graph depending on the rank of vertices pointing to it. The full algorithm can be found in [18]. Here we concentrate only on the most interesting part of the PageRank formula—the random-jump factor is not relevant for our discussion and is therefore omitted. The NotaQL script for computing the PageRank is very close to its mathematical definition (see Fig. 11).

```
IN-FILTER: col_count()>=2,
OUT._r <- IN._c,
OUT.$(IN._r) <-
         IN.children:_v?(@>10);
```

Fig. 10. Parents of persons with two or more children that give more than €10 of pocket money.

The idea is to start with a PageRank value of $\frac{1}{n}$ for each vertex (with n being the number of vertices in the graph) and running some iterations of the formula above until the PageRank values converge. In a wide-column store, the graph is stored in a table with the row-id being the vertex identifier, one column PR in the column family alg with the starting value of $\frac{1}{n}$ and one column for each outgoing edge in the column family edges.

The fraction between the PageRank value and the outdegree of a node y can be used as one addend of the new PageRank values of the nodes x to whom y has an outgoing edge. In our example table, the outdegree is the number of columns

$$PR(x) = \sum_{y|y \to x} \frac{PR(y)}{outdegree(y)}$$

```
OUT._r <- IN._c,
OUT.alg:PR <- SUM(IN.alg:PR/col_count(edges));
```

Fig. 11. The PageRank algorithm

in the column family `edges`. In this transformation, the input and output tables are the same, so there are no steps needed to preserve the graph structure. The results are only updated output cells for the column `PR`. An example: Nodes A (PR: 0.1) and B (PR: 0.3) have one outgoing edge each, namely to node C. So, C's new PageRank value is $\frac{0.1}{1} + \frac{0.3}{1} = 0.4$.

Like updates in SQL, NotaQL transformations have snapshot semantics. This means, logically the full input is read, then all cells are mapped to output cells and at the end the output is written. So writes into the input table during job-execution do not interfere with the remaining transformation process. For our example, the execution framework has to decide after each execution whether more iterations are needed or not. PageRank can be executed iteratively until the changes of the PageRank values are below a specific accuracy value. One approach to control the number of iterations is a change measurement after each iteration. Depending on the amount of changes since the previous iteration, a new run is started or the overall job terminates. Another approach is the usage of an input format that compares the last two versions of each cell value and ignores a row when the changes are below a threshold. Then, the job terminates when the input is empty.

Breadth-First Search. The distance between two vertices in a graph is the number of edges on the shortest path between them. In a weighted graph, it is the sum of (positive) weights of those edges. Breadth-first search [11] can be used to compute the distance from one predefined vertex V_0 to every other vertex. Therefore, a `dist` column is added for start vertex V_0 with the value 0. For all other vertices, the distance is ∞. This can be modeled by the absence of the `dist` column in the column family `alg`.

The NotaQL script in Fig. 12 is executed iteratively until the result does not change anymore. In a connected graph, the number of iterations is equal to the diameter of the graph. In each iteration, neighbors of vertices whose distance are known are updated.

The `IN-FILTER` skips rows with an unknown distance. For the others, the distance of each neighbor vertex is set to the vertex' own distance plus one. If multiple vertices have an edge to the same neighbor, the minimum value is taken. If the algorithm should take weighted edges into account, the `1` in the last line has to be replaced by `IN._v` to add the current edge weight to the own distance.

```
IN-FILTER: dist
OUT._r <- IN._c,
OUT.dist <- MIN(IN.dist+1),
```

Fig. 12. Breadth-first search

3.4 Text Processing

We extended the NotaQL language with a `split` function. It has one input parameter for a delimiter and it splits text values in multiple ones. Figure 13 shows a NotaQL transformation which counts the occurrences of each word in all input

```
OUT._r <- IN._v.split(' '),
OUT.count <- COUNT()
```

Fig. 13. Word-count algorithm

cells. The output is a table where for each word (row-id) a column `count` holds the number of occurrences of the word in all input cells.

With a small modification in the word-count script, one can calculate a *term index* with NotaQL: `OUT.$(IN._r) <- COUNT();` Here, each term row contains a count value for each document that contains the term. These can be used to support an efficient full-text search over large text data. In addition to these examples, many other graph and text algorithms can be expressed in NotaQL. For example, the computation of TF-IDF (term frequency/inverse document frequency) is a chain of three NotaQL transformations.

4   NotaQL Transformation Platform

There are different possibilities to execute NotaQL scripts. They can be mapped to other languages using a wrapper, the direct API to a wide-column store can be used, or one could make use of a framework like MapReduce. In this section, we present a MapReduce-based transformation platform with full NotaQL language support. It is accessed via a command line interface or with a GUI. The GUI can be used to plan, execute and monitor NotaQL transformations [4]. When writing a NotaQL script, the tool immediately visualizes the cell mapping using arrows, as in the figures in Sect. 3. Alternatively, the user can work just graphically by defining arrows between cells. The GUI user can define an update period, i.e. a time interval in which a script will be recomputed.

When a transformation is started, the input table is read row by row. Rows which violate the row predicate are skipped. Each remaining cell fulfilling the cell predicate is mapped to an output cell in the way it is defined in the NotaQL script. Cells with the same identifier are grouped and all its values are aggregated. We used the Hadoop[10] MapReduce framework for the execution because of its advantages for distributed computations, scalability, and failure compensation. Reading and transforming input cells is done by the *Map* function, the Hadoop framework sorts and groups the output cells, and finally, the aggregation and the write of the final output is done by the *Reduce* function.

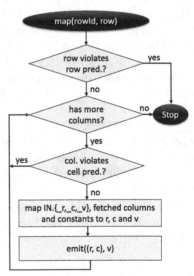

Fig. 14. NotaQL map function

Map. The input for one Map function is one row from the input table that consists of a row-id and a set of columns and values. Figure 14

---

[10] http://hadoop.apache.org.

shows how predicates are evaluated and the map output is produced. The Map-output key is a combination of an output row-id and a column qualifier. So, each Reduce function processes all the values for one specific cell. It is efficient to use a Partitioner function which transfers the data directly to the node which is responsible for storing rows with the given row-id.

Reduce and Combine. Figure 15 shows that the Reduce function just produces one output cell by aggregating all values for one column in a row. Similar to this, a generic Combine function can aggregate existing values as well. So, the network traffic is reduced and the Reducers have to aggregate fewer values for each cell.

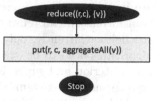

Fig. 15. NotaQL reduce function

	SQL	NotaQL
add/drop columns	(✔)DDL Statements (ALTER TABLE)	✔ OUT.newCol <- ...
check column existence	(✔)col IS NOT NULL; query system catalog	✔ use a predicate
transform data to metadata	✘ only with SchemaSQL [10]/FISQL [22]	✔ OUT.$(IN._v) <- ...
transform metadata to data	(✔)query system catalog; SchemaSQL/FISQL	✔ OUT.xyz <- IN._c
horizontal aggregation	✘ not possible	✔ SUM(IN._v)
graph processing	(✔)many joins over vertex/edge table	✔ see section 3.3
text processing	✔ e.g. regex_split_to_table in PostgreSQL	✔ see section 3.4

Fig. 16. SQL is not well-suited for wide-column stores, 4 easy (4) hard 8 impossible

5   Conclusion

In this paper, we presented NotaQL, a transformation language for wide-column stores that is easy to use and very powerful. With minimal effort, selections, projections, grouping and aggregations can be defined as well as operations which are needed in schema-flexible NoSQL databases like HBase. Each transformation consists of a mapping between input and output cells and optional predicates.

Figure 16 shows the limits of SQL and that NotaQL supports operations which are impossible or difficult to express in SQL. SQL is suitable for well-defined relational schemata, but not for wide-column stores where rows can have arbitrary columns. That's why we introduced the NotaQL language and we showed that it is very powerful. Not only relational operations are supported but also graph and text algorithms. One should choose a language depending on the given data model. No one would use SQL instead of XQuery on XML documents and as NoSQL stands for "Not only SQL", there is a need for new query and transformation languages.

As the title of this paper says, NotaQL is not a query language like SQL or XQuery. On the other hand, one can argue, there is no distinction between a query and a transformation language. But NotaQL is specialized for transformations over large tables and not for ad-hoc queries. NotaQL does not have an API. Queries are executed periodically to perform a data transformation on wide-column stores. The output table can be accessed in the application with a primitive GET API and the up-to-dateness of the data is defined by the query-execution interval.

We are currently working on language extensions for NotaQL to support more complex transformations, e.g. Top-k algorithms. For faster transformations, we are implementing an incremental component in our framework. This means, a transformation can reuse the results from a former run and it has only to read the delta. Currently, only standalone transformations are supported. Iterative algorithms need to be executed through a batch script which checks a termination criterion and supervises the iterations. A language extension for iterative transformations is planned.

Although all experiments are based on the NoSQL database system HBase, NotaQL scripts can be defined on other wide-column stores and other NoSQL and relational databases as well. Next, we will apply our findings to Cassandra because the support of secondary indexes in Cassandra enables better optimizations for NotaQL computations. Our vision is for cross-platform transformations. Then, the input and output of a NotaQL transformation can be any data source from a relational or NoSQL database. So, one can transform a CSV log file into an HBase table, load a graph from HypergraphDB into MySQL or integrate data from Cassandra and a key-value store into MongoDB.

References

1. Buneman, P., Cheney, J.: A copy-and-paste model for provenance in curated databases. Notes **123**, 6512 (2005)
2. Chang, F., Dean, J., Ghemawat, S., Hsieh, W.C., Wallach, D.A., Burrows, M., Chandra, T., Fikes, A., Gruber, R.E.: Bigtable: a distributed storage system for structured data. ACM Trans. Comput. Syst. (TOCS) **26**(2), 1–14 (2008). Article 4
3. Dean, J., Ghemawat, S.: MapReduce: simplified data processing on large clusters. In: OSDI, pp. 137–150 (2004)
4. Emde, M.: GUI und testumgebung für die HBase-schematransformationssprache NotaQL. Bachelor's thesis, Kaiserslautern University (2014)
5. George, L.: HBase: The Definitive Guide, 1st edn. O'Reilly Media, Sebastopol (2011)
6. Gonzalez, J.E., Low, Y., Gu, H., Bickson, D., Guestrin, C.: Powergraph: distributed graph-parallel computation on natural graphs. In: OSDI, vol. 12, p. 2 (2012)
7. Gupta, A., Jagadish, H.V., Mumick, I.S.: Data integration using self-maintainable views. In: Apers, P.M.G., Bouzeghoub, M., Gardarin, G. (eds.) EDBT 1996. LNCS, vol. 1057, pp. 140–144. Springer, Heidelberg (1996)
8. Hernández, M.A., Miller, R.J., Haas, L.M.: Clio: A semi-automatic tool for schema mapping. ACM SIGMOD Rec. **30**(2), 607 (2001)
9. Hong, S., Chafi, H., Sedlar, E., Olukotun, K.: Green-marl: a DSL for easy and efficient graph analysis. ACM SIGARCH Comput. Archit. News **40**(1), 349–362 (2012)
10. Lakshmanan, L.V.S., Sadri, F., Subramanian, I.N.: SchemaSQL-a language for interoperability in relational multi-database systems. In: VLDB, vol. 96, pp. 239–250 (1996)

11. Lin, J., Dyer, C.: Data-intensive text processing with MapReduce. Synth. Lect. Hum. Lang. Technol. **3**(1), 1–177 (2010)
12. Malewicz, G., Austern, M.H., Bik, A.J.C., Dehnert, J.C., Horn, I., Leiser, N., Czajkowski, G.: Pregel: a system for large-scale graph processing. In: Proceedings of the 2010 ACM SIGMOD International Conference on Management of Data, pp. 135–146. ACM (2010)
13. Grinev, M.: Do You Really Need SQL to Do It All in Cassandra? (2010). http://wp.me/pZn7Z-o
14. Sergey, M., Andrey, A., Long, J.J., Romer, G., Shivakumar, S., Tolton, M., Vassilakis, T.: Dremel: interactive analysis of web-scale datasets. Commun. ACM **54**(6), 114–123 (2011)
15. Murray, D.G., Sherry, F.M.C., Isaacs, R., Isard, M., Barham, P., Abadi, M.: Naiad: a timely dataflow system. In: Proceedings of the Twenty-Fourth ACM Symposium on Operating Systems Principles, pp. 439–455. ACM (2013)
16. Olston, C., Chiou, G., Chitnis, L., Liu, F., Han, Y., Larsson, M., Neumann, A., Rao, V.B.N., Sankarasubramanian, V., Seth, S., et al.: Nova: continuous pig/hadoop workflows. In: Proceedings of the 2011 ACM SIGMOD International Conference on Management of Data, pp. 1081–1090. ACM (2011)
17. Olston, C., Reed, B., Srivastava, U., Kumar, R., Tomkins, A.: Pig latin: a not-so-foreign language for data processing. In: Proceedings of the 2008 ACM SIGMOD International Conference on Management of Data, pp. 1099–1110. ACM (2008)
18. Page, L., Brin, S., Motwani, R., Winograd, T.: The pagerank citation ranking: bringing order to the web. Technical report 1999–66, Stanford InfoLab, November 1999. Previous number = SIDL-WP-1999-0120
19. Pike, R., Dorward, S., Griesemer, R., Quinlan, S.: Interpreting the data: parallel analysis with sawzall. Sci. Program. **13**(4), 277–298 (2005)
20. Sato, K.: An inside look at google bigquery. White paper (2012). https://cloud.google.com/files/BigQueryTechnicalWP.pdf
21. Thusoo, A., Sarma, J.S., Jain, N., Shao, Z., Chakka, P., Anthony, S., Liu, H., Wyckoff, P., Murthy, R.: Hive: a warehousing solution over a map-reduce framework. Proc. VLDB Endow. **2**(2), 1626–1629 (2009)
22. Wyss, C.M., Robertson, E.L.: Relational languages for metadata integration. ACM Trans. Database Syst. (TODS) **30**(2), 624–660 (2005)
23. Xin, R.S., Gonzalez, J.E., Franklin, M.J., Stoica, I.: Graphx: a resilient distributed graph system on spark. In: First International Workshop on Graph Data Management Experiences and Systems, p. 2. ACM (2013)
24. Zaharia, M., Chowdhury, M., Das, T., Dave, A., Ma, J., McCauley, M., Franklin, M.J., Shenker, S., Stoica, I.: Resilient distributed datasets: a fault-tolerant abstraction for in-memory cluster computing. In: Proceedings of the 9th USENIX Conference on Networked Systems Design and Implementation, p. 2. USENIX Association (2012)

NoSQL Approach to Large Scale Analysis
of Persisted Streams

Khalid Mahmood[⊠], Thanh Truong, and Tore Risch

Department of Information Technology, Uppsala University,
75237 Uppsala, Sweden
{khalid.mahmood, thanh.truong, tore.risch}@it.uu.se

Abstract. A potential problem for persisting large volume of streaming logs
with conventional relational databases is that loading large volume of data logs
produced at high rates is not fast enough due to the strong consistency model
and high cost of indexing. As a possible alternative, state-of-the-art NoSQL data
stores that sacrifice transactional consistency to achieve higher performance and
scalability can be utilized. In this paper, we describe the challenges in large scale
persisting and analysis of numerical streaming logs. We propose to develop a
benchmark comparing relational databases with state-of-the-art NoSQL data
stores to persist and analyze numerical logs. The benchmark will investigate to
what degree a state-of-the-art NoSQL data store can achieve high performance
persisting and large-scale analysis of data logs. The benchmark will serve as
basis for investigating query processing and indexing of large-scale numerical
logs.

Keywords: NoSQl data stores · Numerical stream logs · Data stream archival

1 Introduction

The data rate and volume of streams of measurements can become very high. This
becomes a bottleneck when using relational databases for large-scale analysis of
streaming logs [1–4]. Persisting large volumes of streaming data at high rates requires
high performance bulk-loading of data into a database before analysis. The loading
time for relational databases may be time consuming due to full transactional consistency [5] and high cost of indexing [6]. In contrast to relational DBMSs, NoSQL data
stores are designed to perform simple tasks with high scalability [7]. For providing high
performance updates and bulk-loading, NoSQL data stores generally sacrifice strong
consistency by providing so called eventual consistency compared with the ACID
transactions of regular DBMSs. Therefore, NoSQL data stores could be utilized for
analysis of streams of numerical logs where full transactional consistency is not
required.

Unlike NoSQL data stores, relational databases provide advanced query languages
and optimization technique for scalable analytics. It has been demonstrated in [8] that
indexing is a major factor for providing scalable performance, giving relational databases a performance advantage compared to a NoSQL data store to speed up the
analytical task. Like relational databases, some state-of-the-art NoSQL data stores

© Springer International Publishing Switzerland 2015
S. Maneth (Ed.): BICOD 2015, LNCS 9147, pp. 152–156, 2015.
DOI: 10.1007/978-3-319-20424-6_15

(e.g. MongoDB), also provide a query language and both primary and secondary indexing, which should be well suited for analyzing persisted streams.

To understand how well NoSQL data stores are suited for persisting and analyzing numerical stream logs, we propose to develop a benchmark comparing state-of-the-art relational databases with state-of-the-art NoSQL data stores. Using the benchmark as test bed, we will then investigate techniques for scalable query processing and indexing of numerical streams persisted with NoSQL data stores.

2 Application Scenario

The Smart Vortex EU project [1] serves as a real world application context, which involves analyzing stream logs from industrial equipment. In the scenario, a factory operates some machines and each machine has several sensors that measure various physical properties like power consumption, pressure, temperature, etc. For each machine, the sensors generate logs of measurements, where each log record has timestamp ts, machine identifier m, sensor identifier s, and a measured value mv. Relational databases are used to analyze the logs by bulk-loading them in table *measures (m, s, ts, mv)* which contains a large volume of data logs from many sensors of different machines [3, 4].

Since the incoming sensor streams can be very large in volume, it is important that the measurements are bulk-loaded fast. After stream logs have been loaded into the database, the user can perform queries to detect anomalies of sensor readings. The following query analyzes the values of mv from sensor logs for a given time interval and parameterized threshold.

```
SELECT * FROM measures WHERE m = ? AND s = ?
     AND ts > ? AND ts < ? AND mv > @th
```

In order to provide scalable performance of the query, we need an index on the composite key of m, s, ts and a secondary B-tree index on mv.

3 Challenges in Analyzing Large Scale Persisted Streams

Analysis of large-scale stream logs in the above application scenario poses the following challenges (C1 to C6) in utilizing relational and NoSQL data stores.

C1. Bulk-Loading: In relational DBMSs, the high cost of maintaining the indexes and full transactional consistency can degrade the bulk-loading performance of large volume of data logs. The loading performance of a relational DBMS from a major commercial vendor, called *DB-C* and a popular open source relational database, called *DB-O* for 6 GB of data logs is shown in Fig. 1. It took more than 1 h in a high performance commodity machine for the state-of-the-art commercial DBMS, DB-C to bulk-load data logs consisting of around 111 million sensor measurements. Some of the data logs consist of more than a billion sensor measurements, which require high-performance bulk-loading. To boost up the performance, weak consistency level of a NoSQL or relational database can be utilized.

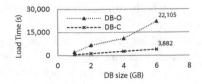 

Fig. 1. Bulk-loading performance of 6 GB logs   **Fig. 2.** Index and database size of 6 GB of logs

C2. Index Size: Fig. 2 shows the index and database sizes for 6 GB of stream logs loaded into the two DBMSs. The size of the index created in both relational DBMSs was larger than the size of the original logs. For high performance and scalable analysis of typical stream logs, hundreds of gigabytes of memory is required in our application. It is interesting to see whether the state-of-the-art NoSQL data store can provide memory efficient indexing strategies. Novel indexing techniques can also be incorporated in order to provide a memory efficient indexing for analyzing persisted streams.

C3. Indexing Strategies: Unlike relational databases and MongoDB, most NoSQL data stores do not provide both primary and secondary indexing, which are essential to scalable processing of queries over data logs. Some NoSQL data stores such as Hbase, Cassandra, Memcached, Voldemort, and Riak do not provide full secondary indexing, which is needed for queries having inequalities over non-key attributes. CouchDB has secondary index, but queries have to be written as map-reduce views [7], not transparently utilizing indexes.

C4. Query Processing: Unlike relational databases, most NoSQL data stores do not provide a query optimizer. Some NoSQL data stores, e.g. MongoDB, provide a query language that is able to transparently utilize indexes. However, the sophistication of query optimizer still needs to be investigated for scalable analysis of data logs.

C5. Advanced Analytics: Relational DBMS features for advanced analytics such as joins or numerical expressions is limited in NoSQL data stores. Therefore, it needs to be investigated how advanced numerical analytics over large-scale data logs could be performed by NoSQL data stores.

C6. Parallelization of Data: NoSQL data stores have the ability to distribute data over many machines, which can provide parallel query execution. However, typical queries for analyzing data logs can generate lots of intermediate results that need to be transferred over the network between nodes, which can be a performance bottleneck. Therefore, the performance of both horizontal and vertical partitioning of distributed NoSQL data stores can be investigated for query execution over numerical logs.

4   Proposed Work

There are several investigations that can be performed for large-scale analysis of numerical stream logs.

Stream Log Analysis Benchmark: Typical TPC benchmarks [9] such as TPC-C, TPC-DS, and TPC-H are targeted towards OLTP or decision support, not for log analysis. To benchmark data stream management systems, the Linear Road Benchmark (LRB) [10] is typically used. However, LRB does not include the performance of persisted streams. Analysis of large-scale data logs often requires scalable queries (e.g. [3, 4]) over persisted numerical logs, which should be the focus the benchmark. In the benchmark, several state-of-the-art NoSQL data stores should be compared with relational DBMSs to investigate at what degree NoSQL data stores are suitable for persisting and analyzing large scale numerical data streams. The performance of bulk-loading capacities of the databases w.r.t. indexing and relaxed consistency should be investigated in the benchmark. The queries should be fundamental to log analyses and targeted to discover the efficiency of query processing and utilization of primary and secondary index of the data logs. The benchmark should analyze and compare the performance differences of loading with relaxed consistency, index utilization, and query execution for both NoSQL and relational databases, which can provide the important insights into challenges C1, C3, C4, and C6.

Query Processing: Supporting advanced analytics using a complete query language with a NoSQL data store requires the development of query processing techniques to compensate for the limitation of the NoSQL query languages, for example lack of join and numerical operators. The push-down of query operators as generated parallel server side scripts should be investigated. Furthermore, it should be investigated how domain indexing strategies [11] in a main memory client-side database (e.g. Amos II [12] developed at UDBL of Uppsala University and [13]) can improve performance of numerical data log analyses of data retrieved from back-end NoSQL databases. These can provide the insights of the challenges C2 and C5.

References

1. Smart Vortex Project. http://www.smartvortex.eu/
2. Zeitler, E., Risch, T.: Massive scale-out of expensive continuous queries. In: VLDB (2011)
3. Truong, T., Risch, T.: Scalable numerical queries by algebraic inequality Transformations. In: DASFAA (2014)
4. Zhu, M., Stefanova, S., Truong, T., Risch, T.: Scalable numerical SPARQL queries over relational databases. In: LWDM Workshop (2014)
5. Doppelhammer, J., Höppler, T., Kemper, A., Kossmann, D.: Database performance in the real world. In: SIGMOD (1997)
6. Stonebraker, M.: SQL databases v. NoSQL databases. Comm. ACM. 53(4), 10–11 (2010)
7. Cattell, R.: Scalable SQL and NoSQL data stores. ACM SIGMOD Rec. 39, 12–27 (2011)
8. Pavlo, A., Paulson, E., Rasin, A., Abadi, D.J., Dewitt, D.J., Madden, S., Stonebraker, M.: A Comparison of approaches to large-scale data analysis. In: SIGMOD (2009)
9. Council, T.P.P.: TPC Benchmarks. http://www.tpc.org/information/benchmarks.asp
10. Arasu, A., Cherniack, M., Galvez, E., Maier, D., Maskey, A.S., Ryvkina, E., Stonebraker, M., Tibbetts, R.: Linear road: a stream data management benchmark. In: VLDB (2004)
11. Gaede, V., Günther, O.: Multidimensional access methods. ACM Comput. Surv. 30, 47–91 (1998)

12. Risch, T., Josifovski, V., Katchaounov, T.: Functional data integration in a distributed mediator system. In: Gray, P.M.D., Kerschberg, L., King, P.J.H., Poulovassilis, A. (eds.) The Functional Approach to Data Management. Springer, Heidelberg (2004)
13. Freedman, C., Ismert, E., Larson, P.-Å.: Compilation in the microsoft SQL server hekaton engine. IEEE Data Eng. Bull. **37**, 22–30 (2014)

Horizontal Fragmentation and Replication for Multiple Relaxation Attributes

Lena Wiese[✉]

Institute of Computer Science, University of Göttingen,
Goldschmidtstraße 7, 37077 Göttingen, Germany
lena.wiese@uni-goettingen.de

Abstract. The data replication problem (DRP) describes the task of distributing copies of data records (that is, database fragments) among a set of servers in a distributed database system. For the application of flexible query answering, several fragments can be overlapping (in terms of tuples in a database table). In this paper, we provide a formulation of the DRP for horizontal fragmentations with overlapping fragments; subsequently we devise a recovery procedure based on these fragmentations.

Keywords: Bin packing problem with conflicts (BPPC) · Data replication problem (DRP) · Distributed database · Fragmentation · Integer linear programming (ILP)

1 Introduction

When storing large-scale data sets in distributed database systems, these data sets are usually *fragmented* (that is, partitioned) into smaller subsets and these subsets are distributed over several database servers. Moreover, to achieve better availability and failure tolerance, copies of the data sets (the so-called *replicas*) are created and stored in a distributed fashion so that different replicas of the same data set reside on distinct servers.

In addition to technical requirements of data distribution, *intelligent query answering* mechanisms are increasingly important to find relevant answers to user queries. Flexible (or cooperative) query answering systems help users of a database system find answers related to his original query in case the original query cannot be answered exactly. *Semantic* techniques rely on taxonomies (or ontologies) to replace some values in a query by others that are closely related according to the taxonomy. This can be achieved by techniques of *query relaxation* – and in particular *query generalization*: the user query is rewritten into a weaker, more general version to also allow related answers.

In this paper we make the following contributions:

– instead of fixing a single relaxation attribute we allow multiple relaxation attributes which lead to several different fragmentations in which fragments from different fragmentations may share common tuples (they "overlap");

© Springer International Publishing Switzerland 2015
S. Maneth (Ed.): BICOD 2015, LNCS 9147, pp. 157–169, 2015.
DOI: 10.1007/978-3-319-20424-6_16

- we devise an m-copy replication scheme for the fragments ensuring the replication factor m by storing overlapping fragments on distinct servers;
- we state the replication problem as an optimization problem minimizing the number of occupied servers;
- we describe a recovery procedure for this kind of replication.

1.1   Organisation of the Article

Section 2 introduces the main notions used in this article and gives an illustrative example. Section 3 defines the problem of data replication with overlapping fragments addressed in this article. Section 4 describes replication and recovery in a practical system. Related work is presented in Sects. 5 and 6 concludes this article with suggestions for future work.

2   Background and Example

We provide background on query generalization, fragmentation and replication.

2.1   Query Generalization

Query generalization has long been studied in flexible query answering [8]. Query generalization at runtime has been implemented in the CoopQA system [5] by applying three generalization operators to a conjunctive query. *Anti-Instantiation* (AI) is one query generalization operator that replaces a constant (or a variable occurring at least twice) in a query with a new variable y. In this paper we focus on replacements of constants because this allows for finding answers that are semantically close to the replaced constant. As the query language we focus on conjunctive queries expressed as logical formulas. We assume a logical language $\mathscr{L}$ consisting of a finite set of predicate symbols (denoting the table names; for example, *Ill*, *Treat* or P), a possibly infinite set *dom* of constant symbols (denoting the values in table cells; for example, *Mary* or a), and an infinite set of variables (x or y). A term is either a constant or a variable. The capital letter X denotes a vector of variables; if the order of variables in X does not matter, we identify X with the set of its variables and apply set operators – for example we write $y \in X$.

A query formula Q is a conjunction (denoted $\wedge$) of literals (consisting of a predicate and terms) with a set of variables X occurring freely; hence we write a query as $Q(X) = L_{i_1} \wedge \ldots \wedge L_{i_n}$. The Anti-Instantiation (AI) operator chooses a constant a in a query $Q(X)$, replaces one occurrence of a by a new variable y and returns the query $Q^{AI}(X, y)$ as the relaxed query. The relaxed query Q^{AI} is a deductive generalization of Q (see [5]).

As a running example, we consider a hospital information system that stores illnesses and treatments of patients as well as their personal information (like address and age) in the following three database tables:

Ill	PatientID	Diagnosis
	8457	Cough
	2784	Flu
	2784	Asthma
	2784	brokenLeg
	8765	Asthma
	1055	brokenArm

Info	PatientID	Name	Address
	8457	Pete	Main Str 5, Newtown
	2784	Mary	New Str 3, Newtown
	8765	Lisa	Main Str 20, Oldtown
	1055	Anne	High Str 2, Oldtown

The query $Q(x_1, x_2, x_3) = Ill(x_1, Flu) \wedge Ill(x_1, Cough) \wedge Info(x_1, x_2, x_3)$ asks for all the patient IDs x_1 as well as names x_2 and addresses x_3 of patients that suffer from both flu and cough. This query fails with the given database tables as there is no patient with both flu and cough. However, the querying user might instead be interested in the patient called Mary who is ill with both flu and asthma. We can find this informative answer by relaxing the query condition *Cough* and instead allowing other related values (like *Asthma*) in the answers. An example generalization with AI is $Q^{AI}(x_1, x_2, x_3, y) = Ill(x_1, Flu) \wedge Ill(x_1, y) \wedge Info(x_1, x_2, x_3)$ by introducing the new variable y. It results in an non-empty (and hence informative) answer: $Ill(2748, Flu) \wedge Ill(2748, Asthma) \wedge Info(2748, Mary, 'New\ Str\ 3, Newtown')$. Another answer obtained is the fact that Mary suffers from a broken leg as: $Ill(2748, Flu) \wedge Ill(2748, brokenLeg) \wedge Info(2748, Mary, 'New\ Str\ 3, Newtown')$ which is however an overgeneralization.

2.2 Clustering-Based Fragmentation

Query generalization at runtime is highly inefficient. That is why we propose a clustering-based fragmentation that preprocesses data into fragments of closely related values (with respect to a relaxation attribute). This clustering-based fragmentation has two main advantages:

- it enables efficient query relaxation at runtime by returning all values in a matching fragment as relevant answers.
- it reduces the amount of servers contacted during query answering in a distributed environment because only one server (containing the matching fragment) has to process the query while other servers can process other queries.

Here we need semantic guidance to identify the set of relevant answers that are close enough to the original query. In previous work [12], a clustering procedure was applied to partition the original tables into fragments based on a *single relaxation attribute* chosen for anti-instantiation. For this we used a notion of similarity between to constants; this similarity can be deduced with the help of an ontology or taxonomy in which the values are put into relation. Finding the fragments is hence achieved by grouping (that is, *clustering*) the values of the respective table column into clusters of closely related values and then splitting the table into fragments according to the clusters found. For example, clusters on the *Diagnosis* column can be made by differentiating between fractures on the one hand and respiratory diseases on the other hand. These clusters then lead to two fragments of the table *Ill* that could be assigned to two different servers:

Server 1:		
Respiratory	PatientID	Diagnosis
	8457	Cough
	2784	Flu
	2784	Asthma
	8765	Asthma

Server 2:		
Fracture	PatientID	Diagnosis
	2784	brokenLeg
	1055	brokenArm

Server 1 can then be used to answer queries related to respiratory diseases while Server 2 can process queries related to fractures. The example query $Q(x_1, x_2, x_3) = Ill(x_1, Flu) \land Ill(x_1, Cough) \land Info(x_1, x_2, x_3)$ will then be rewritten as $Q^{Resp}(x_1, x_2, x_3, y) = Respiratory(x_1, Flu) \land Respiratory(x_1, Cough) \land Info(x_1, x_2, x_3)$ and redirected to Server 1 where only the fragment Respiratory is used to answer the query. In this way only the informative answer containing asthma is returned – while the one containing broken leg will not be generated.

2.3   Data Distribution as a Bin Packing Problem

In a distributed database system data records have to be assigned to different servers. The **data distribution problem** – however not considering replication yet – is basically a Bin Packing Problem (BPP) in the following sense:

- K servers correspond to K bins
- bins have a maximum capacity W
- n data records correspond to n objects
- each object has a weight (a capacity consumption) $w_i \le W$
- objects have to be placed into a minimum number of bins without exceeding the maximum capacity W

This BPP can be written as an integer linear program (ILP) as follows – where x_{ik} is a binary variable that denotes whether fragment/object i is placed in server/bin k; and y_k denotes that server/bin k is used (that is, is non-empty). Moreover, each server/bin has a maximum capacity W and each fragment/object i has a weight w_i that denotes how much capacity the item consumes. As a simple example, W can express how many rows (tuples) a server can store and w_i is the row count of fragment i.

$$\text{minimize} \sum_{k=1}^{K} y_k \qquad \text{(minimize number of bins)} \qquad (1)$$

$$s.t. \sum_{k=1}^{K} x_{ik} = 1, i = 1, \ldots, n \text{ (each object assigned to one bin)} \qquad (2)$$

$$\sum_{i=1}^{n} w_i x_{ik} \le W y_k, k = 1, \ldots, K \text{ (capacity not exceeded)} \qquad (3)$$

$$y_k \in \{0, 1\} k = 1, \ldots, K \qquad (4)$$

$$x_{ik} \in \{0, 1\} k = 1, \ldots, K, i = 1, \ldots, n \qquad (5)$$

An extension of the basic BPP, the Bin Packing with Conflicts (BPPC) problem, considers a conflict graph $G = (V, E)$ where the node set $V = \{1, \ldots, n\}$ corresponds to the set of objects. A binary edge $e = (i, j)$ exists whenever the two objects i and j must *not* be placed into the same bin. In the ILP representation, a further constraint (Eq. 9) is added to avoid conflicts in the placements.

$$\text{minimize} \sum_{k=1}^{K} y_k \qquad \text{(minimize number of bins)} \qquad (6)$$

$$s.t. \sum_{k=1}^{K} x_{ik} = 1, \quad i = 1, \ldots, n \quad \text{(each object assigned to one bin)} \qquad (7)$$

$$\sum_{i=1}^{n} w_i x_{ik} \leq W y_k, \, k = 1, \ldots, K \quad \text{(capacity not exceeded)} \qquad (8)$$

$$x_{ik} + x_{jk} \leq y_k \, k = 1, \ldots, K, \forall (i, j) \in E \text{ (no conflicts)} \qquad (9)$$

$$y_k \in \{0, 1\} \, k = 1, \ldots, K \qquad (10)$$

$$x_{ik} \in \{0, 1\} \, k = 1, \ldots, K, i = 1, \ldots, n \qquad (11)$$

Several results were obtained regarding hardness and approximation of bin packing with conflicts. BPPC can basically be regarded as a combination of a vertex coloring and the basic BPP: first of all, compute a coloring of the conflict graph such that items of different color cannot be placed in the same bin, then solve one classical BPP instance for each color.

3   Overlaps and Multiple Relaxation Attributes

So far, for the taxonomy-based clustering approach only a *single* relaxation attribute has been considered in [12]. There it is proposed that, when doing m-way replication, simply m copies of the fragments obtained for the single relaxation attribute are replicated; this corresponds to solving a BPPC instance where the conflict graph states that copies of the same fragment cannot be placed on the same server. In this paper we want to generalize this procedure to multiple relaxation attributes. This has the following advantages:

– The system can answer queries for several relaxation attributes.
– The intelligent replication procedure reduces storage consumption and hence the amount of servers that are needed for replication.

In order to support flexible query answering on multiple columns, one table can be fragmented multiple times (by clustering different columns); that is, we can choose more than one relaxation attribute. In this case, several fragmentations will be obtained. More formally, if α relaxation attributes are chosen and clustered, then we obtain α fragmentations F_l ($l = 1 \ldots \alpha$) of the same table; each fragmentation contains fragments $f_{l,s}$ where index s depends on the number of clusters found: if n_l clusters are found, then $F_l = \{f_{l,1}, \ldots, f_{l,n_l}\}$.

For example, clusters on the *Diagnosis* column can be made by differentiating between fractures on the one hand and respiratory diseases on the other hand. And additionally, clusters on the patient ID can be obtained by dividing into rows with ID smaller than 5000 and those with ID larger than 5000.

Respiratory	PatientID	Diagnosis
	8457	Cough
	2784	Flu
	2784	Asthma
	8765	Asthma

Fracture	PatientID	Diagnosis
	2784	brokenLeg
	1055	brokenArm

IDlow	PatientID	Diagnosis
	2784	Flu
	2784	brokenLeg
	2784	Asthma
	1055	brokenArm

IDhigh	PatientID	Diagnosis
	8765	Asthma
	8457	Cough

We assume that each of the clusterings (and hence the corresponding fragmentation) is *complete:* every value in the column is assigned to one cluster and hence every tuple is assigned to one fragment. We also assume that each clustering and each fragmentation are *non-redundant:* every value is assigned to exactly one cluster and every tuple belongs to exactly one fragment (for one clustering); in other words, the fragments inside one fragmentation do not overlap.

However, fragments from two *different* fragmentations (for two different clusterings) may overlap. For example, both the *Respiratory* as well as the *IDhigh* fragments contain the tuple $\langle 8457, Cough \rangle$. Due to completeness, every tuple is contained in exactly one of the fragments of each of the α fragmentations: for any tuple j, if α relaxation attributes are chosen and clustered, then in any fragmentation F_l ($l = 1 \ldots \alpha$) there is a fragment $f_{l,s}$ such that tuple $j \in f_{l,s}$.

3.1   Data Replication for Overlapping Fragments

The main contribution of this paper is to analyze intelligent data replication schemes with *multiple* relaxation attributes while at the same time minimizing the amount of data copies – and hence reducing overall storage consumption of the underlying flexible query answering system. The approach is as follows:

- Apply the above clustering heuristics to *any* of the α relaxation attributes.
- Based on each clustering obtain a complete fragmentation of the given table.
- Fragments of different fragmentations (for different clusterings) overlap.
- Ensure replication factor m for tuples by considering these overlaps in BPPC.

While in the standard BPP and BPPC representations usually disjoint fragments and exactly m copies are considered, we extend the basic BPPC as follows:

Conjecture 1. With our intelligent replication procedure, less data copies (only m copies of each tuple) have to be replicated hence reducing the amount of storage needed for replication as opposed to conventional replication approaches that replicate m copies for each of the α fragmentations F_l (which results in αm copies of each tuple).

We argue that m copies of a tuple suffice with an advanced recovery procedure: that is, for every *tuple* j we require that it is stored at m *different*
servers for backup purposes but these copies of j may be contained in different
fragments: one fragmentation F_l can be recovered from fragments in any other
fragmentation F_l' (where $l \neq l'$). From here on we assume that there are **exactly**
m relaxation attributes (that is, $\alpha = m$); in case there are less than m relaxation attributes, some of the existing fragmentations are simply duplicated; in
case there are more than m relaxation attributes, the remaining fragmentations
can be stored on arbitrary servers. We hence consider the following problem:

**Definition 1 (Data Replication Problem with Overlapping Fragments
(Overlap-DRP)).** *Given m fragmentations $F_l = \{f_{l,1}, \ldots, f_{l,n_l}\}$ and replication factor m, for every tuple j there must be fragments f_{l,i_l} (where $1 \leq l \leq m$
and $1 \leq i_l \leq n_l$) such that $j \in f_{1,i_1} \cap \ldots \cap f_{\alpha,i_m}$ and these fragments are all
assigned to different servers.*

We illustrate this with our example. Assume that 5 rows is the maximum capacity W of each server and assume a replication factor 2. In a conventional replication approach, all fragments are of approximately the same size and do not
overlap. Hence, the conventional approach would replicate all fragments (*Respiratory, Fracture, IDhigh, IDlow*) to two servers each. then assign the *Respiratory*
fragment (with 4 rows) to one server $S1$ and a copy of it to another server $S2$.
Now the *Fracture* fragment (with 2 rows) will not fit on any of the two servers;
its two replicas will be stored on two new servers $S3$ and $S4$. For storing the
IDlow fragment (with 4 rows), the conventional approach would need two more
servers $S5$ and $S6$. The *IDhigh* fragment (with 2 rows) could then be mapped to
servers $S3$ and $S4$. The conventional replication approach would hence require
at least six servers to achieve a replication factor 2.

In contrast, our intelligent replication approach takes advantage of the overlapping fragments so that **three** servers suffice to fulfill the replication factor
2; that is, the amount of servers can be substantially reduced if a more intelligent replication and recovery scheme is used that respects the fact that several
fragments overlap and that can handle fragments of differing size to optimally
fill remaining server capacities. This allows for better self-configuration capacities of the distributed database system. First we observe how one fragment
can be recovered from the other fragments: Fragment *Respiratory* can be recovered from fragments *IDlow* and *IDhigh* (because *Respiratory* = (*IDlow* ∩ *Respiratory*) ∪ (*IDhigh* ∩ *Respiratory*)); Fragment *Fracture* can be recovered from
fragment *IDlow* (because *Fracture* = (*IDlow* ∩ *Fracture*)); Fragment *IDlow* can
be recovered from fragments *Respiratory* and *Fracture* (because *IDlow* = (*IDlow*
∩ *Respiratory*) ∪ (*IDlow* ∩ *Fracture*)); Fragment *IDhigh* can be recovered from
fragment *Respiratory* (because *IDhigh* = (*IDhigh* ∩ *Respiratory*)). Hence, we can
store fragment *Respiratory* on server $S1$, fragment *IDlow* on server $S2$, and fragments *Fracture* and *IDhigh* on server $S3$ and still have replication factor 2 for
individual *tuples*.

We now show that our replication problem (with its extensions to overlapping fragments and counting replication based on tuples) can be expressed as an advanced BPPC problem. Let J be the amount of tuples in the input table, m be the number of fragmentations, K the total number of available servers and n be the overall number of fragments obtained in all fragmentations. In the ILP representation we keep the variables y_k for the bins and x_{ik} for fragments – to simplify notation we assume that $i = 1 \ldots n$ where $n = |F_1| + \ldots + |F_m| = n_1 + \ldots + n_m$: all fragments are numbered consecutively from 1 to n even when they come from different fragmentations. In addition, we introduce K new variables z_{jk} for each the tuple j such that $z_{jk} = 1$ if the tuple j is placed on server k; we maintain a mapping between fragments and tuples such that if fragment i is assigned to bin k, and j is contained in i, then tuple j is also assigned to k (see Eq. (15)); the other way round, if there is no fragment i containing j and being assigned to bin k, then tuple j neither is assigned to k (see Eq. (16)); and we modify the conflict constraint to support the replication factor: we require that for each tuple j the amount of bins/servers used is at least m (see Eq. (17)) to ensure the replication factor.

$$\text{minimize} \sum_{k=1}^{K} y_k \qquad \text{(minimize number of bins)} \qquad (12)$$

$$\text{s.t.} \sum_{k=1}^{K} x_{ik} = 1, \quad i = 1, \ldots, n \quad \text{(each fragment } i \text{ assigned to one bin)} \quad (13)$$

$$\sum_{i=1}^{n} w_i x_{ik} \leq W y_k, \quad k = 1, \ldots, K \quad \text{(capacity not exceeded)} \qquad (14)$$

$$z_{jk} \geq x_{ik} \text{ for all } j : j \in i \text{ (tuple } j \text{ in bin when fragment } i \text{ is)} \qquad (15)$$

$$z_{jk} \leq \sum_{(i:j \in i)} x_{ik} \quad \text{for all } j \quad \text{(tuple not in bin when no fragment is)} \quad (16)$$

$$\sum_{k=1}^{K} z_{jk} \geq m \quad \text{for all } j \quad \text{(replication factor } m \text{ on tuples)} \qquad (17)$$

$$y_k \in \{0,1\} \quad k = 1, \ldots, K \qquad (18)$$

$$x_{ik} \in \{0,1\} \quad k = 1, \ldots, K, \ i = 1, \ldots, n \qquad (19)$$

$$z_{jk} \in \{0,1\} \quad k = 1, \ldots, K, \ j = 1, \ldots, J \qquad (20)$$

This ILP will find a valid solution to overlap-DRP.

3.2   Reducing the Amount of Variables

The ILP representation in the previous section is highly inefficient and does not scale to large amounts of tuples: due to the excessive use of z-variables, for large J finding a solution will take prohibitively long. Indeed, in the given representation, we have K y-variables, $n \cdot K$ x-variables, and $J \cdot K$ z-variables where usually $J \gg n$. That is why we want to show now that it is possible to focus on the x-variables to achieve another ILP representation for overlap-DRP: for any tuple j such that j is contained in two fragments i and i' (we assume that $i < i'$ to avoid isomorphic statements in the proof), it is sufficient to ensure that the two fragments are stored on two different servers. In other words, for the $(m \cdot (m-1))/2$ pairs of overlapping fragments i and i', we can make them mutually exclusive in the ILP representation; that is, in the ILP representation we have to satisfy $(m \cdot (m-1))/2$ equalities of the form $x_{ik} + x_{i'k} = 1$ to make them pairwise conflicting.

Theorem 1. *If for any two fragments i and i' such that $i \cap i' \neq \emptyset$ there hold $(m \cdot (m-1))/2$ equations of the form $x_{ik} + x_{i'k} = 1$ where $i < i'$, $i = 1, \dots, n-1$, $i' = 2, \dots, n$ and $k = 1, \dots, K$, then it holds for any tuple j that $\sum_{k=1}^{K} z_{jk} \geq m$.*

Proof. First of all, for every tuple j there are m fragments i such that $j \in i$ due to completeness of the m fragmentations. Now we let I be the set of these m fragments. Then for any two $i, i' \in I$ we have $j \in i \cap i'$ by construction. Due to Eq. (13), for every $i \in I$ there must be exactly one bin k such that $x_{ik} = 1$ and for all other i^* it holds that either $x_{ik} + x_{i^*k} = 1$ (if $i < i^*$) or $x_{i^*k} + x_{ik} = 1$ (if $i^* < i$) so that none of these fragments is assigned to bin k. Hence, m bins are needed to accommodate all fragments in I. Due to Eq. (15), we assure that when $x_{ik} = 1$ then also $z_{jk} = 1$ for the given j and any $i \in I$. Hence $\sum_{k=1}^{K} z_{jk} \geq m$ (Eq. 17) holds.

Instead of considering all individual tuples j, we can now move on to considering only overlapping fragments (with non-empty intersections) and requiring the $(m \cdot (m-1))/2$ equations to hold for each pair of overlapping fragments. We transform the previous ILP representation into the one that enforces a conflict condition for any two overlapping fragments. This coincides with the conventional BPPC representation, where the conflict graph is built over the set of fragments (as the vertex set) by drawing an edge between any two fragments that overlap.

Definition 2 (Conflict Graph for Overlap-DRP). *The conflict graph $\mathcal{G}^{DRP} = (V, E)$ is defined by $V = F_1 \cup \dots \cup F_m$ (one vertex for each fragment inside the m fragmentations) and $E = \{(i, i') \mid i, i' \in V \text{ and } i \cap i' \neq \emptyset\}$ (an undirected edge between fragments that overlap).*

Continuing our example, we have a conflict graph over the fragments *Respiratory*, *Fracture*, *IDlow* and *IDhigh* with an edge between *Respiratory* and *IDlow*, and an edge between *Respiratory* and *IDhigh*, and an edge between *Fracture* and

IDhigh. The ILP representation for overlap-DRP looks now as follows:

$$\text{minimize} \sum_{k=1}^{K} y_k \qquad \text{(minimize number of bins)} \qquad (21)$$

$$\text{s.t.} \sum_{k=1}^{K} x_{ik} = 1, \quad i = 1, \ldots, n \quad \text{(each fragment } i \text{ assigned to one bin)} \quad (22)$$

$$\sum_{i=1}^{n} w_i x_{ik} \leq W y_k, \; k = 1, \ldots, K \quad \text{(capacity not exceeded)} \qquad (23)$$

$$x_{ik} + x_{i'k} \leq y_k \; k = 1, \ldots, K, \, i \cap i' \neq \emptyset \; \text{(overlapping fragments } i, i') \; (24)$$

$$y_k \in \{0, 1\} \; k = 1, \ldots, K \qquad (25)$$

$$x_{ik} \in \{0, 1\} \; k = 1, \ldots, K, \, i = 1, \ldots, n \qquad (26)$$

4   Experimental Study

Our prototype implementation – the OntQA-Replica system – runs on a distributed SAP HANA installation which is an in-memory database system and hence needs a good replication strategy that also reduces the amount of servers needed. The example data set consists of a table that resembles a medical health record and is based on the set of Medical Subject Headings (MeSH [11]). The table contains as columns an artificial, sequential tuple ID, a random patient ID, and a disease chosen from the MeSH data set as well as the concept identifier of the MeSH entry. We varied the table sizes during our test runs. The smallest table consists 56,341 rows, a medium-sized table of 1,802,912 rows and the largest of 14,423,296 rows. A clustering is executed on the MeSH data based on the concept identifier (which orders the MeSH terms in a tree); in other words, entries from the same subconcept belong to the same cluster. One fragmentation (the "clustered" fragmentation) was obtained from this clustering and consists of 117 fragments; these fragments have a column called clusterid. Another fragmentation (the "range-based" fragmentation) is based on ranges of the patient ID and consists of 6 fragments for the small table, 19 for the medium-sized table and 145 for the large table; these fragments have a column called rangeid.

For the replication procedure, first the overlapping fragments (the "conflicts") are identified by using SELECT DISTINCT clusterid, rangeid FROM c_i JOIN c_i ON (r_j .tupleid= r_j .tupleid) for each clustered fragment c_i and each range-based fragment r_j.

Afterwards from the conflicts the overlap-DRP ILP is generated and solved. For the small table, the input had 1820 constraints on 1240 variables; for the medium-sized table, the input had 5720 constraints on 1370 variables; for the large table, the input had 43520 constraints on 2630 variables. Based on the ILP solution, the fragments are moved to different servers by using ALTER TABLE c_i MOVE TO '*severname*' PHYSICAL.

To enable recovery, a lookup table is maintained that stores for each clusterid the tupleids of those tuples that constitute the clustered fragment. The recovery procedure was executed on the range-based fragmentation to recover the clustered fragmentation by running INSERT INTO c_i SELECT * FROM $r_1, \ldots, r_m$ JOIN lookup on (lookup.tupleid = c_i.tupleid) WHERE lookup.clusterid= i for each cluster i. The runtimes obtained are shown in Fig. 1.

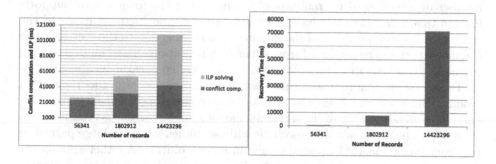

Fig. 1. Runtimes of replication computation and recovery

5   Related Work

There is a long history of fragmentation approaches for the relational data model. Most approaches consider workload-aware fragmentation (see for example, [1,4,9]) that optimize distribution of data for a given workload of queries. However none of these approaches consider semantical similarity of values inside a fragment as is needed for our approach of query relaxation.

Bin packing is one of the classical NP-complete problems and it has been shown to be APX-hard (it is not approximable with a ratio less than 1.5; see [6]). As BPP is a special case of the more general BPPC, these properties carry over to BPPC as well. Some variants of classical bin packing have been surveyed in [2]. One of the primary sources of BPPC is [6]. However, as the number of fragments we consider in our overlap-DRP is comparably low, these complexity theoretic considerations usually do not affect the practical implementation and any off-the-shelf ILP solver will find an optimal solution.

There is also related work on specifying resource management problems as optimization problems. An adaptive solution for data replication using a genetic algorithm is presented in [7]; they also consider transfer cost of replicas between servers. Virtual machine placement is a very recent topic in cloud computing [3,10]. However, these specifications do not address the problem of overlapping resources as we need for the query relaxation approach in this article.

6   Conclusion and Future Work

We presented and analyzed a data replication problem for a flexible query answering system. It provides related answers by relaxing the original query and obtaining a set of semantically close answers. The proposed replication scheme allows for fast response times due to materializing the fragmentations. By solving an ILP representation of the data replication problem, we minimize the overall number of servers used for replication. In this paper the focus lies on supporting multiple relaxation attributes that lead to multiple fragmentations of the same table. A minimization of the number of servers is due to the fact that one fragmentation can be recovered from other fragmentations based on overlapping fragments. The experimental evaluation shows sensible performance results.

Future work has to mainly address dynamic changes in the replication scheme. Deletions and insertions of data lead to changing fragmentations sizes and hence an adaptation of the server allocations might become necessary (similar to [7]). The use of adaptive methods will be studied where (a large part of) a previous solution might be reused to obtain a new solution. Another approach is to compute the common subfragments (intersections) of overlapping fragments and use these subfragments as a unit of replication. Copies of these subfragments will hence be distributed among the servers.

Acknowledgements. The author gratefully acknowledges that the infrastructure and SAP HANA installation for the test runs was provided by the Future SOC Lab of Hasso Plattner Institute (HPI), Potsdam.

References

1. Agrawal, S., Narasayya, V., Yang, B.: Integrating vertical and horizontal partitioning into automated physical database design. In: Proceedings of the 2004 ACM SIGMOD International Conference on Management of Data, pp. 359–370. ACM (2004)
2. Coffman, Jr., E.G., Csirik, J., Leung, J.Y.T.: Variants of classical one-dimensional bin packing. In: Gonzalez, T.F. (ed.) Handbook of Approximation Algorithms and Meta-Heuristics, pp. 33:1–33:10. Francis and Taylor Books (CRC Press), London (2007)
3. Goudarzi, H., Pedram, M.: Energy-efficient virtual machine replication and placement in a cloud computing system. In: IEEE 5th International Conference on Cloud Computing (CLOUD), pp. 750–757. IEEE (2012)
4. Grund, M., Krüger, J., Plattner, H., Zeier, A., Cudre-Mauroux, P., Madden, S.: Hyrise: a main memory hybrid storage engine. Proc. VLDB Endow. **4**(2), 105–116 (2010)
5. Inoue, K., Wiese, L.: Generalizing conjunctive queries for informative answers. In: Christiansen, H., De Tré, G., Yazici, A., Zadrozny, S., Andreasen, T., Larsen, H.L. (eds.) FQAS 2011. LNCS, vol. 7022, pp. 1–12. Springer, Heidelberg (2011)
6. Jansen, K., Öhring, S.: Approximation algorithms for time constrained scheduling. Inf. Comput. **132**(2), 85–108 (1997)

7. Loukopoulos, T., Ahmad, I.: Static and adaptive distributed data replication using genetic algorithms. J. Parallel Distrib. Comput. **64**(11), 1270–1285 (2004)
8. Michalski, R.S.: A theory and methodology of inductive learning. Artif. Intell. **20**(2), 111–161 (1983)
9. Özsu, M.T., Valduriez, P.: Principles of Distributed Database Systems. Springer Science & Business Media, New York (2011)
10. Shi, W., Hong, B.: Towards profitable virtual machine placement in the data center. In: Fourth IEEE International Conference on Utility and Cloud Computing (UCC), pp. 138–145. IEEE (2011)
11. U.S. National Library of Medicine: Medical subject headings. http://www.nlm.nih.gov/mesh/
12. Wiese, L.: Clustering-based fragmentation and data replication for flexible query answering in distributed databases. J. Cloud Comput. **3**(1), 1–15 (2014)

Scalability

Scalable Queries Over Log Database Collections

Minpeng Zhu, Khalid Mahmood, and Tore Risch[✉]

Department of Information Technology, Uppsala University,
75237 Uppsala, Sweden
{minpeng.zhu,khalid.mahmood,tore.risch}@it.uu.se

Abstract. Various business application scenarios need to analyse the working status of products, e.g. to discover abnormal machine behaviours from logged sensor readings. The geographic locations of machines are often widely distributed and have measurements of logged sensor readings stored locally in autonomous relational databases, here called *log databases*, where they can be analysed through queries. A global meta-database is required to describe machines, sensors, measurements, etc. Queries to the log databases can be expressed in terms of these meta-data. FLOQ (Fused LOg database Query processor) enables queries searching collections of distributed log databases combined through a common meta-database. To speed up queries combining meta-data with distributed logged sensor readings, sub-queries to the log databases should be run in parallel. We propose two new strategies using standard database APIs to join meta-data with data retrieved from distributed autonomous log databases. The performance of the strategies is empirically compared with a state-of-the-art previous strategy to join autonomous databases. A cost model is used to predict the efficiency of each strategy and guide the experiments. We show that the proposed strategies substantially improve the query performance when the size of selected meta-data or the number of log databases are increased.

1 Introduction

Various business applications need to observe the working status of products in order to analyse their proper behaviours. Our application is from a real-world scenario [11], where machines such as trucks, pumps, kilns, etc. are widely distributed at different geographic locations and where sensors on machines produce large volumes of data. The data describes time stamped sensor readings of machine components (e.g. oil temperature and pressure) and can be used to analyse abnormal behaviours of the equipment. In order to analyse passed behaviour of monitored equipment, the sensor readings can be stored in relational databases and analysed with SQL. In our application area, data is produced and maintained locally at many different sites in autonomous relational DBMSs called *log databases*. New sites and log databases are dynamically added and removed from the federation. The number of sites is potentially large, so it is important that the query processing scales with increasing number of sites. A global meta-database enables a global view of the working status of all machines on different sites. It stores meta-data about machines, sensors, sites, etc.

© Springer International Publishing Switzerland 2015
S. Maneth (Eds.): BICOD 2015, LNCS 9147, pp. 173–185, 2015.
DOI: 10.1007/978-3-319-20424-6_17

A particular challenge in our scenario is a scalable way to process queries that join meta-data with data selected from the collection of autonomous log databases using standard DBMS APIs. This paper proposes two strategies to perform such joins, namely *parallel bind-join* (PBJ) and *parallel bulk-load join* (PBLJ). PBJ generalizes the *bind-join* (BJ) [4] operator, which is a state-of-the-art algorithm for joining data from an autonomous external database with a central database. One problem with bind-join in our scenario is that large numbers of SQL queries will be sent to the log databases for execution, one for each parameter combination selected from the meta-database, which is slow. Furthermore, whereas bind-join is well suited for joining data from a single log database with the meta-database, our application scenario requires joining data from many sites.

With both PBJ and PBLJ, streams of selected meta-data variable bindings are distributed to the wrapped log databases and processed there in parallel. After the parallel processing the result streams are merged asynchronously by FLOQ.

- With PBJ the streams of bindings selected from the meta-database are bind-joined in the distributed wrappers with their encapsulated log databases. The bind-joins of different wrapped log databases are executed in parallel.
- With PBLJ the selected bindings are first bulk loaded in parallel into a *binding table* in each log database where a regular join is performed between the loaded bindings and the local measurements.

The strategies are implemented in our prototype system called *FLOQ (Fused LOg database Query processor)*. FLOQ provides general query processing over collections of autonomous relational log databases residing on different sites. The collection of log databases is integrated by FLOQ through a meta-database where properties about data in the log databases are stored. On each site the log database is encapsulated by a *FLOQ wrapper* to pre- and post-process queries.

To investigate our strategies, a cost model is proposed to evaluate the efficiency of each strategy. To evaluate the performance we define fundamental queries for detecting abnormal sensor readings and investigate the impact of our join strategies. A relational DBMS from a major commercial vendor is used for storing the log databases.

In summary the contributions are:

- Two join strategies are proposed and compared: parallel bind-join a parallel bulk-load join, for parallel execution of queries joining meta-data with data from collections of autonomous databases using external DBMS APIs.
- A cost model is proposed to evaluate the strategies.
- The conclusions from the cost model are verified experimentally.

The rest of this paper is organized as follows: Sect. 2 overviews the FLOQ system architecture and presents the scenario and queries used for the performance evaluation. Section 3 presents the join strategies and the cost model used in the evaluation. Section 4 presents the performance evaluation for the join strategies. Section 5 describes related work. Finally, Sect. 6 concludes and outlines some future work.

2 FLOQ

Figure 1 illustrates the FLOQ architecture. To analyse machine behaviours, the user sends queries over the integrated log databases to FLOQ. FLOQ processes a query by first querying the meta-database to find the identifiers of the queried log databases containing the desired data, then in parallel sending distributed queries to the log databases, and finally collecting and merging the distributed query results to obtain the final result. Scalable parallel processing of queries making joins between a meta-database and many large log databases is the subject of this paper.

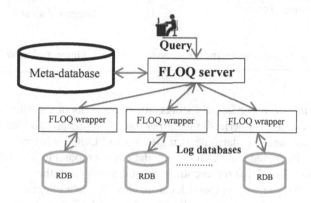

Fig. 1. FLOQ system architecture

Each log database is encapsulated with a *FLOQ wrapper* called from the FLOQ server to process queries over the wrapped log database. A FLOQ wrapper contains a full query processor which enables, e.g. local bind-joins between a stream of bindings selected from the meta-database and the log database. Parallel processing is provided since the FLOQ wrappers work independently of each other. Each FLOQ wrapper sends back to the FLOQ server the result of executing a query as a stream of tuples. The results from many wrappers are asynchronously merged by the FLOQ server while emitting the result to the user. Details of the query processor are described in [10, 13, 14] and are outside the scope of this paper.

2.1 The FLOQ Schema

The schema for the FLOQ meta-database is shown in Fig. 2(a). The table *MachineModel* (*m, mmn, descr, mmanuf*) stores data about machine models, i.e. a unique ma-chine model identifier *m*, along with its name *mmn*, description *descr*, and manufacturer *mmanuf*. The table *MachineInstallation(mi, m, sid)* stores meta-data about each machine installation, i.e. a unique machine installation identifier *mi*, its installed site *sid* and its machine model identifier *m* (foreign key). The table *SensorModel(sm, sname, smanuf)* stores information about sensor models, i.e. a unique sensor model identifier *sm*, the sensor model name *sname*, and its manufacturer *smanuf*. The table *SensorInstallation (si, mi, sm, ev)* stores the sensor installation information, i.e. a sensor installation identifier *si*, the machine installation *mi* of *si*, the sensor model *sm*, and the expected measured value *ev*. The columns *m* and *sid* in table *MachineInstallation* are foreign keys in tables *MachineModel* and *Site*, respectively. The column *mi* in table *Sensor-Installation* is foreign key to *MachineInstallation*.

```
MachineModel(m, mmn, descr, mmanuf)        Measures(mi,si,bt,et,mv)
MachineInstallation(mi, m, sid)                Log table at each site
SensorModel(sm, sname, smanuf)
SensorInstallation(si, mi, sm, ev)   VMeasures(logdb,mi,si,bt,et,mv)
Site(sid, name, logdb)                    Integrated view in FLOQ server
```

Fig. 2. (a). Meta-database schema. (b) Log table at each site. (c) Integrated view in FLOQ server

The table *Site(sid, name, logdb)* stores information about the sites where the log databases are located: a numeric site identifier *sid*, its *name*, and an identifier of its log database, *logdb*. A new log database is registered to FLOQ by inserting a new row in table *Site*. Each site presents to FLOQ its log data as a temporal local relation *Measures (mi, si, bt, et, mv)* (Fig. 2(b)) representing measurements from the sensors installed on the machines at the site, i.e. temporal local-as-view [5] data integration is used. For a machine installation *mi* at a particular site the local view presents the measured readings from sensor installation *si* in the valid time interval *[bt,et)*. The columns *mi* and *si* in *Measures* are foreign keys from the corresponding columns in the meta-database tables *MachineInstallation* and *SensorInstallation*, respectively.

The view *VMeasures* (Fig. 2(c)) in FLOQ integrates the collection of log databases. It is logically a union-all of the local *Measures* views at the different sites. In *VMeasures* the attribute *logdb* identifies the origin of each tuple. Through the meta-database users can make queries over the log databases by joining other meta-data with *VMeasures*. Since the set of log databases is dynamic it is not feasible to define *VMeasures* as a static view; instead FLOQ processes queries to *VMeasures* by dynamically submitting SQL queries to the log databases and collecting the results. In the experiments we populate the meta-database and the log databases with data from a real-world application [11].

2.2   Example Queries

Q1 in Fig. 3 is a simple query that retrieves unexpected sensor readings. It returns machine identifiers *mi* together with the time intervals *[bt,et)* when a sensor on the machine has measured values *mv* higher than the expected values *ev* by a threshold parameter *th* on line 5 marked '?'.

Query *Q1* is used for the basic scalability experiments. It contains a simple numerical expression over the log database view in terms of *th*. On line 6 there is a constraint on the selected machine identifiers *mi* and on line 10 the selected sites *sid* are

```
Q1:
1   SELECT m.mi, m.bt, m.et
2   FROM Measures m, Site s,
3        MachineInstallation mi,
4        SensorInstallation si
5   WHERE m.mv > si.ev+? AND
6        mi.mi > ? AND
7        si.mi = mi.mi AND
8        m.si = si.si AND
9        m.logdb = s.logdb AND
10       s.sid < ?
```

Fig. 3. Query Q1

```
Q2:
1   SELECT count(*)
2   FROM Measures m, Site s,
3        MachineInstallation mi,
4        SensorInstallation si
5   WHERE m.mv > si.ev+? AND
6        mi.mi > ? AND
7        si.mi = mi.mi AND
8        m.si = si.si AND
9        m.logdb = s.logdb AND
10       s.sid < ?
```

Fig. 4. Query Q2

restricted. The experiments are scaled by varying these parameters. The number of log databases is varied by restricting *sid*, the amount of data selected from each log database is varied by *th*, and the number of bindings selected from the meta-database is varied by *mi*.

Query *Q2* in Fig. 4 is similar to *Q1*, the difference being that it applies an aggregate function over *Q1*, i.e. it computes the number of faulty sensor readings. Here only a single value is returned from each log database. The purpose of the query is to investigate the join strategies without concerning the overhead of transferring substantial amounts of data back to the client.

```
Q3:
1   SELECT m.mi, m.bt, m.et
2   FROM Measures m, Site s,
3        MachineInstallation mi,
4        SensorInstallation si
5   WHERE abs(m.mv-si.ev)/si.ev>? AND
6        si.mi = mi.mi AND
7        m.si = si.si AND
8        m.logdb=s.logdb
```

Fig. 5. Query Q3

```
Q4:
1   SELECT m.mi, m.bt, m.et
2   FROM Measures m, Site s,
3        MachineInstallation mi,
4        SensorInstallation si
5   WHERE si.mi = mi.mi AND
6        m.si = si.si AND
7        m.logdb = s.logdb AND
8        ((m.mv>(1+?)*si.ev and si.ev>0) or
9        (m.mv<(1+?)*si.ev and si.ev<0) or
10       (m.mv>(1-?)*si.ev and si.ev>0) or
11       (m.mv>(1-?)*si.ev and si.ev<0))
```

Fig. 6. Transformed Q3

Query *Q3* in Fig. 5 is an example of a more complex numerical query for identifying machine failures. It detects situations where the relative deviation of sensor readings from *ev* is larger than a threshold parameter we denote *rth*. One property of *Q3* is that the query optimizer of the used DBMS cannot utilize an ordered index on the measured value *mv*, so the entire local table *Measures* on each site will be scanned entirely. This query thus has a high query execution cost for searching the log databases.

Query *Q4* in Fig. 6 is a manually transformed version of *Q3* to expose the index column *mv* of *Measures* table for query optimizer of the DBMS for scalable search. Here all parameter occurrences in the query (marked?) refer to the supplied value of *rth*. FLOQ automatically makes this algebraic transformation by utilizing the algorithm in [12]. The difference between *Q3* and *Q4* shows the trade-off between full scan and index scan in the log databases enabled by the rewrite. *Q3* is an expensive query compared to *Q4*.

3   Join Strategies

The two strategies, PBJ and PBLJ, for parallel execution of queries joining data between the meta-database and the log databases are illustrated in Figs. 7 and 8, respectively. With both strategies FLOQ first extracts parameter bindings from the meta-database. The result is a stream of tuples is called the *binding stream B* where each tuple $(i, v_1, v_2, ..., v_p)$ is a *parameter binding*. The elements $v_1, v_2, ..., v_p$ of the binding stream are the values of the free variables in the query fragment sent to the log databases. For example, in Q1 the free variables are *(mi, si, ev)*. Each binding tuple is prefixed with a *destination site, i*, identifying where the log database RDB_i resides. The parameter binding tuples are joined with measurements in the log databases. Thus the binding stream is split into one site binding stream B_i per log database RDB_i, $B = B_1 \cup B_2 ... \cup B_n$, where n is the number of sites. The destination i determines to which site the rest of the tuple $(v_1, v_2, ..., v_p)$, is routed. The join strategies are defined as follows:

PBJ, parallel bind-join: PBJ (Fig. 7) is a generalization of bind-join [4] to handle parallel execution between a common meta-database and a collection of wrapped relational databases RDB_i. On each site i the tuples in the binding stream B_i received by a FLOQ wrapper is bind joined (BJ) with the query σ_i sent to the database RDB_i through parameterized (prepared) JDBC calls. The tuples in the result stream R_i from the JDBC calls are then streamed back to the FLOQ server, where they are merged asynchronously with the result tuples from other sites. With PBJ, a parameterized query is executed many times in each wrapped log database, once for each parameter binding in B_i.

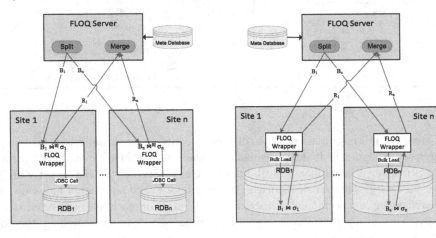

Fig. 7. PBJ   **Fig. 8.** PBLJ

PBLJ, parallel bulk-load join: With PBLJ (Fig. 8) each FLOQ wrapper first bulk loads the entire binding stream B_i into a *binding table* in RDB_i. When all parameter bindings have been loaded, the system submits a single SQL query to the log database to join the loaded binding table with σ_i. As for PBJ, the result stream R_i is shipped back to the FLOQ server through the wrapper for asynchronous merging. Compared to PBJ, the advantage of this approach is that only one query is sent to each log database. It requires the extra step of bulk loading in parallel the entire parameter streams into each log database, which, however, should be less costly compared to calling many prepared SQL statements through JDBC with PBJ. The bulk loading facility of the DBMS is utilized for high performance.

BJ, regular bind-join: If there is a single log database, PBJ is analogous to BJ and is a baseline in our evaluations. With BJ one prepared SQL query per binding is shipped from the FLOQ wrapper to only one log database, RDB_1.

3.1 Cost Model for Join Strategies

The total cost in terms of response times of the proposed join strategies is divided between the cost of execution in the FLOQ server C_{FLOQ} and the maximum site cost C_i.

$$C_{Join} = C_{FLOQ} + max(\{C_i : i = 1,\ldots,n\}) \tag{1}$$

The total cost of the FLOQ server execution is approximately divided between two major components, which are the cost of splitting the binding stream B, C_s, and the cost of merging all result streams R_i, C_m. The cost of the FLOQ server execution is independent of any join strategies, i.e.:

$$C_{FLOQ} = C_s + C_m \tag{2}$$

The variables used in analysing cost models are described in Table 1.

Table 1. Variables used in the cost model

Variable	Description	Variable	Description
C_{Join}	Total cost of a join	C_{FLOQ}	Total execution cost in the FLOQ server
B_i	Binding stream to site i	C_s	Cost of splitting the binding stream B in the FLOQ server
R_i	Result stream from site i	β	A single binding from the binding stream B_i
C_i	Total cost at site i	C_m	Cost of merging result streams R_i in the FLOQ server
C_{σ_i}	Cost of executing $_i$ in RDB_i	C_{JDBC}	Cost of JDBC call for a single binding β
$C_{\bowtie_i}$	Cost of local join at site i	σ_i	The query to RDB_i.
$C_{Bulkload_i}$	Cost of bulk loading in RDB_i	C_{B_i}	Cost of transferring binding stream B_i to site i
C_{σ_β}	Selection Cost for a single binding β	C_{R_i}	Cost of transferring result stream R_i from site i
RDB_i	The relational log database at site i	C_{Net}	Network communication overhead cost for a single binding β

The total site cost C_i is approximately divided between four major cost components: (i) transferring the binding stream B_i from the FLOQ server to the site, C_{B_i}, (ii) executing $_i$ in the log database, C_{σ_i}, (iii) local join $C_{\bowtie_i}$ either in RDB_i ($C_{\bowtie_i}^{LogDB}$ for PBLJ) or in the FLOQ wrapper ($C_{\bowtie_i}^{Wrapper}$ for PBJ), and (iv) transferring the result stream R_i to the FLOQ server, C_{R_i}. Thus the total site cost C_i is defined as:

$$C_i = C_{B_i} + C_{\sigma_i} + C_{\bowtie_i} + C_{R_i} \tag{3}$$

By combining Eqs. (1), (2), and (3), the total cost of a distributed join becomes:

$$C_{Join} = C_s + C_m + max \left(\{ (C_{B_i} + C_{\sigma_i} + C_{\bowtie_i} + C_{R_i}) : i = 1, ..., n \} \right) \tag{4}$$

For each site, the binding stream B_i is significantly smaller than the number of logged measurements in RDB_i:

$$|B_i| \ll |Measures(RDB_i)| \tag{5}$$

For PBJ, the bind-join is performed in each FLOQ wrapper, therefore, the cost of a local join $C_{\bowtie_i}$ can be replaced with the cost of a bind-join in the wrapper, $C_{\bowtie_i}^{Wrapper}$. Also the cost of executing the sub-query σ_i that selects data from a log database, C_{σ_i}, is replaced with the *BJ selection cost*, $C_{\sigma_i}^{Wrapper}$, in the site cost in (3):

$$C_i^{PBJ} = C_{B_i}^{PBJ} + C_{\sigma_i}^{Wrapper} + C_{\bowtie_i}^{Wrapper} + C_{R_i} \tag{6}$$

In PBLJ the joins and selections are combined into one sub-query to each RDB_i. Therefore, the cost of $C_{\bowtie_i}$ and C_{σ_i} and C_{σ_i} in the site cost in Eq. (3) for PBLJ can be replaced with the cost of join and selection in the log database ($(C_{\bowtie_i}^{LogDB}$ and $C_{\sigma_i}^{LogDB})$ and $C_{\sigma_i}^{LogDB}$):

$$C_i^{PBLJ} = C_{B_i}^{PBLJ} + C_{\sigma_i}^{LogDB} + C_{\bowtie_i}^{LogDB} + C_{R_i} \tag{7}$$

In PBJ, the FLOQ server transfers the binding stream B_i to a FLOQ wrapper through the standard network protocol. Therefore, the cost of transferring bindings to each site, $C_{B_i}^{PBJ}$, is the aggregated network communication overhead for each binding, C_{Net}.

$$C_{B_i}^{PBJ} = |B_i| \times C_{Net}, where |B_i| \geq 1 \tag{8}$$

In PBLJ all the bindings B_i are bulk-loaded directly into the log database. The cost of sending all bindings to site $i, C_{B_i}^{PBLJ}$, is the cost of bulk loading the bindings, $C_{Bulkload_i}$.

$$C_{B_i}^{PBLJ} = C_{Bulkload_i} \tag{9}$$

Obviously, the cost of bulk-loading in PBLJ $C_{Bulkload_i}$ is insignificant compared to sending large numbers of bindings to prepared SQL statements in PBJ:
$C_{Bulkload_i} << |B_i| \times C_{Net}$, where $|B_i| \geq 1$; therefore,

$$C_{B_i}^{PBLJ} \leq C_{B_i}^{PBJ} \tag{10}$$

On the other hand, the selection cost of PBLJ is also low compared to PBJ since the cost of selection performed by RDB_i is lower than the combined cost of selection and JDBC overhead for each binding β of a binding stream B_i:

$$C_{\sigma_i}^{LogDB} \leq |B_i| \times (C_{\sigma_\beta} + C_{JDBC}), \text{ where } \beta \in B_i \text{ and } |B_i| \geq 1; \text{ therefore:} \tag{11}$$

$$C_{\sigma_i}^{LogDB} \leq C_{\sigma_i}^{Wrapper} \tag{12}$$

Similarly, a local join in the relational DBMS is efficient compared to the join performed in a FLOQ wrapper since query optimization techniques can be applied inside a relational DBMS where the overhead JDBC calls are eliminated. Thus,

$$C_{\bowtie_i}^{LogDB} \leq C_{\bowtie_i}^{Wrapper} \tag{13}$$

From Eqs. (10), (12), and (13), the total cost at site i for the three components, transferring bindings (C_{B_i}), selection (C_{σ_i}), and join ($(C_{\bowtie_i})$) are lower for PBLJ than for PBJ. The cost C_{R_i} of transferring the result streams R_i to the FLOQ server is equal for both PBLJ and PBJ, therefore, comparing (6) and (7):

$$C_i^{PBLJ} \leq C_i^{PBJ} \tag{14}$$

From Eq. (1), as the cost of the execution at the FLOQ server C_{FLOQ} is equal for both PBJ and PBLJ, by combing Eqs. (1) and (14) it can be stated that the overall cost of join in PBLJ is lower than PBJ:

$$C_{PBLJ} \leq C_{PBJ} \tag{15}$$

3.2 Discussion

According to Eq. (15), PBLJ should always outperform PBJ in every experiment when $|B_i| \geq 1$. Equation (8) and (11) suggest that PBLJ will perform increasingly better than PBJ when scaling the number of bindings $|B_i|$. It is evident from Eq. (4) that, independent the chosen join strategy, when the size of the result stream $|R_i|$ is large, the tuple transfer cost (C_{R_i}) will be a major dominating component in the cost model. Therefore, the performance trade-offs between respective join strategies, are more significant when the number of tuples returned from the log database is small.

To conclude, according to the cost model, the performance evaluation should be investigated by (i) varying the number of tuples returned from the sites, (ii) scaling the number of sites, and (iii) scaling the number of bindings from the meta-database.

4 Performance Evaluation

We compared the performance of the join strategies PBJ and PBLJ based on the queries Q1, Q2, Q3, and Q4. In our real-world application each log database had more than 250 million measurements from sensor readings, occupying 10 GB of raw data.

The following scalability experiments were performed on six PCs (with 4 processors and 8 GB main memory) running Windows 7 while: (i) scaling the number of result tuples | R_i|; (ii) scaling the number of sites, n; and (iii) scaling the number of bindings $|B_i|$.

Scaling the number of result tuples

Figure 9(a) shows the execution times of Q1 for the two join strategies over a single log database, while scaling the number of result tuples $|R|$ by adjusting th. As expected from Eq. (12), PBLJ performs better than PBJ. Since there is only one site, PBJ is equivalent to BJ.

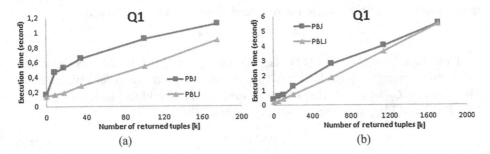

Fig. 9. Q1 (a) with one log database and (b) with six log databases

Figure 9(b) compares the performance of Q1 for six log databases while scaling $|R|$. As expected PBLJ scales better than PBJ. However, as more tuples are returned from the log databases the network overhead is becoming a major dominating factor, making the performance difference of the join strategies insignificant. Notice that the number of returned tuples remains the same for both strategies; thus the network overhead is equal. However, PBLJ will always perform better (even with a small fraction) than PBJ since other overhead is larger for PBJ.

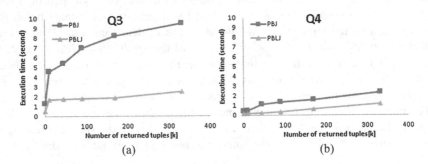

Fig. 10. Execution time for Q3 and Q4 with six log databases

Figure 10 compares PBJ and PBLJ for Q3 and Q4 for six log databases. Q3 is an example of a slow numerical query requiring a full scan of *Measures*, whereas Q4 is faster since it exposes the index on *Measures.mv* for query Q3. It is evident from

Fig. 10 that PBLJ performs better than PBJ for both query Q3 and Q4. Figure 10(b) shows the performance improvement due to index utilization compared to sequential scan in Q3.

To conclude, PBLJ performs better than PBJ when the number of returned tuples is increased, as also indicated by Eq. (15) of the cost model.

Scaling the number of log databases

Figure 11 compares PBJ and PBLJ for Q1 when scaling the number of log databases. In Figs. 11(a) and (b) the total number of tuples returned from a single log database $|R_i|$ is 1 K and 295 K, respectively. Notice that the total number of tuples returned $|R|$ in each figure is multiplied with the fixed $|R_i|$ from each log database.

In Fig. 11(a) $|R|$ is small, so the performance difference between PBJ and PBLJ is dominating over the network cost, while in Fig. 11(b) the higher network cost makes the difference less significant.

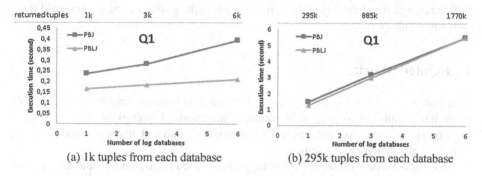

(a) 1k tuples from each database   (b) 295k tuples from each database

Fig. 11. Execution time for Q1 varying number of log databases and selectivity

In summary, the overall performance of PBLJ is always better while scaling number of log databases compared to PBJ.

Scaling the number of bindings

This experiment investigates the performance of PBJ and PBLJ while varying the number of bindings $|B_i|$ from the meta-database. Figure 12 shows the execution times for Q1 and Q2 for PBJ and PBLJ for a single log database.

From Fig. 12(a) it is evident that PBLJ performs significantly better while scaling $|B_i|$. The reason is that in PBJ, the FLOQ wrapper is performing $|B_i|$ bind-joins, so the overhead of the JDBC calls is multiplied with $|B_i|$. In all experiments the extra time for the bulk loading was less than 50 ms irrespective of number of bindings $|B_i|$. This makes it insignificant for this small number of bindings relative to the size of the log databases. This confirms Eqs. (8) and (11) of the cost model that PBJ will not scale compared to PBLJ when increasing the number of bindings. The experimental results of query Q2 that returns a single tuple per site are shown in Fig. 12(b). The reason of the better scalability of PBLJ than for Q1 is because the network communication overhead C_{R_i} in Eq. (4) is negligible since only one tuple is returned from each site.

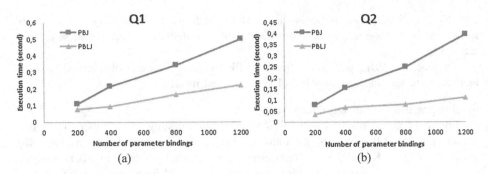

Fig. 12. Execution time for Q1 and Q2

In all experiments, the PBLJ join strategy performs better than PBJ, in particular while scaling the number of bindings $|B_i|$. This confirms Eq. (15) in the cost model. The performance improvement is more significant when the number of tuples returned from each log database is low.

5   Related Work

Bind-join was presented in [4] as a method to join data from external databases [7]. We generalized bind-join to process in parallel parameterized queries to dynamic collections of autonomous log databases. Furthermore we showed that our bulk-load join method scales better in our setting.

In Google Fusion Tables [3] left outer joins are used to combine relational views of web pages, while [6] uses adaptive methods to join data from external data sources. In [9] the selection of autonomous data sources to join is based on market mechanisms. Our case is different because we investigate strategies to join meta-data with data from dynamic collections of log databases without joining the data sources themselves.

Vertical partitioning and indexing of fact tables in monolithic data warehouses is investigated in [1]. One can regard our *VMeasures* view as a horizontally partitioned fact table. A major difference to data warehouse techniques is that we are integrating data from dynamic collections of autonomous log databases, rather than scalable processing of queries to data uploaded to a central data warehouse.

In [2] the problem of making views of many autonomous data warehouses is investigated. The databases are joined using very large SQL queries joining many external databases. Rather than integrating external databases by huge SQL queries, our strategies are based on simple queries over a view (*VMeasures*) of dynamic collections of external databases, i.e. the local-as-view approach [5].

A classical optimization strategy used in distributed databases [8] is to cost different shipping alternatives of data between non-autonomous data servers before joining them. By contrast, we investigate using standard DBMS APIs (JDBC and bulk load) to make multi-database joins of meta-data with dynamic sets of autonomous log databases using local-as-view.

6   Conclusions

Two join strategies were proposed for parallel execution of queries joining meta-data with data from autonomous log databases using standard DBMS APIs: parallel bind-join (PBJ) and parallel bulk-load join (PBLJ). For the performance evaluation we defined typical fundamental queries and investigated the impact of our join strategies. A cost model was used to guide and evaluate the efficiency of the strategies. The experimental results validated the cost model. In general, PBLJ performs better than PBJ when the number of bindings from the meta-database is increased.

In the experiments a rather small set of autonomous log databases were used. Further investigations should evaluate the impact of having very large number of log databases and different strategies to improve communication overheads, e.g. by compression.

Acknowledgments. This work is supported by EU FP7 project Smart Vortex and the Swedish Foundation for Strategic Research under contract RIT08-0041.

References

1. Datta, A., VanderMeer, D.E., Ramamritham, K.: Parallel star join + dataindexes: efficient query processing in data warehouses and OLAP. J. IEEE TKDE **14**(6), 1299–1316 (2002)
2. Dieu, N., Dragusanu, A., Fabret, F., Llirbat, F., Simon, E.: 1,000 tables inside the from. J. ACM VLDB **2**(2), 1450–1461 (2009)
3. Garcia-Molina, H., Halevy, A.Y., Jensen, C.S., Langen, A., Madhavan, J., Shapley, R., Shen, W.: Google fusion tables: data management, integration and collaboration in the cloud. In: SoCC, pp. 175–180 (2010)
4. Haas, L., Kossmann, D., Wimmers, E., Yang, J: Optimizing queries across diverse data source. In: VLDB, pp. 276–285 (1997)
5. Halevy, A., Rajaraman, A., Ordille, J.: Data integration: the teenage years. In: VLDB, pp. 9–16 (2006)
6. Ives, G., Halevy, A., Weld, D.: Adapting to source properties in processing data integration queries. In: SIGMOD, pp. 395–406 (2004)
7. Josifovski, V., Schwarz, P., Haas, L., Lin, E.: Garlic: a new flavor of federated query processing for DB2. In: SIGMOD, pp. 524–532 (2002)
8. Kossmann, D.: The state of the art in distributed query processing. J. ACM Comput. Surv. **32**(4), 422–469 (2000)
9. Pentaris, F., Ioannidis, Y.: Query optimization in distributed networks of autonomous database systems. J. ACM Trans. Database Syst. **31**(2), 537–583 (2006)
10. Risch, T., Josifovski, V.: Distributed data integration by object-oriented mediator servers. J. Concurrency Comput. Pract. Experience **13**(11), 933–953 (2001)
11. Smart Vortex Project. http://www.smartvortex.eu/
12. Truong, T., Risch, T.: Scalable numerical queries by algebraic inequality transformations. In: Bhowmick, S.S., Dyreson, C.E., Jensen, C.S., Lee, M.L., Muliantara, A., Thalheim, B. (eds.) DASFAA 2014, Part I. LNCS, vol. 8421, pp. 95–109. Springer, Heidelberg (2014)
13. Zhu, M., Risch, T.: Querying combined cloud-based and relational databases. In: CSC, pp. 330–335 (2011)
14. Zhu, M., Stefanova, S., Truong, T., Risch, T.: Scalable numerical SPARQL queries over relational databases. In: LWDM Workshop, pp. 257–262 (2014)

ECST – Extended Context-Free Straight-Line Tree Grammars

Stefan Böttcher, Rita Hartel$^{(\boxtimes)}$, Thomas Jacobs, and Markus Jeromin

Computer Science, University of Paderborn, Fürstenallee 11,
33102 Paderborn, Germany
{stb, rst}@uni-paderborn.de,
{tjacobs, mjeromin}@mail.uni-paderborn.de

Abstract. Grammar-based compressors like e.g. CluX [1], BPLEX [2], Tree-RePAIR [3] transform an XML tree X into a context-free straight-line linear tree (CSLT) grammar G and yield strong compression ratios compared to other classes of XML-specific compressors. However, CSLT grammars have the disadvantage that simulating on G update operations like inserting, deleting, or re-labeling a node V of X requires to isolate the path from X's root to V from all the paths represented by G. Usually, this leads to an increased redundancy within G, as grammar rules are copied and modified, but the original and the modified grammar rules often differ only slightly. In this paper, we propose extended context-free straight-line tree (ECST) grammars that allow reducing the redundancy created by path isolation. Furthermore, we show how to query and how to update ECST compressed grammars.

Keywords: Updating compressed XML data · Grammar-based compression

1 Introduction

1.1 Motivation

XML is a widely used, but verbose data exchange and data transmission standard. In order to reduce the volume and costs involved in storage and transmission of verbose XML data, a variety of structure-based XML compression technologies to reduce the size of the structural part of XML documents have been developed. They range from the compression of an XML tree into a directed acyclic graph (DAG) (e.g. [4]) to the compression into a context-free straight-line linear tree (CSLT) grammar (e.g. CluX [1], BPLEX [2], TreeRePAIR [3]). Out of these, compression into a CSLT grammar yields the most strongly compressed still queryable and updateable data format.

While DAG compression shares identical XML subtrees, i.e., repeated occurrences of a subtree are replaced with a reference to the subtree, CSLT grammar-based compression additionally shares similar subtrees having an identical connected fragment of nodes. The identical connected fragment of nodes is represented by a CSLT grammar rule, and different parts of similar subtrees are represented by parameters. However, a CSLT grammar rule can only represent a *connected* fragment of nodes, such that similar subtrees that differ in an inner node or an inner fragment cannot be shared by a single CSLT grammar rule. Our extension ECST overcomes this limitation.

© Springer International Publishing Switzerland 2015
S. Maneth (Ed.): BICOD 2015, LNCS 9147, pp. 186–198, 2015.
DOI: 10.1007/978-3-319-20424-6_18

As a consequence, update operations modifying just one of the shared subtrees expand CSLT grammars and thereby introduce new redundancies, leading to grammars that are more complex to decompress, to query, and to manipulate. We refer to this problem as the *redundant fragment problem* within this paper.

1.2 Contributions

In this paper, we introduce extended context-free straight-line tree (ECST) grammars as a compressed XML data format that overcomes the redundant fragment problem. In particular:

- We define how ECST grammars extend CSLT grammars.
- We show how path isolation which is necessary prior to simulating update operations on grammars works with ECST grammars.
- We demonstrate why using ECST grammars can avoid copying of large parts of rules during the process of path isolation.
- We describe how to evaluate path queries on ECST grammar-compressed data.
- We show how standard update operations can be simulated on ECST grammars.

Altogether, on an ECST grammar G representing an XML tree X, we can not only simulate all query and update operations on X, but also compression to ECST grammars allows keeping the grammars small by avoiding redundant fragments generated by updates of G.

1.3 Paper Organization

In Sect. 2, we define ECST grammars, and we show how relabel, insert, and delete operations of nodes of an XML tree X can be simulated on a compressed ECST grammar G. In Sect. 3, we present an approach to query evaluation and an approach to update processing for arbitrary ECST grammars. Section 4 gives an overview on related research, and finally, Sect. 5 contains a short summary.

2 Grammar-Based Compression and Basic Update Operations

2.1 An Example Using CSLT Grammar-Based Compression

The key idea of CSLT grammar-based compression (e.g., CluX [1], BPLEX [2], or TreeRePAIR [3]) is as follows. Whenever similar subtrees ST1, ..., STk containing an identical fragment F of connected nodes including the root of STi occur within an XML tree X, a grammar G representing X stores only one occurrence A of the fragment F. G replaces all occurrences of such a fragment F in X by a reference to A. This can be implemented e.g. in form of a grammar, where each fragment F of connected nodes multiply occurring in X is stored as a grammar rule A and each subtree STi containing an occurrence of F is represented by a non-terminal symbol representing a call of A.

Differences between the subtrees ST1, ..., STk are represented by providing formal parameters to the grammar rule for A and by providing different actual parameters for different calls of A.

To simplify the presentation and the compression algorithm, we follow [1–3] and, without loss of generality, work on the binary representation of XML trees.

For example, look at the binary XML tree X1 (c.f. Fig. 1) which is represented by the grammar Grammar 1. X1 represents a database of customers together with their orders. For each customer, contact data is stored in form of address, first name, and last name, and for each order, the shipping data is stored in form of address, first name, and last name. Each address might contain an optional sub-element 'isPOB' that defines whether the address represents a post office box. Due to space limitations, we abbreviate the element labels as follows: customer → cu, order → od, address → ad, firstname → fn, lastname → ln, and isPOB → ip.

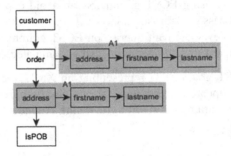

Fig. 1. Binary XML tree X1 corresponding to Grammar 1

```
S           ->    cu(od(A1(ip(-,-)),A1(-)),-)
A1(y1)      ->    ad(y1,fn(-,ln(-,-)))
```

Grammar 1. Example grammar

The repeated fragment consisting of the node with label 'ad', its next-sibling with label 'fn', and this node's next-sibling with label 'ln' is represented by the grammar rule A1. The 'ad'-labeled nodes are the root nodes of the two similar subtrees containing the repeated fragment. The subtrees differ in the first-child of the 'ad'-labeled nodes which is represented by the formal parameter y_1 of rule A1 and by the actual parameter 'ip' for the first subtree in preorder and by the nullpointer as actual parameter for the second subtree. (For readability, we represent the nullpointer by '-'.)

Note that we can reproduce each XML tree X from G by decompression, i.e., recursively applying all rules of G. For this purpose, we would substitute each call of a rule $A(ap_1, ..., ap_n)$ with the right-hand side of the rule A, rhs(A), where we replace A's formal parameters $y_1, ..., y_n$ with the actual parameters $ap_1, ..., ap_n$.

When simulating update operations of a node V of X directly on a CSLT grammar G, i.e., without decompressing G to X, the so called grammar path GP in G representing the path p from X's root to V has to be isolated in G first, such that GP represents only the path p to the node V to be updated.

A grammar path GP = $[A_0, p_0, ..., A_n, p_n]$ is defined as follows (c.f. [5]). Each grammar path GP contains an alternating sequence of non-terminals A_i, $0 \leq i \leq n$, and index positions p_i which refer to a symbol within rhs(A_i), which is a non-terminal calling the next grammar rule A_{i+1} for $0 \leq i < n$, and which is a terminal symbol with the same label as the node V for i = n. A_0 is the start symbol S of grammar G. For example, if we apply the XPath query Q = //od/child::ad to Grammar 1, the selected node can be described by GP1: = [S,3,A1,1]. Thus, GP1 describes a rule call to rhs(A1) at position 3 in rule S. Finally, terminal 'ad' at position 1 in rhs(A1) is selected.

While update operations like e.g. the re-labeling of a single node V with label v to label w is quite simple in the XML document tree X (just change the label of node V from v to w), simulating these operations on grammar-compressed XML documents is more complex for the following reason. In grammar-compressed documents G, in general, a single terminal symbol does not refer to a single node V of a tree X only, but to a set of nodes of X. This means that prior to changing the terminal label, we first have to isolate the grammar path GP addressing node V from G, such that the isolated path represents only the node V to be relabeled. Considering a grammar path GP = $[A_0, p_0, ..., A_n, p_n]$ representing the node V of X, two steps are necessary in order to relabel the terminal v to w. First, we have to copy rule A_n into A_n'. But this is not sufficient. In the second step, we have to copy each rule A_i, $1 \leq i < n$ to A_i', and we have to adjust the calling non-terminal to refer to A_{i+1}' within each copied rule A_i'.

Consider for example Grammar 1 given above and the update operation "relabel // od/child::ad into pob". The terminal 'ad' in rule A1 represents two 'ad'-labeled nodes of the XML tree X1 (shown in Fig. 1), out of which only the first node in preorder (i.e. the node defined by grammar path GP1) is a child of an 'od'-labeled node in X1. In order to update only this 'ad'-labeled node, we have to generate two copies of rule A1. This leads to the following modified grammar, Grammar 2:

```
S               ->    cu(od(A1'(ip(-,-)),A1(-)),-)
A1(y1)          ->    ad(y1,fn(-,ln(-,-)))
A1'(y1)         ->    pob(y1,fn(-,ln(-,-)))
```

Grammar 2. Resulting grammar after performing the update on Grammar 1

As after copying A1 into $\left(A_1'\right)$ only the label 'ad' has been changed into 'pob', the remaining fragments of the right-hand side rhs(A1) of the rule for A1 occur also redundantly in rhs(A1'). Redundancy even increases if the rules to be copied are larger.

This is an example for the *redundant fragment problem* of CSLT grammars invoked by path isolation and subsequent updates: As a CSLT grammar rule can only represent a *connected* fragment of nodes shared by subtrees, subtrees that differ in the root node or in an inner node cannot be shared by a single CSLT grammar rule.

2.2   Extended CSLT Grammars

To overcome the redundant fragment problem, we extend CSLT grammars to ECST grammars. In contrast to CSLT grammar rules, ECST grammar rules not only allow reusing connected fragments of similar subtrees, but also reusing arbitrary tree fragments. ECST's extension to CSLT is that the difference between similar subtrees is represented by a *ranked parameter*, i.e. a parameter that itself has parameters.

ECST grammars are defined as follows. Let T be an alphabet of terminal symbols, $N = \{A_0, \ldots, A_n\}$ be a ranked alphabet of non-terminal symbols, '-' be the nullpointer, and $Z = \{z_1, \ldots, z_m\}$ be a set of ranked alphabet of parameter symbols. The function rank: $N \cup Z \rightarrow N_0$ assigns to each non-terminal symbol and to each parameter symbol a natural number representing its rank. Let the sets T, N, Z, and {-} be disjoint. Let furthermore ID, $LP \in N$ be special non-terminal symbols with the following predefined grammar rules: $ID(y_1) \rightarrow y_1, LP(y_1, y_2) \rightarrow y_2$. Then, a *term* over $T \cup N \cup Z \cup \{-\}$ is

- the nullpointer '-',
- a terminal expression of the form t(fc, ns) where $t \in T$, and fc and ns are terms representing the first-child of t and the next-sibling of t respectively,
- a simple term A_i, $rank(A_i) = 0$, or a non-terminal expression of the form $A_i(t_1, \ldots, t_m)$ where $A_i \in N$, $m = rank(A_i)$ and t_i is a term for $i \in \{1, \ldots, m\}$, or
- a simple parameter z_i of rank 0 or a parameter expression $z_i(t_1, \ldots, t_m)$ where $z_i \in Z$, $m = rank(z_i)$ and t_i is a term for $i \in \{1, \ldots, m\}$.

Then, an ECST grammar is defined as a tuple (T, N, Z, P, S, ID, LP) where T, N, Z, ID, and LP are defined as above. $S \in N$ is the start symbol, and P is a set of grammar rules, where the following constraints must be met:

- For each non-terminal $A_i \in N$, with $rank(A_i) = m$ there exists exactly one grammar rule of the form $A_i(z_{i1}, \ldots, z_{im}) \rightarrow rhs(A_i)$, where $rhs(A_i)$ is a term that contains each symbol $z_{i1}, \ldots, z_{im}$ exactly once in that order, with $z_{ij} \in Z$ and all z_{ij} are distinct. Furthermore, for each non-terminal symbol A_j occurring in $rhs(A_i)$, we have $j < i$ (i.e. calls of grammar rules are acyclic).
- For each rule $A_i(z_{i1}, \ldots, z_{ij}, \ldots, z_{in}) \rightarrow rhs(A_i)$, $rank(A_i) = n$, and each parameter expression $z_{ij}(t_1, \ldots, t_m)$, $rank(z_{ij}) = m$ occurring in $rhs(A_i)$, then in all calls of A_i the appropriate values that can be passed to z_{ij} are a non-terminal expression A_k having $rank(A_k) = m$ or another parameter expression of rank m.

ECST grammars extend CSLT grammars by allowing parameters of arbitrary rank, instead of parameters of rank 0 only, and the special non-terminal symbols ID and LP.

2.3   Isolating the Path to Be Updated

Each update operation on a node V with label v of an XML tree X can be simulated on the grammar G representing X by updates along the grammar path GP representing V in G. No matter, which update operation (relabel, delete, insert) on which node V of X we simulate on G, at first we isolate the grammar path GP representing V in G. Then, we perform the update operation on the isolated grammar path.

Isolation of a grammar path $GP = [S, p_0, A_1, p_1, \ldots, A_n, p_n]$ is implemented as follows.

For the rule $A_n(y_1, \ldots, y_{jk}) \rightarrow rhs(A_n)$, we define a rule $A_n'(y_1, \ldots, y_{jk}) \rightarrow rhs(A_n)$. Then, for $1 \leq m < n$ for the rules $A_m(y_1, \ldots, y_{jl}) \rightarrow rhs(A_m)$, we define a rule $A'_m \left(y_1, \ldots, y_{jl} \right) \rightarrow rhs\left(A'_m \right)$, where $rhs\left(A'_m \right)$ is $rhs(A_m)$ except that the call to A_{m+1} on the grammar path, i.e. at position p_m in $rhs\left(A'_m \right)$, is replaced with a call of A'_{m+1}. Finally, in $rhs(S)$, we replace the call of A_1 at position p_0 in $rhs(S)$, with a call of A'_1.

Grammar path isolation of GP1 leads to the following modified grammar, Grammar 3, which is an intermediate step towards generating Grammar 2:

```
S          ->    cu(od(A1'(ip(-,-)),A1(-)),-)
A1(y1)     ->    ad(y1,fn(-,ln(-,-)))
A1'(y1)    ->    ad(y1,fn(-,ln(-,-)))
```

Grammar 3. Resulting grammar after performing GP isolation on Grammar 1

In case of the relabel operation, only the label 'ad' of the rule A1', i.e. of the last rule A_n' generated for GP1, has to be changed to 'pob'. That is, how we get Grammar 2.

2.4 Basic Update Operations Using Ranked Parameter Symbols

In this section, we define, how the basic update operations relabel, delete, and insert can be performed on rules A_n and A'_n of the grammar path. How to modify and to copy the rules $A'_1, \ldots, A'_{n-1}$ from the rules $A_1, \ldots, A_{n-1}$ is discussed in Sect. 2.5.

Assume that A_n has $rank(A_n) = j$ and assume w.l.o.g. that the position in $rhs(A_n)$ to be modified occurs between the positions of the parameters y_i and y_{i+1}.

To simulate any update operation on G, we first isolate the grammar path to the selected node from G. The further steps differ depending on the operation.

Relabel. Let V be a node in X that shall be relabeled to w, and let v be a terminal in rule $A_n \left(y_1, \ldots, y_j \right) \rightarrow rhs(A_n)$ of G, such that the grammar path GP = $[A_0, p_0, \ldots, A_n, p_n]$ to v represents V (note that other grammar paths to v may represent other nodes of X).

First, we change the call of A_n at position p_{n-1} within $rhs\left(A'_{n-1} \right)$ into a call of $rhs\left(A'_n \right)$.

Second, we create a new rule $A_n * \left(y_1, \ldots, y_i, z, y_{i+1}, \ldots, y_{jk} \right) \rightarrow rhs(A_n*)$, where $rhs(A_n*)$ is $rhs(A_n)$ except that the terminal v at position p_n is replaced by the ranked parameter $z \in Z$, $rank(z) = rank(v) = 2$, and the position of z among the parameters of A_n* is so that the parameter order is preserved. Furthermore, we change $rhs(A_n)$ into $A_n*(y_1, \ldots, y_i, v, y_{i+1}, \ldots, y_j)$, and we change $rhs\left(A'_n \right)$ into $A_n*(y_1, \ldots, y_i, w, y_{i+1}, \ldots, y_j)$.

Grammar 4 shows the result of the second step applied to Grammar 3.

```
S            ->    cu(od(A1'(ip(-,-)),A1(-)),-)
A1(y1)       ->    A1*(ad,y1)
A1'(y1)      ->    A1*(pob,y1)
A1*(z1,y1)-> z1(y1,fn(-,ln(-,-)))
```

Grammar 4. Resulting grammar after combining isolated path and other path

Insert. Let V be a node in X, and let v be a terminal in rule $A_n\left(y_1, \ldots, y_j\right) \rightarrow$ rhs(A_n) of G, such that the grammar path GP = $[A_0, p_0, \ldots, A_n, p_n]$ to v represents V. We want to simulate on G inserting a subtree as the previous sibling of the node V in X. Let the subtree to be inserted be represented by a grammar rule $I(y_1) \rightarrow$ rhs(I), where y_1 represents the next-sibling of the root node of I.

First, we change the call of A_n at position p_{n-1} within rhs$\left(A'_{n-1}\right)$ into a call of A'_n. Let further $y_1, \ldots, y_i$ be the parameters occuring in rhs(A_n) at positions smaller than p_n. Then, we create a new rule $A_n * \left(y_1, \ldots, y_i, z, y_{i+1}, \ldots, y_j\right) \rightarrow$ rhs(A_n*), where rhs (A_n*) is rhs(A_n) except that the term t at position p_n is replaced by the term z(t), where z $\in$ Z is a parameter, with rank(z) = 1, and z's position among the parameters of A_n* is so that the parameter order is preserved. To simulate the insert, the rule $A'_n\left(y_1, \ldots, y_j\right) \rightarrow$ rhs$\left(A'_n\right)$ is replaced with $A'_n\left(y_1, \ldots, y_j\right) \rightarrow A_n * \left(y_1, \ldots, y_i, I, y_{i+1}, \ldots, y_j\right)$, and the rule $A_n\left(y_1, \ldots, y_j\right) \rightarrow$ rhs(A_n) is replaced with $A'_n\left(y_1, \ldots, y_j\right) \rightarrow A_n * \left(y_1, \ldots, y_i, ID, y_{i+1}, \ldots, y_j\right)$.

Grammar 5 shows the result of inserting into Grammar 1 the subtree represented by a rule $I(y_1) \rightarrow$ od(ad$(-, -), y_1$) as previous-sibling of the second 'ad'-labeled node of X1:

```
S               ->    cu(od(A1(ip(-,-)),A1'(-)),-)
A1(y1)          ->    A1*(ID,y1)
A1'(y1)         ->    A1*(I,y1)
A1*(z1,y1)      ->    z1(ad(y1,fn(-,ln(-,-))))
I(y1)           ->    od(ad(-,-),y1)
```

Grammar 5 Insert with the help of ECST and ranked parameter z1

Remark. Note that whenever we want to simulate inserting a subtree or a node as the last child of a node V, we first navigate to the nullpointer representing the non-existence of a next-sibling of the last child of V and perform the above defined operations on the position of that nullpointer. Similarly, if we want to insert a subtree or a node as the only child of V, we first navigate to the nullpointer representing the non-existence of a first-child of V. In both cases, the selected terminal v is a nullpointer.

Delete. Let V be a node in X that shall be deleted including all of its descendants (i.e., V and the subtree rooted in V's first-child are deleted and the pointer to V is replaced by a pointer to V's next-sibling). Furthermore, let v be a terminal in rhs(A_n) of a rule $A_n\left(y_1, \ldots, y_j\right) \rightarrow$ rhs(A_n) of G, such that the grammar path GP = $[A_0, p_0, \ldots, A_n, p_n]$ to v represents V. To simulate this delete operation on G, we change the call of A_n at position p_{n-1} within rhs$\left(A'_{n-1}\right)$ into a call of A'_n Then, we create a new rule $A_n * \left(y_1, \ldots, y_i, z, y_{i+1}, \ldots, y_j\right) \rightarrow$ rhs(A_n*), where rhs(A_n*) is rhs(A_n) except that the terminal v at position p_n is replaced by the ranked parameter z $\in$ Z, rank(z) = rank (v) = 2, and the position of z among the parameters of A_n* is so that the parameter order is preserved. Furthermore, we replace the rule $A'_n\left(y_1, \ldots, y_j\right) \rightarrow$ rhs$\left(A'_n\right)$ with the new rule $A'_n \left(y_1, \ldots, y_j \right) \rightarrow A_n * \left(y_1, \ldots, y_i, \text{LP}, y_{i+1}, \ldots, y_j \right)$ and the rule $A_n \left(y_1, \ldots, y_j \right) \rightarrow \text{rhs}(A_n)$ with the new rule $A_n \left(y_1, \ldots, y_j \right) \rightarrow A_n * (y_1, \ldots, y_i, v, y_{i+1}, \ldots, y_j)$.

Grammar 6 shows the result of simulating on Grammar 1 the deletion of the second 'fn'-labeled node in X1 and replacing it by its next-sibling with label 'ln':

```
S                 ->    cu(od(A1(ip(-,-)),A1'(-)),-)
A1(y1)            ->    A1*(y1, fn)
A1'(y1)           ->    A1*(y1, LP)
A1*(y1,z2)        ->    ad(y1,z2(-,ln(-,-)))
```

Grammar 6 Delete with the help of ECST and ranked parameter z2

Whenever the first-child-term fc of node V contains formal parameters $y_1, \ldots, y_k$, using the rule LP leads to a non-linear rule, as the actual parameters for $y_1, \ldots, y_k$ of rule A'_n 'vanish' when calling A'_n. If an application requires a linear grammar, we propose the following solution: we create rule A'_n as $A'_n \rightarrow \text{rhs}(A'_n)$, where $\text{rhs}(A'_n)$ is a copy of $\text{rhs}(A_n)$ except that the term $v(fc,ns)$ at position p_n is replaced by the term ns. Furthermore, we replace the call of A_n at position p_{n-1} in $\text{rhs}(A'_{n-1})$ with A'_n and delete the actual parameters corresponding to $y_j, \ldots, y_k$ within the parameter list of A'_n. We repeat this for rules A_i, $0 \le i < n$, until we reach a rule $A'_i \rightarrow \text{rhs}(A'_i)$, where we do not have to adapt the list of actual parameters. Then, for the rules $A'_0 \rightarrow \text{rhs} \left(A'_0 \right), \ldots, A'_{i-1} \rightarrow \text{rhs}(A'_{i-1})$, we can use the ranked parameters as proposed in Sect. 2.5.

Thereby, we can avoid using the non-linear rules produced by using LP. As a tradeoff, we cannot use the concept of ranked parameters for the rules $A_i*, \ldots, A_n*$.

2.5 Modifying the Grammar Path

In the previous section, we only considered the last rule of the grammar path. However, whenever a rule A_i occurring in GP is called also from outside GP, we have to create a copy A'_i of rule A_i and modify this copy too. Similarly, as for the rule A_n, the copied rule A'_i ($1 \le i < n$) only differs slightly from the original rule A_i, i.e., we only change the call to A_{i+1} at position p_i in A_i into a call of A'_{i+1}.

To overcome the redundancy caused by the similarity of A_i and A'_i, we again make use of ranked parameters. In order to modify rule A_i, we copy $\text{rhs}(A_i)$ as the rhs of a new rule $A_i*(y_1, \ldots, y_i, z, y_{i+1}, \ldots, y_j)$, and replace the call of A'_{i+1} in $\text{rhs}(A_n*)$ by a parameter $z \in Z$. Furthermore, we create a rule $A'_i \left(y_1, \ldots, y_j \right) \rightarrow A_i * (y_1, \ldots, y_i, A'_{i+1}, y_{i+1}, \ldots, y_j)$ and change the $\text{rhs}(A_i)$ into $A_i*(y_1, \ldots, y_i, A_{i+1}, y_{i+1}, \ldots, y_j)$.

As the start rule S is never called, we do not need to copy rule S, but can modify it directly, as we do not need the original version anymore. For this purpose, we change the call to A_1 at position p_0 in S into a call of A'_1.

For example look at Grammar 6. Assume that S was not the start rule of Grammar 6, but was called from rules that are part of the grammar path in Grammar 6 representing the path from X's root node to the modified node, as well as from other rules. This means, that we need the original version of S, i.e., S $\rightarrow$ cu(od(A1(ip($-,-$)), A1($-$)), $-$) as well as the modified version S' $\rightarrow$ cu(od(A1(ip($-,-$)), A1'($-$)), $-$). In order to avoid this redundancy, we define a rule S $*$ (z) $\rightarrow$ cu(od(A1(ip($-,-$)), z($-$)), $-$) and the two versions S $\rightarrow$ S $*$ (A1) and S' $\rightarrow$ S $*$ (A1'). So again, by using the ranked parameter, we have avoided storing parts of the rules S and S' redundantly.

3 Simulating Queries and Updates on ECST Grammars

Up to now, we have shown how to use ECST grammars to perform updates that lead to fewer redundancies than these updates performed on CSLT grammars. Next, we discuss how query evaluation on an XML tree X and update processing of nodes of X selected by queries can be simulated on an ECST grammar G representing X.

3.1 Assumptions and Problem Definition

Let Q be an XPath query, defining the selected node(s) to be updated, G an ECST grammar representing an XML tree X, and O be an update operation to be simulated on G. In order to simplify the presentation, in this paper, we describe the simulation of queries and update operations on G only for XPath queries Q without predicate filters, i.e., we assume that Q is an absolute XPath query consisting of a single, filter-less path only using the forward axes child, descendant, following-sibling. Note however that like our previous XML database system simulated on CSLT grammars [6], this approach simulating XML queries on an ECST grammar G could be adapted to handle backward axes and predicate filters as well.

Furthermore, in order to simplify the presentation, we describe path isolation only for a single path to a node V to be updated. Note however that the ideas of [5] on how to update multiple paths in parallel can be used for ECST grammars as well.

3.2 Overview of the Query Phase and the Update Phase

First, in the query phase, we simulate on G a preorder walk through X, and for each step, we modify the grammar path to the current context node ccn and generate first-child, next-sibling, or parent events. These events are passed to a query automaton QA that represents the query Q. Whenever QA reaches a final accepting state, i.e., the path through X to a node V matches Q, we store the grammar path GP representing V.

Then, in the update phase, we process each grammar path GP that is a result of the query phase by isolating GP as described in Sect. 2.3 and by simulating the update operation O on the terminal selected by GP as described in Sects. 2.4 and 2.5.

3.3 Simulating a Preorder Walk Through X on an ECST Grammars G

Let GP = [A_0, p_0, ..., A_n, p_n] be the grammar path representing a current context node V of X, and let GP refer to a terminal symbol v at position p_n in the grammar rule A_n.

In order to navigate to the first-child (or next-sibling respectively) of node V represented by GP, we consider the first (or second) parameter fp of v representing V's first-child (or next-sibling respectively) that occurs at position $p_n + i$ in A_n. First, we replace p_n in GP by $p_n + i$ yielding the new grammar path GP = $[A_0, p_0, ..., A_n, p_{n+i}]$.

Then, depending on what kind of symbol the parameter fp is, we proceed as follows:

- If fp is a terminal symbol, we found the first-child (or next-sibling respectively).
- If fp is a nullpointer, there exists no first-child (or no next-sibling), and navigation continues with the next-sibling (or parent) of V.
- If fp is a non-terminal symbol NT, we have to retrieve the terminal that is the root of the subtree created by NT. We determine the root terminal by attaching 'NT,1' to GP, i.e., GP becomes GP = $[A_0, p_0, ..., A_n, p_{n+i}, NT, 1]$, and we examine the first symbol fs of the right-hand side of NT. If fs is a terminal, GP already refers to the symbol that we looked for. If fs is a non-terminal symbol, we recursively determine the root terminal of NT.
- Finally, if fp is a formal parameter z, we have to determine the actual parameter ap provided by GP for z, and then find the root terminal symbol for ap as follows.

In order to determine the actual parameter ap provided by a grammar path GP = $[A_0, p_0, ..., A_{n-1}, p_{n-1}, A_n, p_n]$ for a formal parameter z having rank(z) = 0, we delete the last two entries of GP. If z was the ith formal parameter of rule A_n, we determine the position $p_{n-1} + j$ of the ith parameter of the symbol at position p_{n-1} in A_{n-1}, yielding a new grammar path GP = $[A_0, p_0, ..., A_{n-1}, p_{n-1+j}]$. Then, we determine the root terminal as described above.

In order to explain how we determine the actual parameter ap provided by a grammar path GP = $[A_0, p_0, ..., A_n, p_n]$ for a formal parameter z having rank(z) > 0, we first have to extend the concept of the grammar path slightly: The grammar path GP for an ECST grammar EG might temporarily contain also a so called *virtual non-terminal*, i.e., a non-terminal not defined in EG, together with its rule definition.

For example, GP may contain a virtual non-terminal $A1'$ if a rule for $A1'$ is given.

To determine ap provided by a grammar path GP = $[A_0, p_0, ..., A_n, p_n]$ for a formal parameter z having rank(z) > 0 occurring in A_n, we repeatedly follow GP upwards, until we find a symbol SYM different to a parameter z'. Then we substitute A_n in GP by a virtual non-terminal A_n', and define the rule for A_n' of the rule A_n where we replace z by SYM within the definition of A_n'.

To follow GP upwards one step starting at a parameter z means: if z was the ith formal parameter of rule A_k, we determine the position p_{k-1+j} of the ith parameter of the symbol SYM at position p_{k-1} in A_{k-1}. If SYM is a parameter, we follow the grammar path up one further step. If SYM is no parameter, we return SYM. Finally, we continue in the temporal copy A_n' of A_n in the same way as for arbitrary CSLT grammars.

The non-terminal symbols ID and LP only occur as an actual parameter of a ranked parameter. Whenever we have to replace the parameter z by ID in rhs(A') for any rule $A' \rightarrow$ rhs(A') of a virtual non-terminal A', we replace z by the single parameter of ID. Whenever we have to replace the parameter z by LP in rhs(A') for any rule $A' \rightarrow$ rhs(A') of a virtual non-terminal A', we replace z by the last parameter of LP.

For example, consider the Grammar 7 and the grammar path GP1 $= [S, 1, A1, 1]$ referring to a node V1 with label 'b'. When navigating to V1's first-child V2, we get GP2 $= [S, 1, A1, 2]$ referring to a parameter z1. As z1 is the first formal parameter of rhs(A1), its actual value $av = A2$ is the first parameter of nonterminal A1 at position [S,1]. Therefore, we substitute A1 in GP2 by a virtual nonterminal A1', i.e., we set GP2 $= [S, 1, A1', 2]$, and we define a rule A1' $\rightarrow$ rhs(A1'), where rhs(A1') is equal to rhs(A1) except z1 replaced by A2, such that we get A1' $\rightarrow$ b(A2(a($-, -$), ID), $-$). Now we determine the root terminal for rule A2 resulting finally in grammar path GP2 $= [S, 1, A1', 2, A2, 1]$ representing V2 and referring to a terminal symbol 'd'.

In order to simulate navigating to the next-sibling V3 of V2, we start searching at position GP3 $= [S, 1, A1', 2, A2, 3]$. There, we find the formal parameter z2, having its actual value ID in rule A1 of Grammar 7. Therefore, we substitute A2 in GP3 by a virtual nonterminal A2', i.e. we set GP3 $= [S, 1, A1'2, A2', 3]$, and we define a rule A2' $\rightarrow$ rhs(A2'), where rhs(A2') is equal to rhs(A2) except that we replace z2(A3) by ID(A3) which is simplified to A3, leading to the grammar rule A2'(y1) $\rightarrow$ d(y1, A3). As at the third position of A2', we find the nonterminal A3 which has to be expanded too, the resulting grammar path representing V3 is GP3 $= [S, 1, A1', 2, A2', 3, A3, 1]$ referring to a terminal symbol 'f'.

```
S              -> A1(A2)
A1(z1)         -> b(z1(a(-,-),ID),-)
A2(y1,z2)      -> d(y1,z2(A3))
A3             -> f(-,-)
```

Grammar 7. Example used to show the navigation within ECST grammars

3.4   Computing the Grammar Paths for Answers to a Query Q

We simulate the evaluation of an XPath query Q on an XML tree X represented by a grammar G as follows. We simulate a pre-order walk through the XML tree X on G and thereby modify the grammar path GP that represents the path from X's root to the current context node ccn of X and, in the same steps, produce first-child, next-sibling, or parent events. These events are passed to a query automaton QA that represents the query Q and reaches a final accepting state whenever the event sequence processed by QA represents an answer to Q, i.e. a path through X to a node that matches Q.

QA is implemented in a way that it processes first-child and next-sibling events by changing active states, whereas it processes parent events by using an additional stack as follows. Whenever the simulated preorder walk through X steps from the current context node ccn to its first-child (by a first-child event), QA pushes the set of currently active states on the stack, from which these states are popped and reactivated as soon as the simulated preorder walk through X returns back to ccn by a parent event before visiting the next-sibling of ccn. A detailed description on how to build the automaton, how to produce the events, and how to process the events is given in [7].

Query evaluation simulated on G can be optimized like query evaluation on X as follows. Whenever during query evaluation, there is no active state of QA that can fire for a first-child event, the simulated preorder walk can skip the subtree rooted in the first-child of the current context node ccn and continue query evaluation directly with ccn's next-sibling. While in traditional query evaluation, this optimization allows us to skip parts of X, in the query evaluation simulated on G, we can skip reading and unnecessarily decompressing parts of G.

4 Related Work

There are several approaches to XML structure compression which can be mainly divided into the categories: encoding-based, schema-based or grammar-based compressors.

Encoding-based compressors (e.g. [8–10], XMill [11], XPRESS [12], and XGrind [13]) allow for a faster compression speed than the other compressors, as only local data has to be considered in the compression in comparison to grammar-based compressors which consider different subtrees.

Schema-based compressors (e.g. XCQ [14], Xenia [15], and XSDS [16]) subtract the given schema information from the structural information and only generate and output information not already contained in the schema information.

XQzip [17] and the approaches [18] and [4] belong to *grammar-based* compression. They compress the data structure of an XML document by combining identical subtrees. An extension of [4] and [17] are e.g. CluX [1], BPLEX [2], and TreeRePAIR [3] that not only combine identical subtrees, but recognize similar patterns within the XML tree, and therefore allows a higher degree of compression. The approaches [6], [19] and [20] follow different approaches on how to compute updates on grammar-compressed XML data. A generalization of grammar-based compression to functional programs representing the compressed tree data was presented in [21].

In order to eliminate the redundancies caused by performing updates, a recompression of the updated grammar as proposed in [22] might be performed.

In contrast, we propose using ECST grammars instead of CSLT grammars, such that the overhead can be avoided, instead of eliminating it afterwards.

5 Summary and Conclusions

We proposed extended context-free straight-line tree (ECST) grammars, an extension of CSLT grammars, for compressing XML documents. In contrast to CSLT grammars, ECST grammars allow parameters having a rank greater than 0. They can be used for avoiding redundancies after path isolation which is required for simulating update operations on the grammar.

In this paper, we have not only discussed, how to use ECST grammars to improve the evaluation of updates on grammar-compressed XML data, but furthermore, we presented an approach, how to evaluate queries and updates on ECST grammars.

We assume that ECST grammars are a promising extension of the standard CSLT grammars, allowing in general even better compression ratios.

References

1. Böttcher, S., Hartel, R., Krislin, C.: CluX - Clustering XML sub-trees. In: ICEIS 2010, Funchal, Madeira, Portugal (2010)
2. Busatto, G., Lohrey, M., Maneth, S.: Efficient memory representation of XML documents. In: Bierman, G., Koch, C. (eds.) DBPL 2005. LNCS, vol. 3774, pp. 199–216. Springer, Heidelberg (2005)
3. Lohrey, M., Maneth, S., Mennicke, R.: Tree structure compression with repair. In: DCC 2011, Snowbird, UT, USA (2011)
4. Buneman, P., Grohe, M., Koch, C.: Path queries on compressed XML. In: VLDB 2003, Berlin, Germany (2003)
5. Bätz, A., Böttcher, S., Hartel, R.: Updates on grammar-compressed XML data. In: Fernandes, A.A.A., Gray, A.J.G., Belhajjame, K. (eds.) BNCOD 2011. LNCS, vol. 7051, pp. 154–166. Springer, Heidelberg (2011)
6. Böttcher, S., Hartel, R., Jacobs, T.: Fast multi-update operations on compressed XML data. In: Gottlob, G., Grasso, G., Olteanu, D., Schallhart, C. (eds.) BNCOD 2013. LNCS, vol. 7968, pp. 149–164. Springer, Heidelberg (2013)
7. Böttcher, S., Steinmetz, R.: Evaluating XPath queries on XML data streams. In: Cooper, R., Kennedy, J. (eds.) BNCOD 2007. LNCS, vol. 4587, pp. 101–113. Springer, Heidelberg (2007)
8. Zhang, N., Kacholia, V., Özsu, M.: A succinct physical storage scheme for efficient evaluation of path queries in XML. In: ICDE 2004, Boston, MA, USA (2004)
9. Cheney, J.: Compressing XML with multiplexed hierarchical PPM models. In: DCC 2001, Snowbird, Utah, USA (2001)
10. Girardot, M., Sundaresan, N.: Millau: an encoding format for efficient representation and exchange of XML over the Web. Comput. Netw. **33**, 747–765 (2000)
11. Liefke, H., Suciu, D.: XMILL: an efficient compressor for XML data. In: SIGMOD 2000, Dallas, Texas, USA (2000)
12. Min, J.-K., Park, M.-J., Chung, C.-W.: XPRESS: a queriable compression for XML data. In: SIGMOD 2003, San Diego, California, USA (2003)
13. Tolani, P., Haritsa, J.: XGRIND: a query-friendly XML compressor. In: ICDE 2002, San Jose, CA (2002)
14. Ng, W., Lam, W., Wood, P., Levene, M.: XCQ: a queriable XML compression system. Knowl. Inf. Syst. **10**, 421–452 (2006)
15. Werner, C., Buschmann, C., Brandt, Y., Fischer, S.: Compressing SOAP messages by using pushdown automata. In: ICWS 2006, Chicago, Illinois, USA (2006)
16. Böttcher, S., Hartel, R., Messinger, C.: XML stream data reduction by shared KST signatures. In: HICSS-42 2009, Waikoloa, Big Island, HI, USA (2009)
17. Cheng, J., Ng, W.: XQzip: querying compressed XML using structural indexing. In: Bertino, E., Christodoulakis, S., Plexousakis, D., Christophides, V., Koubarakis, M., Böhm, K. (eds.) EDBT 2004. LNCS, vol. 2992, pp. 219–236. Springer, Heidelberg (2004)
18. Adiego, J., Navarro, G., Fuente, P.: Lempel-ziv compression of structured text. In: DCC 2004, Snowbird, UT, USA (2004)
19. Fisher, D., Maneth, S.: Structural selectivity estimation for XML documents. In: ICDE 2007, Istanbul, Turkey (2007)
20. Fisher, D., Maneth, S.: Selectivity Estimation. Patent WO 2007/134407 A1, May 2007
21. Kobayashi, N., Matsuda, K., Shinohara, A., Yaguchi, K.: Functional programs as compressed data. High.-Order Symbolic Comput. **25**(1), 39–84 (2012)
22. Böttcher, S., Hartel, R., Jacobs, T., Maneth, S.: OnlineRePair: a recompressor for XML structures. In: Poster Paper, DCC, Snow Bird, Utah, USA (2015)

Configuring Spatial Grids for Efficient Main Memory Joins

Farhan Tauheed[2], Thomas Heinis[1], and Anastasia Ailamaki[2(✉)]

[1] Imperial College London, London, UK
[2] DIAS - Data-Intensive Applications and Systems Lab, École Polytechnique
Fédérale de Lausanne (EPFL), Lausanne, Switzerland
anastasia.ailamaki@epfl.ch

Abstract. The performance of spatial joins is becoming increasingly important in many applications, particularly in the scientific domain. Several approaches have been proposed for joining spatial datasets on disk and few in main memory. Recent results show that in main memory, grids are more efficient than the traditional tree based methods primarily developed for disk. The question how to configure the grid, however, has so far not been discussed.

In this paper we study how to configure a spatial grid for joining spatial data in main memory. We discuss the trade-offs involved, develop an analytical model predicting the performance of a configuration and finally validate the model with experiments.

1 Introduction

Spatial joins are an operation of increasing importance in many applications. Whether for spatial datasets from astronomy, neuroscience, medicine or others, the join has to be performed to find objects that intersect with each other or are within a given distance of each other (distance join). An efficient execution of this operation is therefore key to improve overall performance.

In this context main memory joins are becoming increasingly important because many datasets fit into the main memory directly. Even if they do not, and the join has to be performed on disk, a crucial part of a disk-based join is the in memory join. While the strategies of disk-based approaches to partition the data (replication or no replication, space-oriented partitioning or data-oriented partitioning) so it fits into memory differ [1], every approach requires an efficient algorithm to join two partitions in main memory.

The only approaches specifically designed to join spatial data in memory are the nested loop join and plane sweep join approach. The nested loop join technique works by comparing all spatial elements pairwise and is thus computationally very expensive. The plane sweep approach [2] sorts the datasets in one dimension and scans both datasets synchronously with a sweep plane. It has a lower time complexity but compares objects no matter how far apart they are on the sweep plane.

© Springer International Publishing Switzerland 2015
S. Maneth (Ed.): BICOD 2015, LNCS 9147, pp. 199–205, 2015.
DOI: 10.1007/978-3-319-20424-6_19

To speed up the join time over these two slow approaches, tried and tested tree-based indexing techniques on disk have been optimized for main memory. Although these approaches indeed improve performance, recent research shows that a simple grid performs best to join for one-off spatial joins in memory [3]. The problem of configuring the grid optimally, however, is challenging and remains unaddressed to date.

In this paper we therefore develop a cost model that can be used to configure the grid optimally. With experiments we show that the cost model can accurately predict the performance of the join.

2   Grid-Based Spatial Join

Spatial joins are typically split into two phases, filtering and refinement [4]. The filtering phase uses a coarse grained collision detection and finds intersections between approximations of the actual objects. The refinement phase, is used to remove the false positive by using an exact, but time-consuming object-object collision test. The refinement phase is a computationally costly operation with little room for improvement and so, like other approaches for spatial joins [4], the spatial grid-based spatial join focuses on improving the filtering phase.

On a high level, the grid-based spatial join tackles the filtering phase with a three dimensional uniform grid and uses it as an approximate method to group spatially close objects. In the building step we map the MBRs of the objects of both datasets on a grid while the probing step retrieves MBRs from the same cells (which are thus close together) and compares them pairwise.

In the following we first explain the two steps, i.e., building and probing.

2.1   Building Step

The algorithm iterates over both sets of objects and for each object calculates its MBR and maps it on the uniform grid. The mapping process finds the grid cells that intersect with the MBR volume and creates a pointer from each intersecting grid cell to the MBR. By using a uniform grid we simplify the calculation of the mapping of MBR to cell and can calculate the list of intersecting grid cells efficiently as follows. First, we use the minimum and maximum coordinate of the MBR to find the minimum and maximum grid cell intersecting it. Second, we use a nested loop to iterate over all the grid cells bounded by these minimum and maximum grid cell.

The mapping of MBR to grid cells is ambivalent as one MBR can also map to several grid cells. To store this many-many relationship between the MBR and the grid cell we use a hashmap which maps a list of pointers to a grid cell identifier. To map an MBR we access the list of pointers for each intersecting grid cell and insert the pointer in their respective list. Apart from providing a fast access mechanism to the list of pointers the hash table also helps to reduce the memory footprint as only grid cells containing one or more pointers to an MBR require an entry in the hash map and no memory is wasted in storing empty grid cells.

2.2   Probing Step

The probing step of the algorithm retrieves the mapped MBRs of the two objects sets from the grid. The algorithm iterates over all the grid cells and separately retrieves all the MBRs in the cell. For each cell it then compares all MBRs representing objects from the first dataset with all MBRs representing objects from the second dataset.

Because MBRs can be mapped to several cells, intersections between the same pair of MBR's may be detected multiple times. This leads to (a) additional computational overhead (because of additional comparisons) and (b) duplicate results. The spatial grid-based spatial join thus use a global (across all grid cells) set based data structure in a postprocessing step to deduplicate the results before reporting them.

3   Configuring the Grid-Based Spatial Join

As we discuss in the following, the performance of the algorithm we propose for filtering depends on the configuration, i.e., the grid resolution used, as well as the data distribution.

3.1   Impact of Data Skew

Uniform grids are very sensitive to data skew and using them in spatial join algorithm can lead to performance degradation because in dense regions the number of MBRs mapped on a grid cell increases and consequently the number of comparisons required increases too. All MBRs may be mapped to one single grid cell. In this scenario the performance of spatial grid hash join becomes equivalent to a nested loop join because all MBRs need to be compared pairwise and the total number of comparisons is $O(n^2)$. Even worse, all MBRs may be mapped to the same multiple cells and the nested loop is executed comparing the same MBRs several times (resulting in duplicates that need to be eliminated).

The problem of data skew can be addressed by setting a finer grid resolution. With a finer grid resolution also the objects or their MBRs in very dense regions of the datasets will be distributed to numerous grid cells instead of just a few. As we will discuss in the next section, the resolution, however, cannot be set infinitely fine-grained, but reducing the cell size still helps to address the problem of data skew.

3.2   Impact of Grid Resolution

Changing the grid resolution, i.e., making it coarser or finer grained directly affects the performance of the algorithm.

In case of a fine resolution, an MBR is likely to be mapped to many grid cells and the memory footprint therefore increases. This also leads to degraded performance because more comparisons need to be performed in the probing phase. The number of comparisons increases because MBRs mapped to several cells need to be compared more than once.

In case the resolution is coarse, each grid cell contains many MBRs and hence the performance degrades because all MBRs in the same grid cell need to be compared pairwise, thereby increasing the number of comparisons. A coarse resolution, however, lowers the memory consumption of the algorithm because an MBR is less likely to be mapped to many grid cells, thereby reducing duplication (even if pointers are used). Additionally, the probability of comparing the same pair of MBRs several times because they are assigned to several cells (as is the problem of a fine resolution) is considerably reduced, reducing the overall number of comparisons.

Both extremes have advantages and disadvantages and it is difficult to set the resolution intuitively. In the following we therefore develop an analytical model that will predict the optimal grid resolution for two sets of objects in terms of number of total comparisons.

3.3   Analytical Model

To determine the optimal resolution we develop a cost model for predicting the time for the join. Like our algorithm we also split the cost model into building and probing costs.

Building Cost. The building phase loops over the MBR of each of the N_d objects in the first dataset and for each MBR finds the intersecting grid cells using the *getCell* (gC) function. For each cell a *hashLookup* (hL) is performed to obtain the list of pointers that point to the MBR and in the end the pointer of the current MBR is added to the list using *insertPointer* (iP). The resulting cost is summarized in the following equation with C_i as the number of cells an MBR intersects with:

$$BuildingCost = \sum_{i=1}^{N_d} \left\{ gC(MBR_i) + \sum_{j=1}^{C_i} [hL(j) + iP(\&MBR_i)] \right\} \quad (1)$$

The cost of the *getCell* (gC) function is defined as follows:

$$gC(MBR_i) = \sum_{j=1}^{C_i} vertexToGridCell(j)$$

To determine the actual building cost we need to know the duration of each individual operation and the number of iterations of each loop. *vertexToGridCell* and *insertPointer* both are constant time operations and for the sake of simplicity we also assume *hashLookup* to be a constant time operation (this essentially means we use a tuned hash table which is collision-free). The execution time of all these operations heavily depends on the hardware platform they are executed on. We use microbenchmarks to determine their execution time.

N_d, the number of objects in the first dataset, is a given and *Average(C)*, the number of cells an average object's MBR maps to, is calculated as follows (instead of calculating C_i for each object we use an approximation, i.e., *Average(C)*).

Average(C), the number of cells an average MBR_i maps to depends on the average volume of the MBR and on the grid resolution. On average, the MBR of an object particular MBR_i the number of cells it is mapped to, can be approximated by $Volume(MBR_i)/Volume(gridCell)$. This, however, is only an approximation and it underestimates the number of grid cells because the exact number of grid cells intersecting depends on the exact loation of MBR_i relative to the grid cells. If MBR_i is exactly aligned with the grid cell then the combined volume of the grid cell is equal to the volume of MBR_i. If, however, MBR_i is not aligned, then the combined volume of the grid cell is greater than the volume of MBR_i to at most the volume of a single grid cell.

To resolve this issue we expand the volume of MBR_i by half the volume of a single grid cell, to get a better approximation for the average case.

$$Total(C) = \sum_{i=1}^{N_d} \left\{ \frac{Volume(MBR_i) + Volume(gridCell)/2}{Volume(gridCell)} \right\}$$

$$Average(C) = Total(C)/N_d$$

Probing Cost. Similar to the building step, the probing step loops over each object in the second dataset. For each object the algorithm finds the list of cells intersecting the MBR of the object. However, instead of mapping the MBR on the grid, the probing step retrieves the mapped MBRs from the first dataset for testing the overlap.

$$ProbingCost = \sum_{i=1}^{N_a} \left\{ gC(MBR_i) + \sum_{j=1}^{C_i} \left[hL(j) + \sum_{k=1}^{S_j} (oT(i,k) + dD()) \right] \right\} \tag{2}$$

The operations of the probing step are *overlapTest* (oT), which compares two MBRs for overlap, and *deduplication* (dD), which uses a hash based set to remove duplicate results. We consider both these operations as constant time operations, because we assume a near collision free hash set for our estimates. The number of iterations of the loop N_a is the size of the outer data set.

Similar to the building cost model, we use *Average(C)* to approximate the number of grid cells that intersect with the MBRs of the outer data set.

To estimate S_j we use an approximation $Average(S)$. $Average(S)$ is the number of first dataset objects mapped to grid cells, but only the grid cell which intersects the MBRs of objects of the second dataset.

The probing step typically takes the majority of the total time of the join. Setting the resolution optimally therefore has a substantial impact on the performance of the overall algorithm. By using a increasingly fine resolutions, the cell volume decreases, this increases the number of grid cells that intersect the MBR of the outer dataset and hence the performance degrades. At the same time, however, the number of overlap test comparisons decreases because we do not compare objects for overlap which are not located spatially close.

3.4   Optimal Grid Resolution

The sum of both cost models is a concave up curve and the local minimum and hence the optimal value is where the first derivative is equal to zero. To validate the model we have tested it using experiments where we vary the grid cell size. For the experiments we use neuroscience data where 4.5 million cylinders model 1692 neurons and we use the experimental setup described in [5].

In Fig. 1 (a) we measure the individual components (build & probe) as well as the total time of the join. Clearly, for both components there is an optimal (at the same grid cell size) where the join is executed the fastest. The second experiment (Fig. 1 (b)) plots the total execution time against the analytical model and shows that the model can indeed be used to accurately predict the performance and thus to determine the grid configuration.

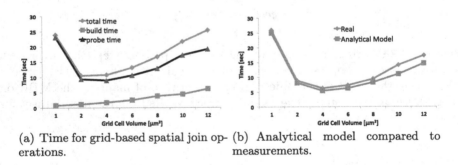

(a) Time for grid-based spatial join operations.   (b) Analytical model compared to measurements.

Fig. 1. Validating the analytical model of the grid-based spatial join.

4   Conclusions

Whether in disk- or in memory spatial joins, the main memory join is a crucial operation. Recent research demonstrated that grid-based approaches outperform tree-based ones in main memory [3], but the question of how to set the optimal resolution remains unaddressed. In this paper we described our implementation of a grid-based spatial join and, crucially, developed and analytical model to predict performance. Our experimental results show that with little information about the datasets to be joined as well as the underlying hardware, the model accurately predicts performance. While it may be difficult to estimate the execution of individual operations, microbenchmarks can be used to find accurate values. Even in the absence of the cost of the operations, the model can still give insight into how to configure the grid for optimal performance.

References

1. Jacox, E.H., Samet, H.: Spatial join techniques. ACM TODS **32**(1), 1–44 (2007)
2. Preparata, F., Shamos, M.: Computational Geometry: An Introduction. Springer, New York (1993)
3. Šidlauskas, D., Jensen, C.S.: Spatial joins in main memory: implementation matters! In: VLDB 2015 (2015)
4. Orenstein, J.: A comparison of spatial query processing techniques for native and parameter spaces. In: SIGMOD 1990 (1990)
5. Tauheed, F., Biveinis, L., Heinis, T., Schürmann, F., Markram, H., Ailamaki, A.: Accelerating range queries for brain simulations. In: ICDE 2012 (2012)

Transactional and Incremental Type Inference from Data Updates

Yu Liu[✉] and Peter McBrien

Department of Computing, Imperial College London, London, UK
{yu.liu11,p.mcbrien}@imperial.ac.uk

Abstract. A distinctive property of relational database systems is the ability to perform data updates and queries in atomic blocks called transactions, with the well known ACID properties. To date, the ability of systems performing reasoning to maintain the ACID properties even over data held within a relational database, has been largely ignored. This paper studies an approach to reasoning over data from OWL 2 ontologies held in a relational database, where the ACID properties of transactions are maintained. Taking an incremental approach to maintaining materialised views of the result of reasoning, the approach is demonstrated to support a query and reasoning performance comparable to or better than other OWL reasoning systems, yet adding the important benefit of supporting transactions.

Keywords: OWL · Incremental reasoning · DBMS transactions · ACID properties · Materialised views

1 Introduction

Many approaches to reasoning over knowledge bases take a query-rewriting approach (e.g. Ontop [1], Stardog [14], DLDB [13]), where a query over the knowledge base is rewritten to a (often complex) query over the base facts in the knowledge base. When the number of queries made on the knowledge base greatly exceeds the number of updates, it might be more efficient to adopt a **materialised** approach (e.g. OWLim [6], WebPIE [17], RDFox [12], Oracle's RDF store [18], Minerva [19]), where the extent of the knowledge base is calculated after updates to the knowledge base, and hence queries are answered directly from the inferred facts.

Even if data is stored in a relational database, such as in Minerva, the reasoning in materialised approaches is normally conducted outside of the core RDBMS engine, and hence fails to provide **transactional reasoning** [7]. In transactional reasoning, the result of reasoning from data is available at the commit of any transaction that inserts or deletes data, and hence reasoning obeys the normal ACID properties of transactions.

This paper considers reasoning over knowledge bases expressed in OWL 2 RL [10]. It restricts itself to consider the issue of efficiently handling ontology

© Springer International Publishing Switzerland 2015
S. Maneth (Ed.): BICOD 2015, LNCS 9147, pp. 206–219, 2015.
DOI: 10.1007/978-3-319-20424-6_20

queries where there are updates occurring to the A-Box (in database terms the data) and not to the T-Box, and the number of queries greatly exceeds the number of updates. Hence, the reasoning performed is **type inference** (i.e. deriving for each instance its membership of classes and properties), and it adopts a materialised approach. This paper sets out to provide transactional type inference for ontologies held in an RDBMS, providing type inference over OWL 2 RL ontologies that can fully integrate with the data of existing RDBMS applications, and maintain the full ACID properties of transactions.

To illustrate the issues addressed, consider a T-Box with three rules:

$$\text{Man} \sqsubseteq \text{Person} \quad (1) \qquad \text{Parent} \sqsubseteq \text{Human} \quad (2) \qquad \text{Person} \equiv \text{Human} \quad (3)$$

which define that (1) every man is a person, (2) every parent is a human, and (3) a person is equivalent to a human. Now suppose that A-Box for the ontology is held as four tables Man, Parent, Person and Human in a database, and four transactions, T_1 inserting **Man(John)**, T_2 inserting **Parent(John)**, T_3 deleting **Parent(John)**, and finally T_4 deleting **Man(John)**, are executed. The expected changes of the database are illustrated in Fig. 1.

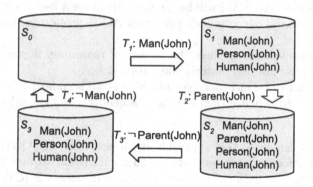

Fig. 1. Example of transactional and incremental type inference

The first transaction T_1 should change the state of the database from S_0 to S_1. After executing T_1, John should be viewed not only from Man but also from Person and Human, because John should be inferred as both a Person and a Human as a result of rules (1) and (3). Transactional type inference requires that any other transaction T_c concurrent with T_1 should view the database either as S_0 or S_1, but not any intermediate state. For example, the query Man(John) $\wedge \neg$Person(John) should always evaluate to false in T_c. With regards to deletes, T_3, which only deletes **Parent(John)**, should not delete inferred facts Person(John) or Human(John), since Man(John) and rules (1) and (3) can still infer them (i.e. the database is changed to S_3). However, the same inferred facts must be deleted when **Man(John)** is deleted in T_4.

Furthermore, we need to reject user attempts to delete implicit facts. For example, when in database states S_1, S_2 or S_3, allowing a user to delete

Person(John) would make the knowledge base inconsistent, and therefore such an update must be rejected.

Our approach is based on **incremental** type inference, and the **Delete & Rederive (DRed)** algorithm [4] for incrementally maintaining materialised views (which might be recursive when considering OWL 2 RL). DRed does not keep any additional information at the stage of materialising derived facts. When deleting explicit facts from base relations which form the materialised view, it first 'over deletes' all facts from the view which can be derived from the deleted facts, and then rederives some facts which are still inferable from the remaining facts. Hence, this algorithm is inefficient when derived facts have many different derivations and have relations to other inferred facts [11]. In this paper, we present a variant of DRed, and outline our implementation of this variant as RDBMS triggers, which support transactional and incremental type inference. Our approach has the following advantages:

- We assign each fact a state when materialising data. Then, deletions over the database invoke triggers to update the state of related facts, which reduces the number of real deletes and reinserts.
- The triggers in the RDBMS will be invoked whenever a user updates the database; consequently, our approach preserves ACID properties over the results of reasoning.
- Since our approach materialises the results of reasoning, it processes queries more efficiently than non-materialising approaches.
- Our approach can be incorporated into almost all standard RDBMS applications, in order to enhance their database schemas with type inference reasoning.

We have implemented this approach as an extension of SQOWL [8], which provided type inference over only inserts to an RDBMS, to now perform type inference over both inserts and deletes. We call our system SQOWL2, and provide this first RDBMS-based system supporting transactional and incrementally materialised type inference. We show that the completeness of query processing is comparable to the same task for other rule-based engines (e.g. OWLim). In addition, SQOWL's query processing is shown to be more efficient than comparable systems (i.e. Stardog and OWLim).

The remainder of the paper is organised as follows. Section 2 demonstrates our approach, especially the process of generating triggers, which are then used for incremental type inference. Section 3 describes the implementation details of our approach in SQOWL and Sect. 4 evaluates this implementation. Section 5 provides a brief summary of similar systems, and finally, Sect. 6 concludes this paper.

2   Our Approach

This section describes what we call an **auto type inference database (ATIDB)**. Our approach separates the T-Box and A-Box reasoning as shown in Fig. 2. Whilst this separation does entail that the reasoning of a system is not complete, it is not uncommon in other large-scale reasoners, and as documented in Sect. 4, the completeness achieved matches that of other approaches.

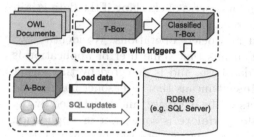

Fig. 2. Approach architecture   **Fig. 3.** Data state transitions

The T-Box of an ontology is firstly classified by a tableaux-based reasoner, in order to obtain complete subsumption relationships w.r.t. the T-Box. For example, a T-Box rule Father ≡ Man ⊓ Parent, can be classified as three subsumption rules: Father ⊑ Man, Father ⊑ Parent and Man ⊓ Parent ⊑ Father.

This classified T-Box is used to establish an ATIDB (with relational tables and SQL triggers). Classes and properties in the classified T-Box are used to generate a basic database schema. Classes are represented as unary relations denoted as C(id) (e.g. Man ⤳ Man(id)), and properties are translated into binary relations denoted as P(domain,range). Axioms in the classified T-Box are used for generating SQL triggers, which here we present as **event condition action** (**ECA**) rules: **when** ⟨event⟩ **if** ⟨condition⟩ **then** ⟨action⟩ associated with the relational tables.

With the triggers created, the ATIDB is ready to accept any A-Box rules as inserts and deletes expressed in SQL. The triggers automatically perform type inference from these updates in the same transaction in which the updates are made. Should the reasoning performed in a trigger discover any inconsistency, then it can perform a rollback, causing the original update to be rejected.

- For inserts to the database, triggers will ignore repeated inserts in order to avoid duplications. It is possible that triggers may cascade, in order to infer additional data from other inferred data.
- For deletes from the database, a **label & check** process is performed to first recursively label all items of data that might be deleted because of this transaction, and then to check as to whether the labelled data can still be inferred or not from unlabelled data. If an item of labelled data is still inferable, then we keep this data item; otherwise, we remove the data.

2.1   The State of Each Data Item

In the ATIDB, each value x in the domain of a class C might become a logical fact C(x). We view C(x) as passing through four states as outlined in Fig. 3.

A fact might not hold and hence is not in the database $(C(x)_\emptyset)$, a fact might be explicitly stored because an explicit A-Box rule asserts it $(C(x)_e)$, or a fact might be implicitly inferred from other facts $(C(x)_i)$. Our method of deleting data introduces a fourth state $(C(x)_d)$, where the data has lost one of the supporting arguments for being in the database, and a process of checking if the data is still inferable from other data is being conducted.

The state can be changed by insert and delete operations. We identify two classes of insert. An **ontology insert** means that some user or application is inserting a new explicit fact into the database, and is detected by the trigger when $C(x)_e$. By contrast, a **reasoner insert** means that a reasoner has derived some implicit fact from the existing facts in the database, and is detected by the trigger when $C(x)_i$. Similarly, an **ontology delete** is some user or application deleting an explicit fact from the database, and is detected by when $\neg C(x)_e$, and a **reasoner delete** is when some supporting evidence for a fact has been deleted, detected in triggers by when $\neg C(x)_i$. Figure 3 gives an overview of the possible state transitions which can occur. For inserts:

- For a data item which is not present in the table, $C(x)_\emptyset$, an ontology insert of $C(x)_e$ updates $C(x)_\emptyset$ to $C(x)_e$, and a reasoner insert of $C(x)_i$ changes $C(x)_\emptyset$ to $C(x)_i$.
- For a data item implicitly stored, $C(x)_i$, further reasoner inserts of $C(x)_i$, do not change the state, so that repeated inference of other facts based on $C(x)_i$ is avoided. However, inserting $C(x)_e$ gives explicit semantics, and thus updates $C(x)_i$ to $C(x)_e$.
- For a data item explicitly stored, $C(x)_e$, inserting $C(x)_i$ does not change the state, in order to avoid duplicated inference. However, to implement normal database semantics, a rollback occurs if further attempts are made to insert $C(x)_e$.

For deletes:

- For a data item $C(x)_\emptyset$, ontology or reasoner deletes are ignored, to match the normal database semantics that deletes of data not present cause no errors.
- For a data item $C(x)_i$, attempting an ontology delete $\neg C(x)_e$ causes inconsistencies since the assertion of being no $C(x)$ conflicts with what can be inferred from other facts, and the transaction should be rolled back. The reasoner delete $\neg C(x)_i$, by contrast, changes $C(x)_i$ to $C(x)_d$, in order to label the data for rechecking.
- For a data item $C(x)_e$, attempting the ontology delete $\neg C(x)_e$ changes it to $C(x)_d$, because the data might still be inferable even after removing the explicit semantics. However, a reasoner delete $\neg C(x)_i$ does not change the state, since only ontology deletes can remove the explicit semantics.

Note that, when the state of $C(x)$ is updated to d, a recursive labelling process is conducted to implicitly delete other data which depends on $C(x)_d$. When the whole labelling process is finished, all data items labelled with d are checked as to whether they are inferable from data in state e or i. If they are still inferable, we change $C(x)_d$ to $C(x)_i$; otherwise, $C(x)_d$ is updated to $C(x)_\emptyset$ (i.e. deleted from the database).

2.2 Transactional and Incremental Type Inference by Triggers

Now, we demonstrate for the example in the introduction how our approach can achieve type inference in an incremental manner.

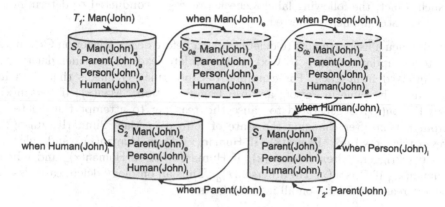

Fig. 4. T_1: insert Man(John) and T_2: insert Parent(John)

Figure 4 first shows the trigger events as the database passes from S_0 to S_1 through two intermediate database states S_{0_a} and S_{0_b}, whilst executing T_1. Firstly, the attempt to insert Man(John)$_e$ is checked by a 'before trigger' (indicated by the $^-$ prefix) **when** $^-$Man$(x)_e$ **if** $\neg$Man$(x)_e$ **then** Man$(x)_e$. Since Man(John)$_\emptyset$ is true, the insert is permitted, and the database enters S_{0_a}. Rule (1) is translated into an 'after trigger' (denoted by the $^+$ prefix) **when** $^+$Man$(x)_{eVi}$ **then** Person$(x)_i$. Thus, after Man(John)$_e$ is inserted, this trigger is invoked to infer a reasoner insert of Person(John)$_i$, updating S_{0_a} to S_{0_b}.

An equivalent relationship between two classes can be treated as two subsumption relations; therefore, rule (3) is translated into two triggers: **when** $^+$Person$(x)_{eVi}$ **then** Human$(x)_i$ and **when** $^+$Human$(x)_{eVi}$ **then** Person$(x)_i$. After the database is updated to the intermediate state S_{0_b}, the insert of Person(John)$_i$ causes the attempt to insert Human(John)$_i$, which changes Human(John)$_\emptyset$ to Human(John)$_i$ (i.e. S_{0_b} is updated to S_1). The insert of Human(John)$_i$ generates the attempt to insert Person(John)$_i$ again because of the after insert trigger on Human. However, the attempt to insert Person(John)$_i$ is ignored, because Person(John)$_i$ is true in S_1 (i.e. the database stays at S_1).

Figure 4 then illustrates the process of executing T_2, which inserts Parent(John) . T_2 first attempts to insert Parent(John)$_e$, which updates the state of Parent(John) from $\emptyset$ to e (i.e. S_1 is updated to S_2). Afterwards, the after insert trigger on Parent generates a new reasoner insert of Human(John)$_i$, which is then ignored by the before insert trigger on Human, since Human(John)$_i$ is already true (i.e. the database stays at S_2).

Attempting ontology deletes of data in state i without removing explicit facts which infer them causes inconsistencies in the database. Thus, from the Person we design a 'before trigger' **when** $^-\neg$Person(x)$_e$ **if** Person(x)$_i$ **then** rollback so that attempting the ontology delete to Person(John)$_i$ results in the rollback of the transaction. In fact, we only allow users to delete explicit facts, C(x)$_e$ or P(x,y)$_e$. As a fact in state e may also be implicitly stated, when executing ontology deletes to such a fact, the following label &check process is conducted to determine if the fact is still implicitly inferred.

Label: when a user attempts to delete C(x)$_e$, a before delete trigger on C changes this to an update of C(x)$_e$ to C(x)$_d$. This update leads to reasoner deletes to data inferred from C(x)$_e$. For example, because rule (1) means that data in Man infers the same in Person, an after triggers **when** $^+$Man(x)$_d$ **if** Person(x)$_i$ **then** Person(x)$_d$ is generated to cause the reasoner to attempt the delete of x from Person after changing the state of x to d in Man. Similarly, rule (2), gives a trigger **when** $^+$Parent(x)$_d$ **if** Human(x)$_i$ **then** Human(x)$_d$, and rule (3) gives two triggers **when** $^+$Person(x)$_d$ **if** Human(x)$_i$ **then** Human(x)$_d$ and **when** $^+$Human(x)$_d$ **if** Person(x)$_i$ **then** Person(x)$_d$. Thus an ontology delete cascades to attempt reasoner deletes on all inferred facts.

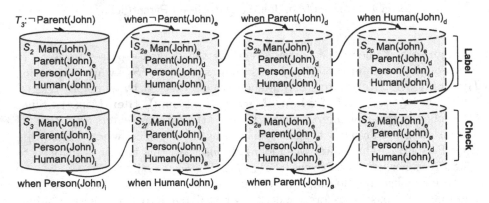

Fig. 5. T_3: delete Parent(John)

Thus, as shown in Fig. 5, T_3, deleting Parent(John), first changes Parent(John)$_e$ to Parent(John)$_d$ as shown from S_2 to S_{2_a}. Then, a reasoner delete of Human(John)$_i$ is generated, which leads to the change of Human(John)$_i$ to Human(John)$_d$ (i.e. S_{2_a} to S_{2_b}). Similarly, after S_{2_b}, the trigger created on Human for labelling causes reasoner delete of Person(John)$_i$, changing its state to Person(John)$_d$. The labelling process is finished as the database becomes S_{2_c}.

Check: All data items with the state d are checked to determine if they can be inferred from the data labelled with i or e. If so, the d is changed to i, otherwise d is changed to ∅. In order to perform the check, we create for each table a datalog-style **inference rule** (with heads $C_{IQ}(x)$ or $P_{IQ}(x,y)$), that contains all the inference logic for the table. The checking is then conducted by the following trigger created on each table: **when** $^+C(x)_d$ **if** $C_{IQ}(x)$ **then** $C(x)_i$ **else** $C(x)_\emptyset$. Obviously, if there is no way to infer data to a table, the inference rule is omitted. For example, when only considering rules (1)–(3), there are no inference rules for tables Man and Parent. The inference rule of Person or Human contains two parts as data can be inferred from the subclass table and the equivalent class table:

$Person_{IQ}(x):- Man(x)_{iVe}$ $Human_{IQ}(x):- Parent(x)_{iVe}$
$Person_{IQ}(x):- Human(x)_{iVe}$ $Human_{IQ}(x):- Person(x)_{iVe}$

In Fig. 5, the checking starts from $Parent(John)_d$ in S_{2_c}. Since $Parent_{IQ}(x)$ is empty, $Parent(John)_d$ is changed to $Parent(John)_\emptyset$ (i.e. S_{2_c} to S_{2_d}). If $Human(John)_d$ is then checked, it is also changed to $Human(John)_\emptyset$ (i.e. S_{2_d} to S_{2_e}), because the state of John in Parent is ∅ and in Person is d. Then, $Person(John)_d$ is checked and then changed to $Person(John)_i$ because of $Man(John)_e$ (i.e. S_{2_e} to S_{2_f}). Because of the 'new' occurrence of $Person(John)_i$, then trigger for inferring $Human(John)_i$ is invoked, to change the database state from S_{2_f} to S_3. Similarly, if we adopt the label &check process to deal with T_4 which deletes **Man(John)**, the database is changed back to the empty one S_0.

2.3   Handling Sub Properties and Transitive Properties

Since space does not permit us to detail how we handle all types of OWL 2 RL axioms, we will outline the general nature of our approach by illustrating how we implement two more constructs. Suppose the ontology contains a SubPropertyOf axiom **hasParent** ⊑ **hasAncestor** and a TransitiveProperty axiom **hasAncestor** ∘ **hasAncestor** ⊑ **hasAncestor.**. These can be implemented as the following triggers:

> **when** $^+hasParent(x,y)_{eVi}$ **then** $hasAncestor(x,y)_i$
> **when** $^+hasAncestor(x,y)_{eVi}$ **if** $hasAncestor(y,z)_{eVi}$ **then** $hasAncestor(x,z)_i$
> **when** $^+hasAncestor(y,z)_{eVi}$ **if** $hasAncestor(x,y)_{eVi}$ **then** $hasAncestor(x,z)_i$

Inserting $hasAncestor(John, Jack)_e$ will infer no additional facts, but inserting fact $hasParent(Jack,Mike)_e$ will infer $hasAncestor(Jack,Mike)_i$, and this addition will continuously infer $hasAncestor(John,Mike)_i$. The inference rule of hasAncestor has two parts:

$hasAncestor_{IQ}(x,y):- hasParent(x,y)_{eVi}$
$hasAncestor_{IQ}(x,z):- hasAncestor(x,y)_{eVi}, hasAncestor(y,z)_{eVi}$

3   Implementation as SQOWL2

In this section, we describe the implementation of our approach, called SQOWL2. It uses the OWL API [5] to load an ontology, and applies Pellet [15] for the

T-Box classification. SQOWL2 currently generates triggers to work on Postgres and on Microsoft SQL Server, and we believe it can be extended to support any mainstream RDBMS.

The state of each data item can be intuitively represented by creating a column st to each relational table. However, exposing such an extra column to users will expose the details of the reasoning implementation to user applications. To avoid this, each ontology has two schemas, a back-end schema S_B which consists of materialised tables storing both data items and their states, and a front-end schema S_F which contains SQL views (i.e. virtual tables) showing only data items stored in S_B. The views and tables are created by using a set of SQL CREATE VIEW and CREATE TABLE statements, based on the following mappings of classes and properties to Datalog rules:

S_F.C(id) :- S_B.C(id,st)

S_F.P(domain,range) :- S_B.P(domain,range,st)

Schema S_F is used for accepting any inserts and deletes. Then, these database operations are transferred to S_B, where the type inference is processed.

SQL BEFORE triggers (PL/pgSQL) or INSTEAD OF triggers (Transact SQL) are used to implement $^-$ events, and SQL AFTER triggers are used for $^+$ events. All triggers are implemented with table-level semantics rather than row-level semantics to improve the performance of type inference. For example, in the physical trigger created on Man in S_B for when $^+$Man(x)$_{eVi}$ then Person(x)$_i$, when a transaction inserts multiple data items to S_B.Man, all inserted items will be inserted to S_B.Person as one reasoner insert rather than inserting each of them separately. When implementing triggers for deletes, the labelling process must be guaranteed to finish before starting the checking process. This is achieved by creating 'before delete' triggers on views in S_F to control the labelling and checking which are really processed in S_B. On each table in S_B, we create SQL DELETE triggers for labelling, and UPDATE triggers for checking.

Finally, we create indices for the column (id) on each class table, and for two pairs of columns (domain,range) and (range,domain) on each property table. These indices improve the query processing performance, both in reasoning, and in user applications.

4   Evaluation

This section[1] compares SQOWL2 to Stardog and OWLim. Stardog is a non-materialising reasoner, while OWLim is a materialising reasoner. They both store their data outside of an RDBMS, and do not provide transactional reasoning.

For the comparison of speed of incremental type inference and query processing, we used the well known **Lehigh University Ontology Benchmark (LUBM)** [3], which covers a university domain. It provides a T-Box of 43 OWL

---

[1] All experiments were processed on a machine with Intel i7-2600 CPU @ 3.40 GHz, 8 Cores, and 16 GB of memory, running Microsoft SQL Server 2014. SQOWL2 uses OWL API v3.4.3 for ontology loading and Pellet v2.3.1 for classification. For comparisons, we used OWLim-Lite v5.4.6486 and Stardog-Community v2.2.1.

classes, 32 OWL properties and approximately 200 axioms. LUBM also offers 14 benchmark queries which we numbered as Q1–Q14, and an A-Box generator to produce data sets of different size. In this section, we use L-n to denote a set of A-Boxes which contains n universities (each university contains approximately 100,000 class & property instances).

To evaluate the completeness of SQOWL2, we compared the results of answering LUBM queries by SQOWL2 to those of Pellet (a complete reasoner), but also used SQOWL2 to process more generic and exhaustive test suites generated by SyGENiA [16]. SyGENiA generates a test suite for a given query and a T-Box. Each test suite contains all possible inference logic that infers answers to this query w.r.t. the T-Box. If a reasoning system successfully passes the test suite, it is complete to answer this query w.r.t. the T-Box and any arbitrary A-Box of data.

4.1   Performance of Incremental Type Inference

Data Loading: We loaded into each system LUBM with four A-Box sizes (i.e. L-25, L-50, L-100 and L-200). Table 1 shows the loading time needed by each system, and Table 2 demonstrates the speed of data loading by them. All systems showed scalable data loading as each system's data loading time grew linearly from L-25 to L-200. The speed of loading different data sets by each system

Table 1. Data loading time (s)

	L-25	L-50	L-100	L-200
SQOWL2	583	1,115	2,133	4,465
OWLim	78	159	335	742
Stardog	14	26	51	-

Table 2. Data loading speed (inserts/s)

	L-25	L-50	L-100	L-200
SQOWL2	5,684	5,966	6,176	5,978
OWLim	42,067	41,623	39,946	35,933
Stardog	242,323	262,752	271,332	-

Table 3. Data deleting speed (deletes/s)

	L-25	L-50	L-100	L-200
SQOWL2	305	587	420	224
Stardog	29,268	28,759	28,903	-

Table 4. Avg. query processing speed (q/m)

	L-25	L-50	L-100	L-200
SQOWL2	1,253	949	519	36
OWLim	446	229	102	42
Stardog	39	17	5	-

Table 5. Detailed query processing time w.r.t. L-100 (ms)

	Q1	Q2	Q3	Q4	Q5	Q6	Q7	Q8	Q9	Q10	Q11	Q12	Q13	Q14
SQOWL2	0	481	0	2	7.2	38	1	112	931	0	14	4.2	5.4	22
OWLim	476	1,969	1	5.4	8	290	2.6	1,368	3,831	1.2	1.8	86	2.4	155
Stardog	57	830	55	90	58	157,022	879	2,178	831	1,106	57	89	57	52

- Stardog-Community cannot handle L-200, as the size of L-200 exceeds the license limitation.

was stable (e.g. Data loading speed of SQOWL2 was around 6,000 inserts/s). Stardog was the fastest, as it does not perform reasoning during data loading. SQOWL2 was the slowest, because it performs type inference as part of database transactions with full ACID properties, and materialises the result of reasoning during inserts. Indeed, due to the overheads associated with providing ACID properties for database updates, even without reasoning (i.e. with SQOWL2 triggers), the speed of data loading for LUBM in the SQL Server database used for testing was around 14,600 inserts/s. Thus, the process of reasoning caused a significant, but not impractical overhead to normal RDBMS database operations.

Data Deleting: After data loading, we used each system to execute a number of random deletes translated from A-Box data. Table 3 only shows the average speed of handling deletes by SQOWL2 and Stardog, as the Lite version of OWLim performs the whole reasoning again after deleting any facts. Again, as Stardog does not consider reasoning when inserting or deleting facts, its speed of data deleting was stable over different datasets, and was much faster than SQOWL2. As expected, the label & check process meant that the speed of handling deletes by SQOWL2 decreased when processing deletes from larger data sets, except from L-25 to L-50. The reason for this improvement was the RDBMS switching to a more efficient query plan when moving from L-25 to L-50. Due to the cost of the reasoning process, SQOWL2 caused a significant overhead when comparing with the speed of processing deletes without considering reasoning (but with indicies created), which is at about 20,000 deletes/s.

4.2   Performance of Query Processing

Completeness: We used SQOWL2 to process the 14 LUBM queries over L-1, and our experiment shows that SQOWL2 generated exactly the same answers as Pellet; therefore, SQOWL2 is sound and complete for processing the 14 queries over L-1. However, since the LUBM benchmark data is not very exhaustive [2], we further used our system to process the test suites generated by SyGENiA for the LUBM T-Box and the 14 queries. SQOWL2 passed all test suites, and therefore is complete for the 14 queries w.r.t the T-Box and any arbitrary LUBM A-Boxes. In [16], the most complete system out of four tested was found to be OWLim. Our tests show even now it provides incomplete answers for Q6, Q8 and Q10 with completeness 0.96, 0.93 and 0.96 respectively (the completeness level of processing each test suite is calculated as dividing the number of passed inference cases in this test suite by the number of all inference cases contained in this test suite). For example, Q6 is incomplete, since OWLim does not totally handle reasoning which includes existential quantification.

Efficiency: We used the three systems to answer queries over different LUBM data sets and recorded the time used for executing each of the queries. Table 4 shows the average speed when processing queries (i.e. how many queries on average can be processed per minute) by each of the three systems. The speeds of query processing by SQOWL2 or OWLim were much faster than Stardog,

because the two systems store explicit and implicit data at the data loading stage. For example, the average speed for executing queries over L-100 by
SQOWL2 was about 100 times as fast as Stardog. When only comparing the
two materialisation-based systems, SQOWL2's average speed was significantly
faster than OWLim for L-25, L-50 and L-100, and was comparable to OWLim
for L-200. The average speed of query processing by SQOWL2 dropped sharply
from L-100 to L-200 due mostly to Q2 (which needed 0.48 s over L-100 but 21 s
over L-200). The query plans used by the RDBMS show that it chose Nested
Loops for joining tables when processing Q2 over L-200, which is less efficient
than the Hash Match used over L-100. We intentionally did not tune the database
to solve this problem, but note that as in any RDBMS application, larger data
sets may require certain queries to be manually tuned by a database adminis-
trator.

A more detailed query processing time needed for executing each query by
three systems w.r.t. L-100 is shown in Table 5. SQOWL2 outperformed OWLim
when answering 12 of 14 queries, (i.e. SQOWL2 was slightly slower when processing Q11 and Q13). SQOWL2 was much faster than Stardog when processing all
LUBM queries, except Q9, which was just slightly slower than Stardog. Stardog
was significantly slower when answering Q6 and Q10 than both SQOWL2 and
OWLim, since these two queries are very complex to rewrite and compute the
answers (169 and 168 inference cases are respectively contained in the test suites
generated by SyGENiA for Q6 and Q10).

5 Related Work

Reasoning over large scale data can be classified as dynamic and materialised
approaches. Systems using the former approach (e.g. DLDB [13], Stardog [14]
and Ontop [1]) store only explicit facts and conduct reasoning only when there
is a query executed over the ontology (i.e. query rewriting methods), where no
incremental type inference is required. DLDB can be considered as transactional
reasoning system, as it uses temporal views inside an RDBMS as a manner to
rewrite executed queries. Reasoning systems based on materialised approaches
store both explicit and implicit data, in order to provide a fast query processing
service [9]. Most systems tend to perform reasoning outside an RDBMS (i.e. not
proper transactional reasoning), even though they still choose an RDBMS as a
possible data container. WebPIE [17], as a sample inference engine, applies the
MapReduce model and builds the reasoning mechanism for RDFS and OWL
ter Horst semantics on top of a Hadoop cluster. WebPIE only supports incremental data loading but not deleting. OWLim [6] is another triple-store system,
which uses a file system instead of an RDBMS as a container for storing semantic data. Its standard and enterprise versions support incremental data loading
and deleting, but not in a transactional manner. RDFox [12] adopts a so called
Backward/Forward algorithm (can be more efficient than DRed in some cases)
to achieve incremental reasoning without using an RDBMS, and it is not a
transactional reasoning system. Minerva [19] only uses an RDBMS to hold the

materialised results generated by an extra reasoner outside the RDBMS, so we do not consider it as a transactional or incremental reasoning system. Oracle's RDF store [18], by contrast, loads the explicit data in advance, and then uses inference rules to generate an inference closure of the loaded data. Although the reasoning is inside the database, it is not performed in an incremental manner.

6   Conclusion

We have demonstrated an approach using SQL triggers which extends an RDBMS to have type inference capabilities. We are the first approach to provide transactional and incremental type inference from both inserts and deletes of A-Box data, and holding data in an RDBMS allows ontology reasoning to be integrated into mainstream data processing. The evaluation shows that our SQOWL2, compared to two fast reasoners, is faster at query processing, and the completeness of query answering is comparable to or better than the same task for other rule-based engines. Of course, the approach is unsuited to applications where the inferred data is very large, and queries are relatively infrequent compared to updates. As our approach is built as a separate layer over the RDBMS, our work has not yet addressed the key issue of optimising the efficiency of handling updates to be as fast as the other engines which are specially designed for triple store (e.g. OWLim and RDFox), which is the subject of our future work.

References

1. Bagosi, T., Calvanese, D., Hardi, J., Komla-Ebri, S., Lanti, D., Rezk, M., Rodríguez-Muro, M., Slusnys, M., Xiao, G.: The ontop framework for ontology based data access. In: Zhao, D., Du, J., Wang, H., Wang, P., Ji, D., Pan, J.Z. (eds.) CSWS 2014. CCIS, vol. 480, pp. 67–77. Springer, Heidelberg (2014)
2. Grau, B.C., Motik, B., Stoilos, G., Horrocks, I.: Completeness guarantees for incomplete ontology reasoners: theory and practice. J. JAIR **43**(1), 419–476 (2012)
3. Guo, Y., Pan, Z., Heflin, J.: LUBM: a benchmark for OWL knowledge base systems. J. Web Semant. **3**(2–3), 158–182 (2005)
4. Gupta, A., Mumick, I.S., Subrahmanian, V.S.: Maintaining views incrementally. In: Proceedings of SIGMOD, pp. 157–166 (1993)
5. Horridge, M., Bechhofer, S.: The OWL API: a Java API for owl ontologies. Semant. Web **2**(1), 11–21 (2011)
6. Kiryakov, A., Ognyanov, D., Manov, D.: OWLIM-a pragmatic semantic repository for OWL. In: Proceedings of WISE, pp. 182–192 (2005)
7. Liu, Y., McBrien, P.: SQOWL2: transactional type inference for OWL 2 DL in an RDBMS. In: Description Logics, pp. 779–790 (2013)
8. McBrien, P.J., Rizopoulos, N., Smith, A.C.: SQOWL: type inference in an RDBMS. In: Parsons, Jeffrey, Saeki, Motoshi, Shoval, Peretz, Woo, Carson, Wand, Yair (eds.) ER 2010. LNCS, vol. 6412, pp. 362–376. Springer, Heidelberg (2010)
9. McBrien, P., Rizopoulos, N., Smith, A.C.: Type inference methods and performance for data in an RDBMS. In: Proceedings of SWIM, p. 6 (2012)
10. Motik, B., Grau, B.C., Horrocks, I., Wu, Z., Fokoue, A., Lutz, C.: OWL 2 web ontology language profiles. W3C Recommendation **27**, 61 (2007)

11. Motik, B., Nenov, Y., Piro, R., Horrocks, I.: Incremental Update of Datalog Materialisation: The Backward/Forward Algorithm. AAAI Press, California (2015)
12. Motik, B., Nenov, Y., Piro, R., Horrocks, I., Olteanu, D.: Parallel materialisation of datalog programs in centralised, main-memory RDF systems. In: Proceedings of the AAAI, pp. 129–137 (2014)
13. Pan, Z., Zhang, X., Heflin, J.: DLDB2: a scalable multi-perspective semantic web repository. In: Proceedings of WI-IAT 2008, pp. 489–495 (2008)
14. Pérez-Urbina, H., Rodrıguez-Dıaz, E., Grove, M., Konstantinidis, G., Sirin, E.: Evaluation of query rewriting approaches for OWL 2. In: Proceedings of SSWS+ HPCSW, vol. 943 (2012)
15. Sirin, E., Parsia, B., Grau, B.C., Kalyanpur, A., Katz, Y.: Pellet: a practical owl-dl reasoner. J. Web Semant. **5**(2), 51–53 (2007)
16. Stoilos, G., Grau, B.C., Horrocks, I.: How incomplete is your semantic web reasoner? In: AAAI (2010)
17. Urbani, J., Kotoulas, S., Maassen, J., Van Harmelen, F., Bal, H.: WebPIE: a webscale parallel inference engine using mapreduce. J. Web Semant. **10**, 59–75 (2012)
18. Wu, Z., Eadon, G., Das, S., Chong, E.I., Kolovski, V., Annamalai, M., Srinivasan, J.: Implementing an inference engine for RDFS/OWL constructs and user-defined rules in oracle. In: Proceedings of ICDE, pp. 1239–1248 (2008)
19. Zhou, J., Ma, L., Liu, Q., Zhang, L., Yu, Y., Pan, Y.: Minerva: a scalable OWL ontology storage and inference system. In: Mizoguchi, R., Shi, Z.-Z., Giunchiglia, F. (eds.) ASWC 2006. LNCS, vol. 4185, pp. 429–443. Springer, Heidelberg (2006)

Author Index